Religion in West European politics

RELIGION IN
WEST EUROPEAN POLITICS

RELIGION IN WEST EUROPEAN POLITICS

Edited by
Suzanne Berger

FRANK CASS

First published 1982 in Great Britain by
FRANK CASS AND COMPANY LIMITED
Gainsborough House, 11 Gainsborough Road,
London E11 1RS, England

and in the United States of America by
FRANK CASS AND COMPANY LIMITED
c/o Biblio Distribution Centre
81 Adams Drive, P.O. Box 327, Totowa, N.J. 07511

British Library Cataloguing in Publication Data

Religion in West European Politics.
  1. Europe—Politics and government
  2. Europe, Western—Politics and government
  I. Berger, Suzanne   II. Western European Politics
  261.7   JN94.A2 '

ISBN 0-7146-3218-X

This group of studies first appeared in a Special Issue on
'Religion in West European Politics' of *West European
Politics*, Vol. 5, No. 2, published by Frank Cass & Co. Ltd.

Typeset by Method Ltd., Woodford Green, Essex
Printed and Bound in Great Britain by
John Wright & Sons (Printing) Ltd. at The Stonebridge Press, Bristol

Contents

Notes on the Contributors

Suzanne Berger is a Professor of Political Science at the Massachusetts Institute of Technology. She has recently published *Dualism and Discontinuity in Industrial Societies* (1980) (with Michael Piore) and edited *Organising Interests in Western Europe: Pluralism, Corporatism and the Transformation of Politics.*

Annick Percheron is a *chargé de recherche* at the Centre National de la Recherche Scientifique, Fondation Nationale des Sciences Politiques, Paris, France. She has written widely on political socialisation, including *L'Univers politique des enfants* (1975) and *Les 10–16 ans et la politique* (1978).

Eusebio Mujal-León is Assistant Professor of Government at Georgetown University in Washington, D.C. He has written widely on Spanish and Portuguese politics, and his book *Communism and Political Change in Spain* will be published later this year by Indiana University Press.

Renaud Dulong is a *chargé de recherche* of the Centre National de la Recherche Scientifique. Among his other works are *L'Eglise cassée* (1971) and *La Question bretonne* (1975).

Jean-Marie Donegani is an *attaché de recherche* at the Centre National de la Recherche Scientifique, Fondation Nationale des Sciences Politiques, Paris, France. He is the author, among other articles, of 'Itinéraire politique et cheminement religieux', *Revue française de science politique*, vol. 29, no. 4–5, August–October 1979.

Douglas Wertman is a Research Analyst in the West Europe/Canada Unit of the Office of Research of the United States International Communication Agency. He has written on Italian politics, including chapters in both *Italy at the Polls* volumes, West European attitudes on security issues, and the European Community.

Brian H. Smith is an Assistant Professor in Political Science at the Massachusetts Institute of Technology. His book *The Church and Politics in Chile: Challenges to Modern Catholicism* (Princeton University Press) will appear this year.

Mady A. Thung is Professor of Sociology of Religion in the Department of Theology, Leyden, Netherlands.

John Madeley is a Lecturer at the London School of Economics and has written widely on religion and politics in Western Europe.

Kenneth Medhurst is Professor of Political Studies at the University of Stirling. His recent publications include *The Basques and Catalans (1977)* and 'Religion and Politics—a Typology', *Scottish Journal of Religious Studies*, 1981.

George Moyser is Lecturer in Government at the University of Manchester. Among his writings are articles in *Government and Opposition*, and (with K. Medhurst) a contribution to K. Jones, *Living the Faith* (1980).

Introduction

Suzanne Berger

Viewed through the simplifying lens of Left-Right conflict, the politics of religion in Western Europe has been remarkably stable over the two centuries since the French Revolution. Catholic and Protestant churches alike have been the bulwarks of social and political order. The religiously observant populations of Western Europe have been among the staunchest supporters of right-wing politics. There have been exceptions to this alliance of religion with the defenders of the status quo, or of reaction, and some of the deviant cases have been very important: French Protestant support for the Republic; radical millenarian movements in Italy; Catholic support for Irish nationalism; and so forth. But the dominant pattern has been a tight association between religion and the Right, as demonstrated in an extensive scholarly literature on local, national, and cross-national settings, with analyses of data from historical, electoral, opinion survey, and case studies, all converging on the same general conclusions.

Considered together, the essays in this volume tell a common story: that these old and close ties between religion and conservatism are unravelling and that possibilities for new politics are beginning to unfold. The two principal features of this development—a striking decline over the past two decades in traditional forms of religious practice and a significant expansion of Left political attitudes and behaviour—recur to a greater or lesser degree in all of the national cases analysed here. What the causes are of the simultaneous appearance of these two processes in Western European societies that are in so many other respects diverse is far from obvious. The simple notion that these changes can be attributed to modernisation, industrialisation or some other process at work across all advanced societies is apparently refuted by the case of the United States. In that country over the same decades there has been a religious groundswell, with 50 million Americans in 1976 describing themselves as 'born-again Christians'. Moreover, the role of religious groups in the Republican victories of the 1980 presidential and congressional elections testifies to the existence of powerful new links between the Right and religion in the United States.[1]

Thus the origins of the new relationships between religion and politics in Western Europe apparently must be sought out, not in the general features of modern society, but in the national and religious specificities of European historical experience.[2] As the chapters on the various countries of Catholic and Protestant Europe describe, there are multiple causes of these shifts. Some of them lie in the impact on the churches of societies experiencing rapid and profound social and economic transformations in the post-war period. Others reflect an internal evolution of religion, catalysed sometimes by pressures from the environment, but often pursuing, with considerable autonomy, a logic deriving from the Church's own inner life and spirit.

Why and how the two processes—decline of practice and shifts to the Left—are linked is complex. It should be noted that the impact of changes in religion has not only, and not everywhere, worked for the Left. In some countries old patterns have been reinforced. In others, the same set of causes has apparently worked to produce a mobilisation on the Right, as, for example, in the case of the Italian group *Comunione e liberazione*. Moreover, the shift to the Left of groups that were once reservoirs of support for the Right involves two different phenomena. The Left has benefited, first of all, from an overall decline in religious observance. Although the proportion of the population identifying with a given religion remains very high across Western Europe, the proportion that practises regularly has been falling. Sunday church attendance is decreasing and there are parallel declining trends for the performance of such rites as confession and communion and for participation in institutions closely associated with the churches (church schools, youth movements, devotional circles, and so forth). Regular religious practice and Right politics are highly correlated in most of Western Europe, and so the 'conversion' of some fraction of the church-going population into infrequent or non-practising Christians tends to bring a virtually automatic dividend to the Left. When once highly observant groups reduce their practice, their voting patterns tend to realign in distributions closer to average national distributions. This 'nationalisation' of politics as a result of an evening-out of rates of religious participation in a downward direction thus profits the Left far more than the Right, even in countries where the association between religious practice and Right politics remains a very tight one.

The Left has benefited in another way from religious changes in Western Europe: from the shift to the Left of groups who retain deep religious attachments. Even if one considers those whose connections to the Church, as measured by the conventional criteria of regular practice, are closest and whose distance from Left politics has historically been the greatest, there have been significant changes over the past several decades. In the case of the clergy, Kenneth Medhurst and George Moyser's work on Anglican bishops, reported in this volume, and Christel Peyrefitte's surveys of French priests,[3] to mention only two of the most recent studies, clearly show growing support for the Left. The trend is most pronounced among younger generations of clerics. But even for older generations and for the higher ranks of the hierarchy where rates of Left identification are much lower, there is willingness to live and let live and even to co-operate with Left groups that marks a real break with the past.

Indeed, the new openness of the Church to the Left goes beyond the sympathies of its individual members to a growing institutional acceptance of the legitimacy of Left politics and to an agreement, if not to advance or ally with the causes of the Left, at least not to block them. Just how far the official churches will move toward peaceful coexistence and collaboration is a matter of great importance for the prospects of Left parties in much of Western Europe. The question is particularly salient in France, where the position of the Church may be critical for the Left over the next few years. Whether or not the projects for social transformation that the Socialist government proposes will provoke a counter-mobilisation on the Right, may well depend on whether the Church joins up, once again, in an alliance of conservative forces. This, in turn, may hang on the Socialists' approach to the Church's traditional concerns, and above all, to Church schools, which Socialist programmes promised to integrate into a single national system.

On these questions about the potential for cooperation, coexistence and conflict between the Church and the Left, the experience of a Latin American state, in which the Left came to power with considerable acceptance from the official Church, reveals both the degree of flexibility in the Roman Catholic Church's approach to the Left and its limits. The limits, Brian Smith shows in his article on the 'lessons of Chile' in this volume, were reached when the Allende government threatened the traditional interests of the Church, particularly in education. The analogy with the French case is suggestive. The implications of the 'lessons of Chile' for Left political alliance strategies have generated major controversies in the Western European Socialist and Communist parties, for the latter have seen pre-figured in this case their own futures in situations in which they may win electoral victories without achieving a sufficiently broad social consensus to survive in power. Because the symbolic weight of this experience has had so great an impact on debate over Left strategies, we thought it useful to include an account of the Chilean outcome alongside the contributions on Western European societies.

Just how far the churches *can* move to the Left is determined not only by the politics of the shepherds but also by the politics of the flock. The regular church-going laity are in many Western European countries more conservative politically than their pastors and remain overwhelmingly attached to Right and Centre parties, despite the churches' greater acceptance of political pluralism and the example of their own clergy. When the Left has made important inroads in regions considered bulwarks of religion and Right politics, closer analysis has often revealed that the gains reflect a decline in practice, not a shift from Right to Left of regular church-goers. Thus Philippe Braud has shown that the Socialist advance in Brittany in the 1970s did not so much result from a higher proportion of Socialist voters among practising Catholics but from a higher proportion of non-practising Catholics in the population.[4] There are, however, some signs that even the practising laity may be less tightly committed to the Right than before. In the 1981 French presidential elections, for example, surveys showed that 'only' 81 per cent of the regular church-goers voted for a candidate of the Right whereas in 1974, 90 per cent of them had voted for the Right. On balance, though, even the 1981 results underscore the great gap between the politics of the practising and non-practising.

Measuring changes in the politics of Christians by their votes for parties of the traditional Left may, however, suggest a degree of continuity in attitudes and behaviour that is deceptive. As Annick Percheron demonstrates in her contribution to this volume, there has been a massive shift in values relating to everyday private life. Even those young French Catholics whose religious practices and political choices in the narrow sense are close to their parents, diverge widely from them on issues such as abortion, the Pill, working women, and cultural liberalism in general. These questions have been central to new political mobilisations over the past fifteen years. Indeed, in so far as what is at stake is a new perception of the boundaries of the political and acceptable limits of social intervention in individual choices, the worker self-management, ecology, anti-nuclear, and ethnic movements also reflect this new sensibility. The old parties of the Left have been slow to pick up on these problems; and new single-issue groups have sprung up to identify these issues and to mobilise around them. While these social movements are not integral parts of Left parties, they do gravitate to the Left's magnetic field, and the attraction of their themes may pull into the Left, broadly conceived, a generation of practising Christians who would not otherwise be likely to participate in or perhaps even to vote for Left parties. Looking at how the values of regular church-goers have shifted on the issues around which these new groups have organised suggests, then, a far greater Leftward shift than revealed by electoral surveys on voting intentions. But in the long run if these value changes and support for the new single-issue social movements of the Left turn out to be way-stations to Left politics *tout court*—and some of the research reported in this volume suggests this—then significant electoral realignments may be in the offing.

Alongside clergy and laity a third group with strong ties to religion can be distinguished: the activists in church-affiliated organisations. The mass of Christian recruits to left-wing politics have been drawn from this population as studies on Italy, Spain, and France show. Jean-Marie Donegani, Renaud Dulong, and Eusebio Mujal-Leon describe in their contributions in this volume how the Catholic Action movements have, since the end of the 1960s, been strongly influenced by Marxism, and activists who served organisational 'apprenticeships' in these religious organisations have moved in large numbers into left-wing trade unions and parties. Although the activists are only a minority of the Christian laity, they are doubly important, first, because in some segments of the population participation in such organisations has come to replace regular church attendance as the normal mode of religious expression and of connection to the Church. In France, for example, the presence of the Church in the working-class world is primarily ensured by working-class Catholic Action and not by the traditional parish, and a realistic measure of working-class attachment to the Church might be rates of participation in these groups rather than frequency of attendance at mass. Secondly, the Left politics of the activists, like those of the clergy, are significant because of the strategic position in society of the activists. They not only have a disproportionate influence within the world of the religiously faithful, they also man the bridges between this world and the outside, and by a selective channelling of the 'traffic' between these worlds, they are able to exercise a far greater influence than their numbers alone would suggest.

Finally, the essays in this volume raise questions about the effects that the detachment of religion from its traditional moorings may have on politics in Western European states. One obvious difference this may make is in electoral outcomes, as the redistribution among parties of the rapidly enlarging group of those who no longer practise regularly and the political realignment of a small but growing fraction of those still attached to the Church both work to increase Left tallies. In France and Italy these two processes have already combined to tilt the balance of power between Left and Right sufficiently to make Left victories possible, though hardly inevitable.

But will the entry of Christians into the electorates and the parties of the Left do any more than swell the troops available to the same leaders, in the same organisations, for the same projects? Does the integration into the Left of once or still-religious groups have any impact on the characteristics of the Left? Is the issue at stake simply an alteration in the Left's chances of coming to power? Or do these realignments create the potential of a transformation of the Left by its new recruits of religious origin? On this critical question, there is no agreement at all among the authors in this collection or indeed in the larger literature on politics and religion. Perhaps the most widely-held view is that the new recruits are indeed absorbed into political structures that remain essentially unchanged by their presence. And the proof of the claim that the Christians make no specific contribution to the Left would, from this perspective, be that Christians scatter themselves among Left organisations, thus revealing the absence of any special affinity for particular values, projects, or programmes. In France, for example, it is frequently observed in support of this view that Socialists and Communists whose political trajectories start from Catholic Action, end up in all factions of the Left. Both the CERES, the wing of the Socialist Party that is closest to the Communists, and the group around Michel Rocard, whose political platform is furthest from orthodox Marxism, have been heavily populated by activists of Christian origin. If the political recruits from Christian backgrounds have anything at all in common, in this perspective, it is their relative lack of power and influence within the Left. For to the extent that they are marked at all by their Christian origins, they have traits—political naiveté, obsession with purity and keeping one's hands clean, distaste for conflict and zeal for reconciliation—that are hardly serviceable qualities in a political organisation.

There is, however, another and diametrically opposed view of the difference that the shift of Christians to the Left may make in Western European politics. This position has been formulated in an extremely provocative fashion by Alain Besançon in *La Confusion des Langues* but is held in more or less moderate forms by others on the Left as well as on the Right.[5] The central notion here is that the political migration of Christians represents a transfer of passions, religious intensity, of a sense of transcendent mission, and of faith from the God of Christian belief onto the gods of secular political faiths, in a word, to Marxism. The underlying assumption is that a religious need is a permanent part of human nature. When such needs are channelled into traditional religious institutions—as they are in the United States and England, as they once were on the Continent—a liberal and stable polity can be preserved in a modern democratic society. But when religious energies and aspirations are directed into politics, the result is the revolutionary, ultimately totalitarian politics of the Jacobins, the Bolsheviks, and the Maoists. The effort to realise transcendent aims on earth, the urge to achieve a unity between one's religious and political selves, the translation of absolute values into criteria for political action—all these tendencies are held to characterise Christian recruits to the Left, who supposedly pour into politics the energies and aspirations they once directed to religion.

In the strongest versions of this case, such characteristics are supposed to propel Christians toward political groups that propose wholesale social and political transformation, that demand high degrees of discipline and self-abnegation from members, and that have little respect for human liberties. Thus the Christian entry into Left politics would reinforce the most extreme and intolerant groups within it. As translated into a French joke of the 1970s, this view predicts that 'the last Marxist-Leninist in Europe will be a Breton priest'. In more positive presentations of the case, the specifically Christian responses to politics are seen as offering a certain protection against totalitarian parties and states: for the Christian who judges his politics by his faith, so the argument goes, remains in a critical stance, unwilling to allow the ends to justify the means, uninterested in power for its own sake, committed no matter what the regime or the party to condemn violations of human freedom and dignity.

However opposed these two accounts of the consequences of a shift of Christians to the Left, they agree in dismissing the possibility that the world-view which Christians bear with them into new forms of political commitment might still have significant autonomy, vitality, and efficacy. They both assume that the political and cultural legacy of religion has been exhausted; thus when Christians move into politics—whether into the Left, as one set of theories predicts, or scatter across Left, Centre, and Right—they are simply absorbed by their new destinations and become indistinguishable from those who arrived at the same destinations but started from non-religious origins.

The articles in this collection point to quite different conclusions. They show the persistence and vitality of political values and attitudes linked to religious commitments in society at large, even as traditional forms of religious practice decline and the traditional political connections between the Right and religion are loosened. The Dulong and Donegani contributions suggest that even in the critical limiting case of the Christians who join Marxist movements, the stamp of their religious formation appears, if not indelible, at least remarkably resistant in an environment which should have effaced its traces. The role of religion in contemporary politics appears from these studies to be not only a residue and a drag factor but also a force capable of generating new effects. The concerns, values, and ways of looking at the world that are rooted in Christian responses to modern society have nourished a new set of demands in European politics. The broad movement for democracy in the workplace and for greater citizen access to power at all levels of the state; a questioning of the values of productivity and growth shared by both liberals and Marxists; an internationalism focusing on the interdependence of the peoples of rich and poor, or Northern and Southern, countries; these and other new issues reflect the sensibilities and contributions of Christians. These perspectives are not, of course, uniquely Christian. The demand for democratising the factory, for example, has deep roots in the traditions of secular trade unions. But within the union movement, the demands for worker self-management that had once been raised by anarcho-syndicalism, for example, have over time been relegated to obscurity by programmes inspired by socialist and Marxist understandings of the industrial world. The specific impact of Christians on this issue, as well as on many of the others that figure on the new agenda of Western European politics, has been to illuminate problems that were barely visible in either the liberal or the Marxist visions. The infusion of Christians into politics across the entire Left-Right spectrum has thus had the effect of raising and giving new content to aspirations for transforming aspects of advanced industrial societies that both liberals and Marxists had been treating as inevitable constraints.

The implications of this collection of essays about the prospects of profound changes in Western European politics have, undoubtedly, been skewed by the volume's focus on new forms of Christian political participation. Examining the cases of Christian groups with long experience in the governing coalitions of European states—particularly Christian Democracy in Western Germany and in Italy—might have suggested a far more conservative set of outcomes from the entry of new cohorts of Christians into politics.[6] And, indeed, however different the activists of Christian background of the 1970s and 1980s from earlier generations of Christian Democrats, the former, too, may respond to the temptations and disappointments of power by accommodation to the system or even retreat from it, rather than by a persevering effort to change it. Yet another factor that may cause these new pressures for political reform to abort may be growing difficulties of recruitment. If religious practice and membership in Christian organisations continue to decline, if the subcultures that once produced the militants now moving into the politics of the larger society disappear, can the socialisation of future generations be assured? If the new politics draws on a stock of traditional values and institutions, how can it be sustained, once the reservoir is drained?

NOTES

1. On the role of religion in recent American politics and on the failure of the 'secularisation thesis' to account for trends in religion in the United States, see Walter Dean Burnham, 'The 1980 Earthquake: Realignment, Reaction or What?' in Thomas Ferguson and Joel Rogers (eds), *The Hidden Election*. New York: Pantheon, 1981, particularly pp. 132-40.
2. For a development of this argument over a far longer historical period see David Martin, *A General Theory of Secularization*. Oxford: Blackwell, 1978.
3. A preliminary statement can be found in Christel Peyrefitte, 'Contraintes du catholicisme', *Faire*, (March 1981).
4. Philippe Braud, 'Les élections législatives de mars 1978 dans la région Bretagne', *Revue française de science politique*, Vol. 28, No. 6, (December 1978).
5. Alain Besançon, *La Confusion des Langues*. Paris: Calmann-Levy, 1978, and Juan Miguel Garrigues, 'L'Eglise catholique et l'Etat libéral', *Commentaire*, no. 8, (Winter 1979-80).
6. For a recent survey of the situation of Christian Democracy, see R.E.M. Irving, 'Christian Democracy in Post-War Europe: Conservatism Writ-Large or Distinctive Political Phenomenon?', *West European Politics*, Vol. 2, No. 1, (January 1979).

Religious Acculturation and Political Socialisation in France

Annick Percheron

Sociologically speaking, France remains predominantly Catholic: 90 per cent of all French are baptised;[1] of these, 80 per cent spontaneously describe themselves as Catholic.[2] Social science research and surveys conducted at election times show that no variable accounts better for French political attitudes than the degree of religious integration.[3] Even today, in all age groups and for every social class, for both males and females, a vote for the Right and conservative attitudes increase with the frequency of church attendance. This constant in attitudes and behaviour reflects old historical and geographical continuities. Left and Right France today coincide in large part with the 'red' and 'white' France of the Revolution. This continuity conceals, however, certain recent developments: diminished church attendance and the evolution of voting patterns in favour of the Left. These changes, which are appreciable throughout the population, are particularly clear, as shown in Figures 1a and b, in the youngest age groups. Some have interpreted this dual evolution as the sign of change in Catholic political attitudes. Others insist that the statistical link between religious practice and voting remains intact, and that if the Left is progressing, it is not because Catholics are changing, but rather because there are fewer and fewer practising Catholics.[4]

The history of Catholicism in other countries shows that there is no necessary link between this religion and political conservatism.[5] Historical factors may explain the origins of the situation in France. The persistence of this specificity, however, involves both the critical role of inter-generational transmission of political and religious attitudes and also the close interdependence between religious acculturation and political socialisation. Broadly speaking, children apparently inherit a given system of politico-religious attitudes. But transmission does not mean identical reproduction. The current evolution of religious and political situations may indicate a weakening of the role of inter-generational transmission of political and religious attitudes; direct inheritance would seem to be less frequent. These shifts may also reflect a change in the message as a result of the disjuncture, erosion, or transformation of the links among the various religious and political components in it. To put it another way, the content of the inheritance may be altered, even distorted.

Despite the importance of the subject in any attempt to understand French political life, there has been no empirical study of the twin phenomena of religious and political socialisation in childhood and adolescence. Our aim is to fill this gap by answering three sets of questions. First, of political and religious attitudes, which are formed earlier, which are transmitted first and best? Are political and religious attitudes modified with age, and if so, how?

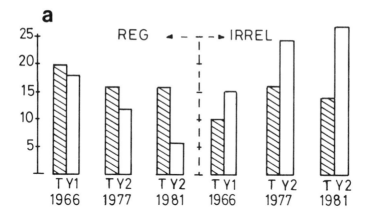

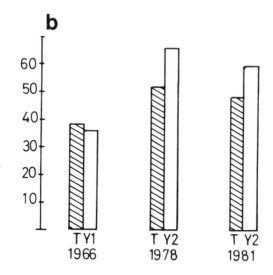

Figure 1

a Frequencies of regular practitioners and irreligious among the whole population (*T*) and the youngest class of age (Y1 = 21–4 years old, Y2 = 18–24 years old).

b Frequencies of Left preferences among the whole population and the youngest class of age.

1966: IFOP survey, data kindly provided by G. Michelat
1977: SOFRES survey
1981: SOFRES survey, unpublished data kindly provided by J. Jaffré

Next, what is the influence of parental religiosity in the formation of political preferences in children and adolescents? Finally, are the links between religious and political attitudes observed in adults already present in childhood?

Our study will be based on data collected in two surveys: one carried out in November-December 1975, with a representative and matched sample of parents and adolescents (one child of between 13 and 18, one parent per family); the other conducted in December 1979-January 1980 with a representative sample of children in the 8-14 age range.[7]

Before discussing the analyses in detail, three points should be made:

(1) Of all the agents of socialisation, this study emphasises the parents. This is a reasonable hypothesis, given what we know from other research in the field of religion[8] and politics[9], but this choice, we realise, still leaves important questions open. One of the sources of the weakening of the transmission of values from parents to children, for example, is competition with other agents of socialisation, for example, the media. In a simplified form, the following diagram seems to us to account for the essential mechanisms at work between parents and children; it also illustrates the different stages of our study.

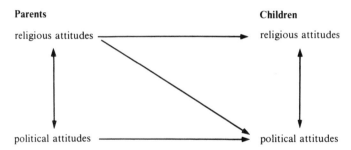

(2) For lack of data, and despite the importance of this aspect of the subject, we shall not pose the question of the transmission of faith or beliefs within the family unit, but shall confine our study to the transmission of habits of religious practice.[10] Our hypothesis is, however, that the transmission of practice can be considered as an indicator of the transmission of a wider set of religious values and beliefs. Michelat and Simon have shown that the degree of religious practice is, in adults, a good indicator of belief-systems for, if belief unaccompanied by a minimum of worship is infrequent, regular church-going with lack of belief is extremely rare.[11] We believe that this situation can be generalised to include childhood and adolescence and the phenomena of parent-child transmission.

(3) The number of political attitudes taken into consideration will also be limited. Essentially the mechanisms involved in the formation and transmission of ideological preferences will be studied.[12] But here again, it is known that these preferences are, in the case of adults, strongly correlated with electoral behaviour, and that, more generally, they go hand in hand with a set of opinions and attitudes that are characteristic of the Left or Right.

TRANSMISSION OF THE LEVEL OF RELIGIOUS INTEGRATION AND IDEOLOGICAL PREFERENCES WITHIN THE FAMILY

The transmission of church-going habits seems more efficient than that of ideological preferences. Such is the initial indication of the correlation coefficients (tau.b) of the distribution of these habits and preferences for adolescents and their parents. The coefficients are significant in both cases, but they are much higher for religious integration (0.59) than for ideological preferences (0.27). Detailed examination of children's attitudes relative to those of their parents (see Tables 1 and 2) suggests that, whatever their degree of practice or ideological preferences, parents have a good chance of seeing their children adopt the same patterns. But there are significant differences: left-wing parents pass on their preferences somewhat better (48 per cent left-wing children) than right-wing (43 per cent) or centrist (37 per cent) parents. Non-religious parents bring up more children in their own image (74 per cent) than do regular church-goers (67 per cent) or non-church-goers (54 per cent) or those who practise infrequently (59 per cent). In a sense, the more parents have a clear and defined ideological position, the better their chances of passing it on to their children.

TABLE 1

DEGREE OF RELIGIOUS INTEGRATION AMONG CHILDREN ACCORDING TO THE DEGREE OF RELIGIOUS INTEGRATION OF THEIR PARENTS

Children's religious integration as percentage of parents'*

Parents' religious integration	regular	irregular	non-practising	irreligious
regular	67	26	6	2
irregular	13	59	23	5
non-practising	4	29	54	13
irreligious	—	5	22	74

*In this and subsequent tables, discrepancies in percentage totals are due to rounding up or down of some figures.

TABLE 2

IDEOLOGICAL PREFERENCES OF CHILDREN ACCORDING TO THE IDEOLOGICAL PREFERENCES OF THEIR PARENTS

Children's ideological preferences as percentage of parents'

Parents' ideological preferences	no answer	Left	Centre	Right
no answer	53	17	17	13
Left	22	48	24	6
Centre	25	21	37	18
Right	19	12	25	43

These observations are insufficient, however, for there are three factors liable to influence these patterns of transmission: sex, level of education, and the parents' social group. More women than men go to church regularly, but men are more often interested in politics. There are signs or traces of a traditional division of the masculine and feminine roles that influence children's education, leading to the notion that religious upbringing stems from the mother, but that political initiation is the father's responsibility.[13] In the United States, studies such as those carried out by Jennings and Niemi have shown that in all cases, mothers have as much chance as fathers of passing on their partisan preferences to children.[14] What is the situation in France, as regards both the religious and the political spheres? The coefficients of association between the distributions of ideological preferences or the level of religious integration of adolescents and their fathers and mothers show that neither the mother in the religious sphere, nor the father in the political sphere, has any real advantage over the other (see Table 3). This holds true, regardless of the level of religious integration and kinds of ideological preferences at stake. In other words, neither father nor mother plays specific roles in the religious or political spheres; moreover, no greater rate of transmission can be attributed to greater or lesser degrees of practice or to particular types of ideological preference. Mothers who are regular church-goers and left-wing fathers (to confine ourselves to the most obvious examples) do not form their children 'in their own image' any more than other parents do.

TABLE 3

CORRELATION (τ_b OF KENDALL) BETWEEN THE DEGREE OF RELIGIOUS INTEGRATION AND IDEOLOGICAL PREFERENCE OF PARENTS AND THAT OF THEIR CHILDREN, ACCORDING TO SEX, LEVEL OF EDUCATION AND OCCUPATION OF THE PARENT

Sex	Male	Female			
Religious integration	0.55 (373)*	0.60 (539)			
Ideological preferences	0.31	0.21			

Level of education	Primary	Secondary	Technical	University	
Religious integration	0.56 (489)	0.66 (239)	0.57 (112)	0.51 (69)	
Ideological preferences	0.26	0.30	0.20	0.37	

Occupation	Peasant	Craftsmen	Shop-keeper (high level)	White collar (high level)	White collar (low level)	Employees	Blue collar
Religious integration	0.62 (85)	0.58 (32)	0.60 (31)	0.66 (53)	0.61 (66)	0.66 (187)
Ideological preferences	0.34	0.40	0.31	0.21	0.28	0.28

*Size of the group is given in brackets

Educational level plays a decisive role in the formation and expression of political opinions and attitudes.[15] It was therefore natural to imagine that this factor would also be crucial in the parents' capacity to pass on their value systems to their children: the higher the parents' level of education, the better they would transmit their religious and political attitudes. This hypothesis was not validated. The correlations between the respective distributions of the religious and political attitudes of parents and children remain the same whatever the parents' level of education (see Table 3). A detailed analysis, educational level by educational level, of the positions of adolescents with respect to the education of their parents, does however show a special transmission pattern for those parents who have received higher education. Whereas in all the other cases, non-religious and regularly practising parents, and left-wing and right-wing parents, are about equally effective, in the case of parents with higher education, irreligious and left-wing parents are more successful in passing on their own ideas.

Analysis of the role of social milieu does not simply repeat that of the educational variable. Social position is synonymous with unequal levels of education; it also implies different historical and cultural traditions, class situations, exposure to politics and various kinds of educational experience. Our results take these specific factors into account. Once again, globally speaking, the coefficients of association between the political and religious attitudes of parents and those of adolescents hardly vary from one social group to the next (see Table 3). But detailed analysis of adolescents' political preferences, or of their degree of religious integration relative to that of their parents, reveals divergent models of socialisation according to social group.

In the case of executives and workers, irreligious and left-wing parents are most likely to pass their attitudes on to their children. Since irreligious attitudes and Left identification go hand in hand with a greater interest in politics, the parents' level of politicisation may account for this difference. It is important to underline the fact that this phenomenon holds true for groups both with the highest (executives) and lowest (workers) educational levels; the latter group no doubt compensates for the scholastic handicap by the concrete experience of militancy or political struggle.[16]

In more traditional milieux (farmers, shopkeepers, and artisans) it is, on the other hand, regular church-goers or right-wing parents that have the greatest influence on their children. Here we rediscover phenomena that we have already noted.[17] In traditional milieux, which are not generally highly politicised, but in which the predominant group norms are regular church attendance and a Right vote, these are the norms that are reproduced best from one generation to the next.

Analysis of educational level, and above all of social group, thus obliges us to question the idea of an oversimplified model in which all parents would have an equal chance of passing on their value systems. The analysis also reveals points of convergence between certain ideological preferences and given levels of religious integration. Irreligion and left-wing tendencies, regular church attendance and right-wing preferences, are best transmitted in the same social groups. But these affinities do not affect the initial result, which remains the most significant: regardless of social group, educational level or the parent's gender, religion is better transmitted than politics.

IMPORTANCE OF RELIGION AND POLITICS IN CHILDHOOD

Optimal transmission of the religious message can be explained by the relative importance of politics and religion in childhood. Religious acculturation and political socialisation are mechanisms for anchoring the child in a social group by the acquisition of the value systems and symbolic codes that define group identity and underpin group relationships. These two processes go hand in hand, but, in France, they take very different forms and channels.

Even today, 78 per cent of the adult population consider baptism to be indispensable for their children: 98 per cent of regular church-goers but still 83 per cent of those with no religion; 94 per cent of persons on the Right but still 83 per cent of the Communists and 68 per cent of the extreme-Left supporters; almost as many (73 per cent) think children should be sent to catechism classes.[18] The Church clearly remains a positive point of reference in children's education, even for non-practising families. It is clear that not all these parents expect their children to be taught the faith. Baptism, communion, church marriage, remain marks of social recognition and constitute positively-valued rites of passage. But they represent more than this.

What parents hope from religious instruction—and this is perhaps the decisive factor in the formation of political and social values—is the acquisition of 'good habits' and a code of behaviour. This fact emerges clearly from different surveys carried out with adults on the role of catechism,[19] as well as in the definition children give of a Christian (see Table 4).

TABLE 4

DEFINITION OF WHO IS A CHRISTIAN GIVEN BY 8–14 YEAR OLD CHILDREN, ACCORDING TO THEIR
DEGREE OF RELIGIOUS INTEGRATION

Percentage responses of children going to Church:

A Christian is:	very often, often	not very often	never	irreligious
someone who is good, generous	36	32	22	29
someone who tries with others to make life beautiful	24	29	21	11
someone who prays alone or with others	13	10	19	14
someone who speaks about Jesus and God	27	28	33	43
No answer	1	1	—	4
Total sample (N)	335	221	184	28

Paradoxically, the non-practising and irreligious children give the most 'religious' answers; Catholic children usually give the most positive definitions, but ones which essentially describe types of social behaviour: 'A Christian is someone with a lot of heart' and 'who works with others to make life more beautiful'. 'Good habits' constitute another aspect which is just as decisive: the acceptance of authority, and a certain degree of submission that goes with it. When asked to give a definition of God, regular church-going children choose equally 'God as love' and 'God as supreme authority' (see Table 5). It is significant that the younger the children are, the more often they choose the latter definition. 'God knows all, sees all' is chosen by 50 per cent of children in the 8–10 age range; by 37 per cent of the 13–14 range. 'God cares about you, no matter what' is chosen by 46 per cent of children from 8–10 years, and by 57 per cent of children from 13–14 years old.

TABLE 5

DEFINITION OF GOD BY 8-14 YEAR OLD CHILDREN, ACCORDING TO THEIR DEGREE OF RELIGIOUS INTEGRATION

Percentage responses of children going to Church:

For you, who is God?	very often, often	not very often	never	irreligious
Someone who knows, who sees everything	45	36	33	7
Someone who cares about you and loves you whatever	51	47	24	11
Someone created by men	1	7	26	43
No answer	4	10	18	39

Thus religious education is the more likely to have a profound impact because it is not simply based on mastering texts but on gestures and rituals whose rhythm and content are prescribed. The form of religious transmission is just as important as its content: words and gestures are transmitted in an authoritative form by adults whose power is set in a hierarchical context that is clearly identifiable.

Indeed religious acculturation is completely programmed and structured. It is the product of a system. In contrast, the absence of religion depends almost entirely on belonging to an irreligious family and on declaring oneself as 'having no religion', a declaration difficult for young children who may belong to irreligious families even though they have been baptised. Although precise measurement is impossible, it seems that children hesitate for a long time between announcing that they are non-practising and announcing that they are non-believers. In many cases it is only at adolescence that the philosophical and ideological implications of the declaration of irreligion assume their full significance.

Catholics, on the other hand, have at their disposal a complex apparatus of religious instruction. It is the parents who very early on (and early timing is important) teach their children to pray and take them to mass: 67 per cent of children in the 8–10 range say that they pray. Before the age of eight, children are accompanied to mass, and the studies of Boulard and Rémy have shown the importance of the parental example.[20] In 1962, in cases where both parents were regular church-goers, almost all children between the ages of 15 and 24 still attended church. But parents are not the only agents of religious socialisation. Sooner or later they are assisted, equally visibly, by catechism instructors, the clergy, youth movements and Catholic private schools. Although nearly two-thirds of all children attend catechism classes, only a minority attend Catholic private schools (16 per cent of the 8–14 age group in the survey) or participate in youth movements. Religious 'capital' is therefore unequally distributed. It is, moreover, difficult to appreciate the influence of each actor. Attendance at catechism classes, participation in a youth movement or going to private school are first and foremost marks of the parents' greater degree of religious integration. Are we observing the effect of exposure to a greater number of messages or to more frequent repetition of the same messages, due to the influence of a greater degree of religious integration of the family? Quite possibly both. In any case, the system contributes strongly to reinforcing the child's religious integration: 20 per cent of all children aged 8–14, as opposed to 47 per cent of those who attend catechism classes, go to private schools, pray, and claim that they attend mass regularly (see Figure 2). This is not a transient effect. A survey of adults in 1978 showed that there were three times as many regular church-going Catholics among those who had attended private school than among those who had attended public, state schools.[21]

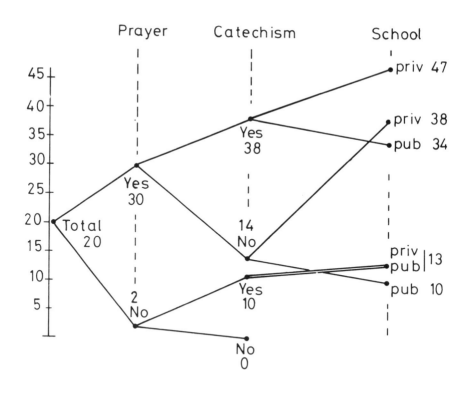

Figure 2

Frequencies of regular religious practice among 8–14 year old children when they pray; when they pray and attend catechism; and when they pray, attend catechism and a private school.

The conditions of political socialisation are different in many ways. In brief, politics is something that the family is reluctant to discuss, and ideological preferences are transmitted despite the educational ideals affirmed by most parents. Three principles form the basis of parents' attitudes: childhood and politics should not be mixed; religion and politics should not be mixed; and, *a fortiori*, childhood, religion and politics should not be mixed.

The extremely ambiguous attitude of parents with respect to politics and childhood we have discussed elsewhere, and here we shall simply recall certain essential aspects of the problem.[22] The first important fact is that parents wish to be the sole authority in the political education of their children.[23] This makes concerted action between family and school impossible. Politics does not belong in school. The demand for scholastic neutrality is the convenient pretext for this exclusion and is based on three types of reasons: the first is a certain mistrust of teachers whom parents feel (and not without reason) to be more left-wing than themselves. The second is that for parents, political and moral education are indissociable. This entails, for them, a natural distribution of tasks between school and the family: the production of knowledge, together with a certain technical baggage, is the school's job; the formation of opinions and of a value system is the natural domain of the family alone. The third reason, and perhaps the most decisive, has to do with the extremely negative image that parents have of politics. To claim the exclusive right to the political education of one's children in the family is tantamount to an attempt to exclude it from the family itself. For parents, politics is something cold, impure, and sterile, an important source of division and conflict. This means that the child must be protected against politics.

The best form of protection against politics is not to discuss it. The vast majority of French people 'say' they rarely or never talk about politics in the family.[24] The results of the two studies echo this: 72 per cent of the children aged between 8 and 12, and 63 per cent of those aged 13 and 14, claim they do not discuss political programmes they see on television with their parents. Only 27 per cent of parents with children between the ages of 13 and 15, and 32 per cent of those with children aged 16–18, claim that they often or very often discuss politics with children. Moreover, in 68 per cent and 52 per cent of these cases, respectively, the same parents consider their children to have no political opinions. Is this a sincere reflection of certainty or rather a desire not to destroy an idealised image of childhood? It should be noted, in any case, that 33 per cent of adolescents in the 13–15 age range cannot or will not classify themselves on the Left-Right axis, but that this percentage falls to 16 per cent (contrasted with 11 per cent in the case of their parents) for the 16–18 year olds.

This situation is complicated by the parallel refusal to mix religion and politics. On this point everyone, whether church-goer or not, left-wing or not, agrees, but for different reasons: the irreligious and left-wingers reject religion; and practising Catholics and right-wingers reject politics.[25] Michelat and Simon have shown the depth of the Catholic rejection of the politics of politicians and parties.[26] It is, moreover, significant that the vast majority of adults accept the idea that religion should influence their family life, but not their political opinions.[27] From these premises it follows, *a fortiori*, that childhood, religion, and politics should not be mixed, and that one may hypothesise that Catholic parents will talk politics less often with their children than others. Table 6 verifies this hypothesis by showing that the cleavage here is between irreligious parents and all Catholics, whatever their degree of practice.

TABLE 6

FREQUENCY OF POLITICAL DISCUSSION BETWEEN PARENTS AND CHILDREN, ACCORDING TO THE DEGREE OF RELIGIOUS INTEGRATION OF PARENTS

Percentage responses according to degree of religious integration:

Do you often discuss politics with your children?	regular	irregular	practising	irreligious
Very often, often	36	22	29	53
Not very often	43	38	31	18
Never	21	38	38	27
No answer	—	2	2	2

The relative importance of politics and religion in childhood explains the differences observed at the level of the transmission of religious integration and ideological preferences. This does not mean that ideological preferences are not shaped or transmitted. Indeed, we have shown elsewhere that children need neither to 'know' their parents' opinions, nor to be capable in themselves of formulating political choices for there to be formation and transmission of ideological preferences.[28] But the differences between the religious and political spheres are patent. In the first case, the formation of religious opinions is orchestrated, organised and has a positive image. In the second, the formation of opinions and attitudes is less positively valued, the transmission of political choices as such is less willingly accepted, and the family, which considers itself uniquely responsible for education in this domain, often cloaks it in a moral guise. At the level of the formation of political attitudes, this means that delays and discrepancies are likely. A comparison between the percentages of non-response to questions concerning religious identification and those on ideological preferences is revealing (see Table 7). Nearly two-thirds of the 8 year olds have no 'declared' ideological preferences, but at the same age less than a fifth of them are unable to say what religion they are. By the age of 14, the ratio is 1:5 between the 'no response' replies on the two questions.

TABLE 7

FREQUENCIES OF 'NO ANSWER' ON THE QUESTION OF RELIGIOUS AND IDEOLOGICAL PREFERENCES BY AGE

	Age in years						
	8	9	10	11	12	13	14
On the question: What is your religion?	22	14	18	18	12	10	6
On the index of ideological preferences	59	47	42	37	26	32	30

These results pose a certain number of questions. If, for ideological preferences, it is simply a question of lag or of difficulty of expression, the level of transmission of ideological preferences from parents to children should increase with age. On the other hand, the level of transmission of religious integration should remain stable. But this would be to ignore both the role of social convention in the church-going habits of some young people, and the importance of the evolution of society as a whole. Once religious instruction is finished (after confirmation or first communion, today at around 13), once the direct influence of private school is over (end of compulsory schooling, today at 16) young people, because of the retreat of religion in society as a whole, and because of the competition of agents of socialisation other than church or family (work environment, peers, the media) are liable to 'drop out' of religion.

EROSION WITH AGE OF CHURCH ATTENDANCE IN YOUNG PEOPLE, AND
REINFORCEMENT OF PREFERENCES FOR THE LEFT

The studies of Boulard and Rémy, using parish censuses of the 1950s, showed that there was an initial abrupt fall-off practice between the ages of 12 and 14, after first communion and the end of compulsory schooling, followed by a more gradual erosion phase until the age of 25.[29] The data of the 1975 and 1979 surveys, concerning the age ranges in question (up to 18), reveal comparable phenomena (see Figure 3a): irregular church attendance and irreligion increase regularly with age; regular church attendance drops sharply between 13 and 14, and continues to decline in favour of non-practice. The age at which this drop takes place suggests a correction of Boulard and Rémy's interpretations: what seems to trigger this decline is the carrying out of the social ritual of first communion or confirmation, and not the end of compulsory schooling, which today does not occur before the age of 16. It is not a consequence of a change in the conditions of life but the end of a certain practice motivated by social convention and necessity: regular worship and catechism are indispensable for communion. It is not, therefore, surprising to learn that the drop in catechism attendance takes place at the same ages: 37 per cent at age 13, 17 per cent at age 14. On the other hand, erosion of the frequency of prayer is much less marked: 65 per cent at ages 12–13 and 52 per cent at age 14. This is important, for it emphasises the fact that though the instances of 'public' worship decrease, not all the signs of membership in the Catholic community disappear at the same time.

During the same period, in accordance with our hypothesis (see Figure 3b), expressions of ideological preferences for the Right and especially for the Left increase in number.

This evolution has repercussions on the levels of transmission of religious and political attitudes from parents to children. In general, as the coefficients of association show, the results move in the expected direction: with age, the coefficients of association become stronger for ideological preferences (0.24 for the 13–15 age group, 0.33 for 16–18 years) and are less marked for religious integration (0.67 and 0.48 respectively). At the same time, the disparities between the levels of transmission of ideological preferences and the degrees

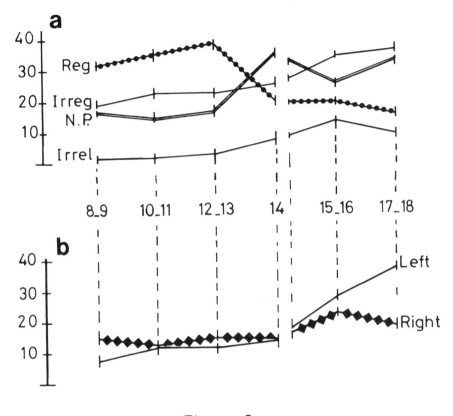

Figure 3

a Degree of religious integration,
b Ideological preferences, by age (8–14 years old 1979 survey; 16–18 years old 1975 survey).

of religious integration tend to diminish sharply. More precisely, where only parents and children who place themselves on the Left-Right axis are considered and the 'no response' replies are excluded, the coefficients of association between ideological preferences of parents and children become 0.47 for ages 13–15 and 0.44 for ages 16–18. For the group of 16–18 year olds, the disparities between religion and politics disappear and we find levels of transmission of ideological preferences comparable with those observed in other countries, notably those most similar in their religious and political structures: in Italy the coefficient of association is 0.45 between the ideological preferences of parents and children at the same ages.[30]

Consideration of the levels of integration and of ideological preferences of children relative to those of their parents enables us to deepen the analysis. For religious practice, up to the age of 14, children tend to be more observant than their parents, but subsequently the movement is reversed. At the ages of 16–18, 28 per cent are religiously less integrated than their parents. This shift from practice to non-practice is observable in all social groups. In all cases, the number of 'irreligious' doubles between the parents' generation and that of 16–18 year olds.

The development of ideological preferences is different. There is no abrupt change here between one age and another, but rather a progressive increase, year by year, of choices in favour of the Left or of the Right. Whatever the children's age, some are more Left, Centre or Right than their parents. There is no uni-directional shift, but rather a continual movement of exchanges. But the fact remains that, if we add up the movements from Left to Right (excluding centrist positions) and from Right to Left, the latter outnumber the former, and the gap between these two types of exchange grows wider with age. The result is that for 16–18 year olds, 20 per cent are more left-wing than their parents.

In these results there are signs of an evolution comparable with that of the whole population: a drop in practice and an increase in left-wing preferences. We know, moreover, that processes begun in adolescence do not stop at age 18. Boulard and Rémy's studies indicate that erosion of practice persists up to the age of 25. We also know that young people are only slowly and progressively integrated into their electoral role. Not until the age of 25 are all, or almost all, enrolled on the electoral register.[31] There are more electoral abstentions in the youngest age groups, and in opinion polls the 18–24 age group give the most non-responses concerning their voting intentions or their position on the Left-Right axis.

Our results show, moreover, that the decline in rates of practice is greater than the increase in the number of preferences for the Left. If, as some sociologists have insisted, the Left is progressing because the number of practising Catholics is diminishing, the gains of irreligion do not all benefit the Left. In our survey it can be seen that 63 per cent of irreligious children with irreligious parents prefer the Left, which is true of only 54 per cent of the irreligious children with more religiously integrated parents. Of course, it remains true that the number of Left preferences may increase as the effect of primary socialisation into the Catholic religion wears off. But the effects never totally disappear. Opinion polls of adults appear to indicate that the irreligious descendants of irreligious families are more often communist than those of Catholic families. And as we know, anti-communism is one of the fundamental aspects of Catholic culture.[32]

INFLUENCE OF PARENTS' AND CHILDREN'S RELIGION UPON THE FORMATION AND TRANSMISSION OF IDEOLOGICAL PREFERENCES

Comparison of the transmission of ideological preferences and of degrees of religious integration has revealed points of convergence between irreligion and Left preferences and between regular practice and Right preferences: they seem to appear together in the same families. If this is so, it must be because the level of the parents' religious integration plays an equally important role in the transmission of both religious attitudes and of ideological preferences. Our last remark concerning the role of parents' irreligiosity in their children's declarations of preferences for the Left seems to confirm this. But the analysis must be extended to include the totality of ideological preferences and all levels of religious integration.

In general, whatever the degree of children's religious integration, the same correlations are observed between parents' and children's ideological preferences: 0.26 for regular church-goers, 0.25 for irregular ones, 0.21 for non-practising children and 0.24 for irreligious children. But this apparent uniformity conceals extremely unequal degrees of success in transmitting preferences for the Left or Right according to the level of religious integration (see Table 8). Certainly, in each case the same phenomenon is observed: the more Left the parents are, the more likely it is that their children will be Left; conversely, the more Right the parents are, the more likely their children will be on the Right. The decisive influence of political preferences should not, however, mask the clear division between irreligious parents, on one side, and Catholic parents, on the other, regardless of the latter's practice: when parents are Right, 70 per cent of the children of regular church-goers, 68 per cent of the children of irregular church-goers, and 67 per cent of those of non-church-goers are not left-wingers, as against 50 per cent of the children of irreligious parents. Here the division is simple and the degree of practice is not at issue.

TABLE 8

IDEOLOGICAL PREFERENCES OF CHILDREN ACCORDING TO THE IDEOLOGICAL PREFERENCES AND
THE DEGREE OF RELIGIOUS INTEGRATION OF THEIR PARENTS

	Children (parents regular)				Children (parents irregular)		
Parents:	*no answer*	*Left*	*non-Left*	*Parents:*	*no answer*	*Left*	*non-Left*
Left oriented	9	53	38	Left	27	38	35
'Centre'	11	24	66	'Centre'	24	21	56
Right	19	11	70	Right	20	12	68

	Children (parents non-practitioners)				Children (parents irreligious)		
Parents:	*no answer*	*Left*	*non-Left*	*Parents:*	*no answer*	*Left*	*non-Left*
Left oriented	25	46	30	Left	16	75	9
'Centre'	31	18	52	'Centre' }			
Right	22	11	67	Right }	25	25	50

On the Left, the frequency with which children make the same choices as their parents varies even more widely according to whether parents are Catholic or irreligious (a difference of between 22 and 37 points); but these differences also subsist among Catholics. It is significant that regular church-going families have more left-wing children (53 per cent) than do irregular church-going families (38 per cent) or non-practising ones (46 per cent). Among Catholics, left-wing, regular church-goers occupy a unique position. These left-wing church-goers are known to have often a strong interest in politics: 62 per cent (against 39 per cent of right-wing regular church-goers) describe themselves as very interested in politics. A high degree of politicisation together with Left preferences and, probably, a higher level of education, tend to counterbalance the effect of strong religious integration.

Parents' religious and ideological choices are so important in determining children's ideological preferences that one may wonder whether the children's own religious practice has any autonomous effect. In fact, this variable plays a role that is far from negligible (see Figure 4 a and b), but here again there are differences: the level of children's religious integration is important essentially in Catholic families and plays a much more important role in the case of preferences for the Left. Within these limits, variation is perfectly simple: when the parents are left-wing, the proportion of children with left-wing preferences is higher for those children whose church-going habits are less assiduous than their parents'. When the parents are not left-wing, the relationship is inverse: equal or more frequent church attendance on the part of children entails more frequent choices outside the Left. Whatever the parents' degree of religious integration, preferences for the Left are more common in irreligious or non-practising children than in others, and right-wing preferences are more frequent in regular or irregular church-going Catholic children.

These phenomena are crucial. They act as a reminder that there is no such thing as 'blind' determinism or transmission. Children have their own systems of preference and choice and these weigh heavily in the construction of their own value systems. There is transmission from the parents, but this does not imply simple reproduction. Inherited values and attitudes contribute to building a world-view in which values, opinions and attitudes are both renewed and refashioned for each generation.

These results, moreover, again reveal the specificity of the cases of irreligion and Catholic religion. The situation is simplest for irreligiosity, and here the transmission of ideological preferences is most successful. The child's room for manoeuvre is extremely limited: children born into irreligious families have every chance of being irreligious themselves, and if the parents are left-wingers (as is most often the case), in three cases out of four they will also inherit these political preferences. In the case of Catholics, the children's own religious attitudes play a more important role, above all when their politics tend towards the Left, i.e. when they move in the opposite direction to the norm. In cases where there is contradiction or reinforcement between parents' and children's religious practice, the interplay of the socialisation mechanisms is more complex, and the influence of a wider network of agents is seen. It is significant that, when the children are more regular church-goers than the parents, the fall in the number of preferences for the Left is greater than its rise in the converse situation. Where the parents are regular church-goers and have Right or Centre politics, the dropout effect of less assiduous religious practice on the part of the children is less marked. This underscores the importance of the affinities between Catholicism and the Right and the importance of the system that shapes the child's religious views. The survey of

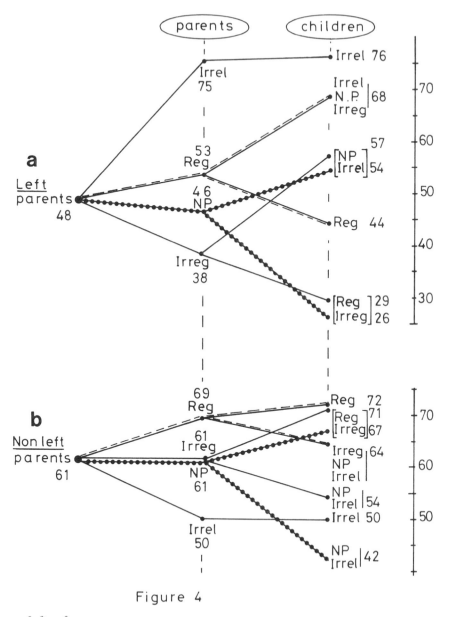

Figure 4

a Left preferences,
b Non-Left preferences, among children according to the ideological preferences of their parents; the ideological preferences and the degree of religious integration of their parents; the ideological preferences, the degree of religious integration of the parents and the degree of religious integration of the children themselves.

the 8–14 age groups furnishes an example of this. We have seen that the frequency of church attendance increases for children who pray, attend catechism, and above all, go to Catholic private schools. It is possible to show, in the same way, that whereas 14 per cent of the 8–14 age group express Right preferences, this rises to 20 per cent for children who practise regularly and to 30 per cent for those who practise regularly and also attend private schools.

The relationship between religion and politics is not, however, one way only. It is clear that political stances entail certain judgements on religion and a certain questioning of the beliefs and values proposed by the Church. This is true from early childhood, as witnessed by the different definitions of God in the 8–12 age group, depending on whether they are right- or left-wing: for 43 per cent of the former and 33 per cent of the latter, God is 'someone who knows all and sees all'; for 41 per cent of the former and 30 per cent of the latter, God is 'someone who loves you whatever happens'; for 8 per cent of the former and 22 per cent of the latter, God is 'a human invention'.

DOES THE RELATIONSHIP BETWEEN RELIGIOUS INTEGRATION AND POLITICAL ATTITUDES PERSIST IN THE NEW GENERATION?

Our analysis demonstrates the strength of the influence of parents' and children's religious integration upon the formation of ideological preferences in children. Does this mean that, from one generation to the next, the relationships between religious and political attitudes remain unchanged? If so, there would be no transformation of political attitudes in Catholic groups.

In fact, our results seem to indicate a close reproduction of the relationship between political preferences and level of religious integration, and it is hardly surprising to find the same curves in graphs showing the left- and right-wing orientations of parents and children as a function of their respective levels of religious integration (see Figures 5a and b). What is more unexpected is that, whatever the age of the children, the curves are parallel. At the outset, the relations between ideological preferences and religious attitudes are immediately apparent. With age the frequency of the expression of ideological preferences increases, and gradually the curves approach those of adults. This appears to show that religious and political attitudes are two interdependent elements in the construction of a social and cultural identity, which influences the choices made in both spheres.

The slope of the curves, according to age, also show a certain disparity in the formation and expression of left-wing and right-wing preferences. The latter benefit from the support of a coherent and powerful educational system. It should not be forgotten, moreover, that in 1975 and in 1979, France was governed by the Right. All these factors favour a more precocious development of preferences for this political camp.

Can the similarities between the stances of the two generations according to their degree of religious integration be generalised beyond ideological preferences? The answer is affirmative for other political dimensions, witness the case of parents' and children's interest in politics (see Figure 5c). For both groups, the same U-curve is seen: whatever the age, strong interest in politics is less frequent in irregular and non-church-goers, but more common in regular church-goers, and above all, for those who are irreligious.

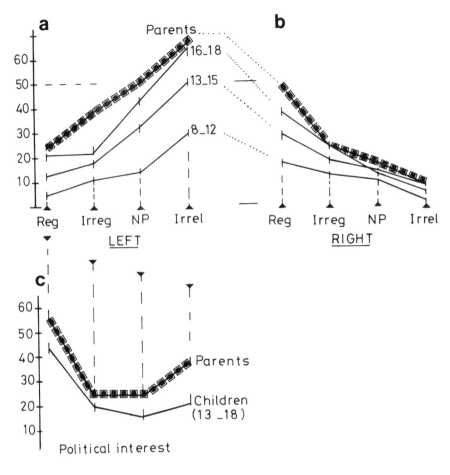

Figure 5

a, b Left and Right preferences among parents and children by age.
c High degree of political interest among parents and children.

To go further, what happens if we expand our definition of politics? A sphere that Rokeach would call peripheral values[33] and that Fichter would classify as 'fluctuating value-norms'[34] appears of interest: the realm of everyday morals. It is in fact a link between religion and politics. The issues surrounding the liberalisation of culture and morality (women at work, the Pill, cohabitation and so forth) are at the heart of debate over society's evolution, and, in recent years, they have become political issues. These are clearly matters that call into question Christian morality, and thus have discussion within the Church itself. The construction of two comparable scales showing the liberalisation of everyday values in children and their parents enables us to compare their respective attitudes relative to their degree of religious integration.[35] This comparison is extremely fruitful and suggests conclusions radically different from those drawn from the case of ideological preferences or political interest (see Figures 6 a and b). Only in irreligious families are the positions of parents and children extremely close, and practically identical as far as everyday morality is concerned. In Catholic families, on the other hand, and whatever their degree of practice, parents and children hold diametrically opposed positions. The vast majority of Catholic parents are hostile to the liberalisation of morals, and the young, whatever the degree of their religious integration, are largely favourable to it. In Catholic groups, solidarity with those of the same age is far more important than inter-generational solidarity.

This comparison is of prime importance, since, first, it shows the coherence and strength of value systems in the irreligious group. In this group only, the transmission of political choices and socio-cultural values seems to be equally successful; only in this group is there no divergence between political choices and social attitudes. The comparison reveals, moreover, the zones of strength and weakness within the Catholic value systems, and perhaps enables us to speculate on how this system of attitudes may be transformed. If parents and children differ more on the scale of liberalisation of morals than in the expression of political preferences, it may be because Catholic parents' conservative values go against the evolution of society itself, and thus encounter strong competition from other agents of socialisation. One may hypothesise that in the new generation, the transformation of socio-cultural attitudes will, in the long run, lead to a change in ideological preferences. Given the strength of the primary socialisation process, the transformation of Catholics' political attitudes would not begin with the transformation of their ideological preferences. Rather, the modification of these latter would proceed, by contagion, from a less political towards a more political dimension. Similar indications can be found in Donegani's studies on the life-histories of left-wing Catholic political activists.[36] He shows that a break with the family's religious heritage and a subsequent commitment to the Left must be preceded in early adulthood by some challenge to patterns of everyday personal life (moving, divorce, serving in colonial wars, and so forth).

What conclusions can be drawn from these results? The most significant is the crucial role of filiation in the religious and political spheres. One is almost sure to be irreligious if one is born into an irreligious family; those born into a practising family have a good chance of being practising Catholics themselves. Similarly the probabilities for being Left or Right are high when one's parents are Left or Right. Chances are lower in this second domain, except when both aspects occur together. Irreligion and regular practice constitute decisive reinforcements in the successful transmission of ideological preferences. But heredity is not all. The child's personal choices, born of other encounters and of his own social experiences, reinforce or contradict the effects of transmission, and in any case, mould them into a specific whole that is much more than the sum of its parts.

Our study also shows the gulf separating irreligious groups from Catholics. It is true that, among the Catholics, there are differences of degree. But the

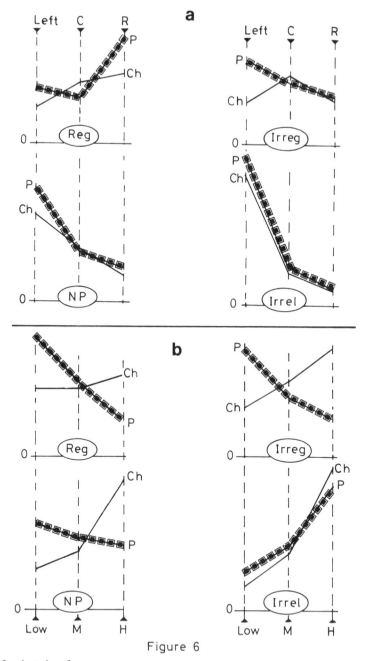

Figure 6

a Left oriented preferences
b Degree of socio-cultural liberalisation, among parents and children according to their degree of religious integration.

irreligious families are quite another matter. It is useful and justified to speak in their case of zero religious integration since they are not Catholics at all. But this would only account for what they are not, and would say nothing about what is powerful and original in their value system. Along with regular church-going Catholics on the Left, but far ahead of them, the irreligious are those who have the most coherent value system and who best succeed in passing it on to their descendants, even without the support of any specific institution.

Finally, our results confirm the analyses of those who claim that the affinities between regular church-attendance and a Right vote, and irreligion and a Left vote, are not merely phenomena of the past. If there are more and more people on the Left, it is because there are fewer and fewer regular church-goers. It should also be noted that the gains on one side do not equal the losses on the other. The importance of the primary socialisation process is such that some may stop going to church without moving to the Left. Nonetheless, a breach can now be seen in the effectiveness of the transmission of the Catholic value system from one generation to the next. However successful in the sphere of ideological preferences and political interest, this transmission is a total failure in the case of the norms and values of day-to-day morality. Perhaps the transformation of Catholic political attitudes will in the long run depend on this failed transmission in everyday life.

NOTES

1. In a SOFRES survey for *Le Nouvel Observateur* in 1977, 14 per cent said they had been baptised, 82 per cent said they had been baptised and had had first communion, and only 4 per cent had neither been baptised nor taken first communion. Boulard in *Sondages*, Nos.3 and 4, (1977), pp. 7-13, using religious census data estimated that 70 per cent were baptised.

2. To the question 'Can you tell me what religion you are?' 82 per cent of the French in 1979 (as against 84 per cent in 1975) said Catholic. See the Louis Harris survey for TF1 in October 1979.

3. See the work of Michelat and Simon, in particular, Guy Michelat and Michel Simon, *Classe, religion et comportement politique*. Paris: Presses de la Fondation Nationale des Sciences Politiques/Editions Sociales, 1977; Guy Michelat and Michel Simon, 'Religion, Class, and Politics', *Comparative Politics*, Vol. 10, No. 1, (October 1977), pp. 159-86; Guy Michelat and Michel Simon, 'Niveau d'intégration religieuse et comportements politiques', *Religion et politique*, Venise: Actes de la 15e conférence internationale de sociologie religieuse, August 1979. We borrow from these authors the notion of religious integration. On measuring it, see note 10. See also J.M. Donegani, 'Itinéraire politique et cheminement religieux', *Revue française de science politique*, Vol. 29, Nos. 4-5, (August-October 1979), pp. 693-738.

4. On this subject see Christel Peyrefitte, 'Religion et politique', *L'Opinion française en 1977*. Paris: Presses de la Fondation Nationale des Sciences Politiques, 1978, pp. 117-34.

5. On these issues, see David Martin, *A General Theory of Secularization*. New York: Harper Colophon Books, 1978.

6. A representative survey with a national sample carried out under our direction by IFOP for IFOREP, with 916 pairs of parents and children.

7. A representative survey with a national sample carried out by SOFRES for several subscribers, including *Le Pélerin* and *Le Nouvel Observateur*. The results of the religious part of the survey appeared in *Le Pélerin*, 4 March 1979. The political section we prepared and have commented on in *Le Nouvel Observateur*, 19 February 1979. We thank J. Jaffré and the SOFRES for allowing us to carry out secondary analysis of the data and to relate the political and religious data.

8.   See for France, F, Boulard, J. Rémy with the assistance of M. Decreuse, *Pratique religieuse urbaine et régions culturelles*, Paris: Editions Ouvrières, 1968, especially Ch. VI, pp. 121-56; see also L. Voye, 'Liaison entre la religion et les fonctions culturelles de la famille', *Social Compass*, Vol. 16, No. 3 (1961), pp. 355-69.

9.   For France, see Annick Percheron *et al.*, *Les 10-16 ans et la politique,* Paris: Presses de la Fondation Nationale des Sciences Politiques, 1978; Annick Percheron, 'Tel père, tel fils', *Projet*, No. 115, (May 1977), pp. 532-46.

10. For the survey of parents and children (1975). Our indicator of religious integration and of religious practice was built with responses to the question, 'Are you Catholic?' (If yes) 'Do you go to church, every Sunday, several times a year, or never; other religion; no religion.' The 'other religion' responses were excluded, and the study considered only Catholics. We constructed the following categories. Level zero of religious integration: those who responded 'no religion' and whom we call *irreligious*; level 1 of religious integration: those who 'never' go to church, and whom we call *non-practising*; level 2 of religious integration: those who go to church several times a year, and whom we call *irregular church-goers*; and level 3 of religious integration: those who go to church every Sunday, and whom we call *regular church-goers*. For the survey on the 8-14 year olds (1979), the indicator of religious integration was made up from responses to two questions: 'What is your religion; are you Catholic, Protestant, Jewish, other, no religion, don't know'; (if Catholic) 'Do you go to mass very often, rather often, not often, never.' The children responding Protestant, Jewish, or other were excluded. We considered as *irreligious* those children who described themselves as having no religion; as *non-practising*, those who were Catholics who never go to mass; as *irregular church-goers*, those who do not go often or rather often to mass; and as *regular church-goers*, those Catholics who attend mass very frequently.

11. See Michelat and Simon (1979), p. 124.

12. In the parent-child survey (November 1975), ideological preferences were measured by self-location on a Left-Right scale with seven positions. The calculation of the coefficients of association between the ideological preferences of parents and those of children used the totality of possible responses, including the 'no responses'. Because of the limited number of cases, however, for a certain number of tables and figures, we have collapsed the seven positions into four: no response, Left (positions 1,2,3), centre of the scale, which does not, however, correspond exactly to 'centre' in its usual political sense (4), and Right (positions 5,6,7). Sometimes we considered only the basic cuts of no response, Left (1,2,3), and non-Left (4,5,6,7). The ideological preferences for the 8-14 year olds (1979) were measured by combining their answers to 'Do you like the Left?' (yes, no, no response); 'Do you like the Right?' (yes, no, no response). We classified as having a preference for the Left all those children who replied 'I like the Left and I don't like the Right'; and as having a Right preference, those who responded 'I like the Right and I don't like the Left'. On the importance and reliability of this indicator see A. Percheron, 'Ideological Proximity among French Children: Problems of Definition and Measurement', *European Journal of Political Research,* No. 5, (1977), pp. 53-81.

13. See, in a SOFRES survey carried out for *La Croix*, December 1974, the responses to questions about whether the man or the woman in the family should be in charge of educating children about politics, educating them about religion, and educating them about sexual matters.

14. K. Jennings and R. Niemi, *The Political Character of Adolescence: The Influence of Families and Schools*. Princeton: Princeton University Press, 1974.

15. See P. Bourdieu, *La Distinction: Critique sociale du jugement*. Paris: Editions de Minuit, 1979, particularly Ch. 8, pp. 463-541.

16. We have considered similar phenomena in the case of the political apprenticeship of children of the same social milieu in A. Percheron, *L'Univers politique des enfants*. Paris: Presses de la Fondation Nationale des Sciences Politiques, 1975.

17. See Percheron (1978), particularly Ch. 3, pp. 139-202.

18. SOFRES survey for *Le Nouvel Observateur*, November 1977.

19. See the responses to a question about which of the functions of the Church is most important: to create a more just world; to provide children with moral principles; to help the sick and the poor; to bring the gospel to the world. (SOFRES survey for *Le Pélerin* and *La Croix*, December 1971.) See also the responses to the question of why children should be sent

to catechism classes in a Louis Harris survey for TF.I, October 1979.

20. See Boulard and Rémy, op. cit.

21. The data on mass attendance comes from an IFOP survey, February 1978, for *Témoignage Chrétien*.

22. See Percheron (1978), particularly the introduction.

23. See the answers to the question of whether youth should receive a political education in the family or in high school (*lycée*) in an IFOP survey, 1968.

24. See the IFOP survey for *La Vie Catholique* in 1978 which asked whether politics was discussed in the family; 62 per cent answered 'never' or 'rarely'.

25. See the SOFRES survey, 1977, cited by Christel Peyrefitte, 'Contraintes du catholicisme', *Faire*, (March 1981). The majority of Catholics of all degrees of practice and of various ideological persuasions agreed that religion and politics should not be mixed; the greatest support for not confusing the two spheres came from non-practising right-wing Catholics, whereas only 68 per cent of the practising left-wing Catholics agreed to this proposition.

26. See Michelat and Simon (1977).

27. See the responses to a question about the impact of religion on family life, on professional life, and on political opinions in a 1971 SOFRES survey for *Le Pélerin-La Croix*.

28. See Percheron (1977).

29. See Boulard and Rémy, op cit.

30. See A. Percheron and K. Jennings, 'Political Continuities in French Families: A New Perspective on an Old Controversy', *Comparative Politics* (1981).

31. M. Sineau, 'L'abstentionnisme parisien aux élections municipales (1965-1967)', pp. 55-72; J. Mossuz-Lavau and M. Sineau, 'Sociologie de l'abstention dans huit bureaux de vote parisiens', pp. 73-101; and M.F. Toinet, 'Remarques sur l'inscription et la participation électorales à Paris', pp. 102-17, in *Revue française de science politique*, Vol. 28, No. 1, (February, 1978).

32. See Michelat and Simon (1977).

33. See M. Rokeach, *The Open and Closed Mind*. New York: Basic Books, 1960.

34. J.H. Fichter, 'Religious Values and the Social Personality', *American Catholic Sociological Review*, Vol. 17, No. 2, (June 1956), pp. 109-17.

35. We measured attitudes on the liberalisation of morals and on everyday ethics with two scales constructed by Loevinger's method, asking both parents and children whether parents should advise a daughter to use the Pill, whether they should let their children see them nude, about cohabitation, about using someone else's property without permission, and about buying prepared foods instead of cooking at home.

36. See Donegani, op. cit.

The Left and the Catholic Question in Spain

Eusebio Mujal-León

Conflict between the Left and Catholicism has played a major role in twentieth-century Spanish politics. The Church in Spain, as elsewhere 'in its historic heartlands',[1] has served as the bulwark of order, representing one of the most important obstacles to the legitimation of the parties of the Left and to their accession to power. Controversy over its place in society contributed decisively to the outbreak of the Civil War. After the Franco victory in 1939, the Church and Catholicism served as the principal ideological pillars of the regime. Despite the important socio-structural changes of the last four decades,[2] the Catholic Church's presence and influence continue to generate tension in Spain. Thus, even today, as Juan Linz has noted, 'religion continues to be the decisive variable in accounting for the moderate and conservative electoral choices of the voters. In fact, it is a more important factor than social class.'[3]

The Left has been forced to devise a strategy for dealing with the Catholic phenomenon in Spain. A first line of attack, in line with the anti-clerical tradition of its Latin European counterparts, was a call for a frontal assault on the Church. The Anarchists, Communists and Socialists pursued this strategy in the years preceding the Civil War and for the first two decades of the Franco regime. Eventually, under the impetus of changes taking place in Spanish society and among Catholics, as well as of lessons learned from having allowed the Right to exploit religion in its favour, a less conflictual alternative emerged. Socialists and Communists—the Anarchists having lost their prominence in the Left by the 1950s—inclined their parties toward more flexible postures. As we shall see, the degree of interest and innovation in policy was not the same among the two parties, but both sought to break the marriage between Catholicism and social/political conservatism.

This essay will analyse the evolving policies and attitudes of the Socialists (PSOE: Partido Socialista Obrero Español) and Communists (PCE: Partido Comunista de España) with respect to Spanish Catholicism. The first section explores the role of the Church and subculture in Franco Spain and discusses the reasons for and extent of their evolution. The second section focuses on the PSOE and PCE analysis of and response to that phenomenon, and the final section assesses the efficacy of those policies and the place of the Catholic Church and subculture in Spain today.

THE ROLE OF THE CHURCH IN FRANCO'S SPAIN

Catholicism has consistently been one of the principal bulwarks of opposition to change in nineteenth- and twentieth-century Spain. Struggling, as elsewhere in Latin Europe, against the secularising trends of Liberalism and Socialism, Spanish Catholicism was a reservoir of moral and political support for conservative forces. Historically, the link between Catholicism and the State has been very close in Spain: the Church had an exalted role in the *reconquista* from the Moors and galvanised subsequent crusades against Jews and heretics domestically, and against Protestantism in Europe more generally.[4] As cement for the Castilian monarchs and their successors in building the Spanish nation, Catholicism became indissolubly linked to the national identity.

At the same time, cleavage along religious lines deepened in Spanish society, especially during the first decades of this century. The battle intensified after 1931 with the establishment of the Second Spanish Republic. Profoundly monarchist, most members of the Catholic hierarchy never more than grudgingly accepted the Republic. The few chances for an accommodation evaporated when the Republican Constitution, approved in late 1931, adopted an openly anti-clerical tone. Rejecting the more moderate proposals of a juridical commission, the Republican majority in the *Cortes* refused to grant the Church any special status and, in the now famous Article 26, called for the closure of convents and religious schools and the ending of subsidies for the clergy.

Although Catholic estrangement from and hostility to the Republic contributed heavily to polarisation, an equal share of the responsibility for that development belongs in the Republican camp. Anarchists and Socialists, drawing on an anti-clerical tradition which in Andalucia, Asturias and Cataluña led to the burning of convents and churches and attacks on the clergy, did little to temper this volatile situation.

Distinguishing 'socialist' from 'bourgeois' anti-clericalism, the PSOE adopted a belligerent attitude toward the Church and its doctrines.[5] The Socialists supported the disestablishment of Catholicism, the dissolution of religious orders and the confiscation of their properties, the expulsion of the Jesuit order, the prohibition of any church role in education (public or private), and state control over all schools. The Communists, whose political presence was slight in the years prior to the Civil War, shared these sentiments but their anti-clericalism appeared mild in comparison to the virulence of some Republicans and others on the Left. In part, this relative moderation on the Catholic question had its roots in the view that too militant an atheism—one which led to terrorism, for example—was undesirable in so far as it would detract from other more important political tasks. Moreover, the Popular Front strategy followed by the PCE and other Latin European parties during the 1930s at the instigation of Moscow, caused those parties to adopt a much less radical posture than that which party members or leaders if given free rein would have chosen. This was true on the Catholic question as on other issues. For the most part the Spanish Communists followed a policy of the 'outstretched hand' articulated by the French Communist leader Maurice Thorez.

The moderation of the PCE on the Catholic question was relative and eminently tactical. Certainly, the tone which comes through the speeches and writings of prominent Spanish Communists during the 1930s could hardly be described as sympathetic to the Church. On more than one occasion the party justified attacks on churches and religious houses, and in fact (although the party subsequently toned down its opinion on this matter) in 1935 the PCE demanded the expropriation of all church properties without any compensation.[6] These attitudes were shared by others on the Left. Churches and religious beliefs, PCE leaders felt, would inexorably disappear as Spanish Catholics were shown the error of their ways. The PCE nevertheless showed a more sophisticated sense of political realism than others on the Left, distinguishing between Catholics supporting the Republic and those opposing it. The Communists went further, differentiating the reflexive anti-Republican stance of most Catholics in Spain from the reasoned political/social opposition of the hierarchy.

The failure of the putative Catholic party, the *Confederación Española de Derechas Autónomas* (CEDA), and of its leader José María Gil Robles to block the ascent of the Left and Republican forces in the elections of early 1936, led the church hierarchy to look elsewhere for a vehicle to guarantee the Catholicity of Spanish society. Victimised in the form of church burnings and other violence in 1931, 1934 and again in 1936, the Church enthusiastically greeted the Nationalist uprising led by Franco in July 1936, and most members of the hierarchy signed a collective pastoral letter a year later, in which they lamented the 'great national catastrophe' Spain had suffered but endorsed without hesitation the battle against the 'enemies of God'.[7] As a reward for lending the Civil War the overtones of a crusade in support of Western civilisation and ensuring Vatican support for him, Franco granted the Church a privileged institutional position with respect to the State after 1939, codifying that relationship in the August 1953 Concordat.

Much has been written about Church-State relations in Franco Spain. Here we simply suggest that there are various competing interpretations: at one pole, its characterisation by Max Gallo in the first decades of the new regime as a *total confianza recíproca*; at the other pole, views such as that of the sociologist Juan José Ruíz Rico, stressing essential coincidences and the role played by the Church as ideological pillar, but also insisting on the competitiveness within the relationship[8]; and that the latter is more convincing and relevant for understanding the subsequent shift of the hierarchy toward a more neutral position *vis-à-vis* the State in the last years of the Franco regime.

Catholic support for Franco during and after the Civil War was decisive, both in consolidating the regime domestically and in breaching its international isolation. When the tide of World War II turned against the Axis powers and the threat of Allied intervention in Spain became real, Franco employed his Catholic connection to the full. Thus, in 1945 a government reshuffle put a prominent lay Catholic, Martín Artajo, at the head of the vitally important Ministry of Foreign Affairs, and other members of the ACNP were also placed in strategic positions—all this at a time when the Falange was being shunted aside. The Francoist cause was not hurt, either, by the presence of powerful Christian Democratic parties in France, Germany and Italy or the tacit support it received from the Vatican.

The Church was not, however, entirely at ease in Franco's coalition. Its ideological convictions were profoundly reactionary, conservative, and anti-modern, with none of the revolutionary qualities associated with Fascism or its Spanish variant, Falangism. The Catholic hierarchy hoped for the restoration of the sixteenth-century theocratic 'National Catholic' state and thereby of its own influence over Spanish society. Franco offered that prospect, but the Church was deeply apprehensive about the intentions and influence of the Falange. Full implementation of its statist ideology would curtail church privileges, particularly in education and the spiritual formation of youth. The verdict of World War II and the unwillingness of Franco to permit the Falange to develop into a real state party helped settle the argument. In exchange for support for the regime, Franco granted the Catholic Church a series of privileges. The Concordat established the confessionality of the State, exempting the clergy from taxation and church publications from the official censorship. The agreement allowed church schools, granted a subsidy to religious personnel, and gave the hierarchy the right to supervise doctrinal instruction in the public schools. Apostolic labour organisations like the HOAC (*Hermandades Obreras de Acción Católica*) and JOC (*Juventud Obrera Católica*) were permitted to function independently of (though presumably parallel to) the official syndical structures. In exchange, the Church made express its commitment to the Franco regime and put the considerable weight of its prestige behind the government. Breaking a tradition it had observed since the late nineteenth century, the Vatican also agreed to allow the Spanish state indirectly to fill vacant bishoprics.[9]

The Concordat—which some bishops feared left too much room for state intervention in church affairs—marked the high-point in Church-State collaboration in Franco Spain. Restoring Catholicism to a position it had last enjoyed four centuries before, and decisively bolstering the legitimacy of the regime, the agreement appeared to usher in a new era in Spanish history. This proved illusory. Profound changes in Spanish social structure associated with industrialisation, along with international events like the Second Vatican Council and some of the Cold War, caused the Spanish Church to begin extricating itself from the embrace of the State over the next two decades.

There was little ambiguity over church support for Franco either before or after 1939. However, one of the characteristics of the authoritarian system that Franco fashioned was a relative institutional pluralism within the regime, and, within the diversity of the victorious coalition, the Church was deeply engaged in an incessant struggle to maintain the influence it had acquired after the Civil War. Paradoxically, its defence of the privileges accorded it led the Church increasingly to mark its distance from the regime.

Nowhere is this process more evident than with respect to apostolic labour organisations like the HOAC and JOC. The Catholic labour groups were not formally syndical organisations. Like the ACLI in Italy and Catholic Action movements in Europe, the Spanish apostolic labour organisations started out as service-oriented movements whose objective was the 'recuperation of the worker world for Christ'.[10] The Church hierarchy saw these organisations as filling a void created by the elimination of the Left. Catholicism would thus have an unprecedented opportunity to penetrate into a milieu, that of the working class, where Socialist and Anarcho-syndicalist ideas had always had preponderance. Founded in the late 1940s at a time of economic prostration, these organisations also provided an outlet for Catholics with a social concern.

The HOAC and JOAC (the latter changed its name to JOC in 1956) became key actors in the struggle for influence between the Falange and the Church. Although supposed to work in harmony with the *Organización Sindical* run by the Falange, those organisations were the only ones allowed by the terms of the August 1953 Concordat to break the organisational monopoly which the *sindicato vertical* exercised over the labour movement. Armed with their own newspapers, bulletins, and independent financial backing, the HOAC and JOC slowly moved away from their original service orientation and became a direct competitor of the OS.

The radicalisation of the apostolic labour organisations or, to be more precise, of some of their most active members, placed the Spanish Catholic hierarchy in an awkward position. Clearly, it opposed politicisation of the apostolic labour organisations and their growing competition with the OS, but the bishops also had very strong reasons to defend these organisations against critics within the regime. To some extent, by expressing a social concern, Catholic labour activists were simply picking up on a refrain of various episcopal statements of the period. The bishops were likewise sensitive to a continuing need to ensure Catholic influence in Spanish society as a whole, and especially in the working class.

This concern had been evident already in the early 1950s. Uncomfortable with the Falange both over its doctrine and the control it exercised over the OS, the hierarchy stepped up its support for Catholic Action. By 1960, the argument over just how representative the *sindicatos verticales* were, culminated in an exchange of letters between the HOAC leadership and the Minister of the *Movimiento*, José Solís. The HOAC leaders complained about irregularities in syndical elections and obstacles placed in the way of some activists, and Solís harshly rebutted the charges and criticised the HOAC.[11] The various Catholic Action movements exerted their greatest influence in the decade after 1956. Their growing estrangement from the Franco regime caused problems for the Spanish hierarchy, leading most of the bishops eventually to move away from close identification with the regime. At the same time, relations between the hierarchy and the apostolic labour organisations became more and more tense.

Another aspect of the problem was the radicalisation of priests and clergy who worked either in working-class areas or where regionalist sentiment ran high, as in the Basque country or Cataluña. The phenomenon of worker priests had been imported from France in the 1950s and, not surprisingly, sharing the lives of workers and experiencing the repression of labour activists by the regime, or factory owners in collusion with the OS, helped radicalise many priests in the industrial belt around Madrid, Barcelona and other large cities. The involvement of individuals from religious orders in opposition activities became a serious problem for church and civil authorities beginning in the early 1960s. At first, the problem related simply to the use of parish halls and buildings as meeting places for organisations like the *Comisiones Obreras* and neighbourhood associations where opposition influence was predominant. Entry into church property was formally possible only with the permission of the priest or the bishop of the diocese. Symptomatically, the first national meeting of the *Comisiones Obreras* organisation took place at a religious house in June 1967 and when, five years later, police arrested the principal leaders of the CC.OO., they did so at a retreat house. Later, priests and members of religious orders lent more than logistical support to groups in opposition; they finally became members of these organisations. By 1968, arrested clergy were sent to a special ecclesiastical prison.

The radicalisation of clergy and Catholic Action militants was evident throughout Spain, but particularly in the Basque country and Cataluña where regional or separatist sentiment overlapped with more general anti-Franco sentiment. The politicisation of priests and clergy—their alienation aggravated by the presence of non-Basque, extremely conservative bishops— achieved dramatic proportions in the Basque country. A significant number of religious became actively involved in ETA groups and many others helped hide and otherwise protect the activists of the extreme Left. By the late 1960s, as the government responded to acts of terror and political demonstrations by declaring martial law and treating Euskadi more and more as an occupied territory, the situation worsened, resulting not only in the radicalisation of many Catholics but in the growth of tension between the national Church and the State.

The politics of opposition practised by Catalan Catholics, clergy and labour activists, who grew disaffected with the Franco regime, was more traditional and had a unique cultural component missing in the Basque country. As in other parts of Spain, churches and parish halls, particularly in the towns composing the industrial belt around Barcelona, became meeting places for *Comisiones Obreras* among others. Again, with many Catholics opting for opposition politics, the national hierarchy and the bishops of Cataluña had to defend those privileges the Church had been granted. This meant protecting those people who fell under the Catholic umbrella while avoiding a direct confrontation with the State.

Defending its privileges led to significant frictions between Church and State. The Catholic hierarchy gradually lost control and influence over many of the institutions fostered by it, as well as over important segments of Catholic opinion. What were some of the reasons for the change in the Catholic mentality in Spain? Of major importance were the profound social and economic changes which Spain experienced from the late 1950s. These changes turned Spain from a predominantly agrarian and rural country to one in which, by the early part of this decade, three-quarters of the active labour force was employed in the industrial or service sectors. Economic development led to dramatic shifts in demographic patterns and to tensions and psychological changes associated with modernisation. Millions of people migrated from the countryside to cities in Spain and throughout Europe with a significant decline in religious patterns. The Church did not maintain or develop a very effective presence in the working-class *barrios* which sprang up around the major cities. Indeed, in 1957 a HOAC survey among Spanish workers showed that 90 per cent of those answering described themselves as anti-clerical and only 8 per cent attended mass regularly.[12]

Those venturing into such areas, whether clergy or members of the apostolic labour organisations, were soon drawn into the vortex of social struggle. For them, the evident contradiction between church social doctrine on the one hand and the political/social reality of the Franco regime on the other, fuelled a profound sense of shame which gradually led to a commitment to opposition politics. Feeling their Church had betrayed the poor and working class, many Catholic activists joined one of the myriad Left and extreme Left groups of the 1960s.

If the Church and its related organisations could not help but be affected by the development and transformation of Spanish society, the effects were magnified by the role it played and the privileges it enjoyed under Franco. Considered a 'perfect' society, that is, one which functioned independently of the State, under the terms of the Concordat, the Church enjoyed freedom under the regime. This circumstance posed no real problem so long as the groups covered by that institutional umbrella were loyal to the State. But individual members of these groups moved away from the regime and the hierarchy lost control over entities like the apostolic labour organisation and the movement known as *Justicia y Paz*. Because of its broad social base and its privileges, the Church and the organisational network it had developed after 1939 had become a place where otherwise repressed social and political ideas could be raised and defended.[13] The hierarchy was thus caught in an irresolvable quandary over whether to defend organisations under its aegis which identified less and less with the Franco regime, or to reaffirm loyalty to the government as required under the terms of the Concordat.

Further impetus for change came from the Second Vatican Council which represented a clear break on the part of the international Church with what Avery Dulles has called its 'institutional model'. The shift away from identification with conservative social and political systems and toward the reassertion of church independence even from the most 'Catholic' of states had a profound impact on Spanish Catholicism. Spanish bishops had seen their support for the Francoist cause during and after the Civil War as an opportunity to enshrine in the mid-twentieth century the principles proclaimed centuries earlier by Rome, which were also the core of the values of the Spanish-led Counter-Reformation. The doctrines emanating from the Council and the various encyclicals issued by John XXIII and Paul VI undermined the authority of the Spanish hierarchy and gave critics within the Church authoritative sources upon which to base their attacks on the existing state of affairs.

THE PCE, THE PSOE AND THE CHURCH

Having described and analysed the evolution of the Catholic Church in Spain, we can turn our focus now to the efforts of the PCE and PSOE to deal with the Catholic question. Earlier, in discussing the Communist attitude toward the Catholic world during the Civil War, we emphasised the relative moderation of the PCE. However tactically inspired, this moderation continued in the aftermath of the Civil War, as the PCE maintained its broad-front orientation and calls for collaboration with Catholics. Fundamentally hostile to Catholicism, the Spanish Communists nevertheless looked for points of contact with representatives of the *sector católico* in their search for anti-fascist unity during World War II. In this, of course, they were neither innovative nor unique. Collaboration between Communists and Catholics was the order of the day among the Latin European Communist parties, not only in France and Portugal but even more in Italy where Catholic participation with Communists and Socialists in the Resistance after the signing of the September 1943 Armistice was an important political event. In Italy a *Movimento dei Cattolici Comunisti* emerged,[14] one of whose guiding lights, Franco Rodano, would be important in developing Italian Communist strategy toward the Christian Democratic party and in formulating 'the historic compromise'. The Spanish Communists looked more to their French counterparts for political guidance, but considered the Italian experience as a certain precursor of possibilities for their own country. The title of a 1947 article in *Nuestra Bandera* urged: 'Con los Católicos que quieren liquidar el fascismo en España, podemos y debemos estar unidos'.[15]

This was wishful thinking in Spain of the late 1940s. More favourable circumstances would emerge only in the wake of the definitive consolidation of the Franco regime and of the renovation of leadership and strategy in the PCE brought on by de-Stalinisation. The first uncertain steps in this direction came at the Fifth PCE Congress in November 1954 when delegates approved a reference to the effect that 'given the religious sentiment of a great part of the population' the party promised its support for a continuation of the state subsidy to the Church in the post-Franco era.[16] Nevertheless, anyone who took the trouble (if they could find a copy of it) to read the report delivered by Dolores Ibárruri in the name of the Central Committee, would have noticed that she stressed that the party was not and could not be neutral on the question of religion. 'We make and will make propaganda against religious prejudices,' she said, 'because religion goes against science and against progress and because the ruling classes have used religious beliefs to keep the workers and the popular masses under their domination.'[17]

The call for National Reconciliation issued by the PCE in June 1956 on the thirtieth anniversary of the Civil War represented a more significant step. The *Declaración del PCE por la Reconciliación Nacional* was a very important document: it was the first salvo fired by a newly dominant faction associated with Santiago Carrillo, the first real step taken by the Spanish Communist party to put the past behind and concentrate on building its presence in the post-Franco era. Its emphasis on overcoming the divisions of the Civil War, healing its scars and reconciliation, eventually struck a responsive chord in more liberal religious circles and among Catholics who desired restoration of political liberties.

The Communists did not greet the incorporation of Catholics in the opposition with unrestrained enthusiasm. They viewed the more moderate Christian Democratic groups (such as the *Unión Democrática Cristiana* founded in October 1956) and figures like the recently deposed Minister of Education, Joaquín Ruíz Giménez, with a mixture of approval, concern, and disdain. The PCE interpreted them as a sign of advanced decomposition in the Franco coalition, considering that their commitment to the anti-Franco opposition was shallow and that they would settle for cosmetic changes in the system as long as this included their legalisation. PCE leaders viewed more radical groups like the *Frente de Liberación Popular* (FLP) in a similar way.

They welcomed its participation in the anti-Franco struggle as further evidence that church support for the regime was wavering. But the PCE may have been stung by criticisms from the FLP that the Communist party was not revolutionary enough, and warned the working class not to be fooled by radical rhetoric.

In its search for contact with Catholics, the PCE did not hesitate to take advantage of what Santiago Carrillo called the 'guilt complex' of many Catholics about the Church's identification with the regime.[18] On the one hand, the Communist party was the *coco* (a Spanish expression signifying the forbidden fruit or a taboo subject); all Spaniards were warned of it as soon as they reached political maturity. The Franco regime lost no opportunity to brand all opposition activity, within the country as well as outside, as the product of a Communist conspiracy. This approach was effective in some ways but, at the same time, this contributed to a certain fascination with the Communists and, because of the supposed omnipresence of the PCE, that party became for many the symbol of opposition to the regime. Just as anti-Communism helped define those who supported Franco, so pro-Communism, or at least a sense of sympathy for the PCE, often characterised those Catholics who eventually moved into the ranks of the opposition. Indeed, as time went by, for many of those Catholics who were particularly anxious to purge themselves for the support their Church had lent Franco, there was no better way of demonstrating anti-regime convictions than by joining, supporting, or collaborating with the PCE.

Collaboration between Catholics and Communists in the labour movement was important for the PCE for two reasons. It allowed the party to develop an organisational structure and presence in a crucial sector of Spanish society, encouraging also a more flexible posture *vis-à-vis* the Catholic world as a whole. Members of the leadership or party intellectuals could publish articles in *Cuadernos para el Diálogo* edited by Ruíz Giménez, or have prominent Catholic lawyers defend them at their trials, but what really had an impact on otherwise sectarian working-class militants was the visible successes achieved through cooperation in the nascent *Comisiones Obreras*. While militants might not be particularly happy about dealing with Catholic labour activists, as good Leninists and therefore as political realists, they could hardly deny the benefits to the party. However grudging that admission, it allowed people like Santiago Carrillo, whose role in the development and evolution of PCE policy was vitally important, to press further in their quest for alliance with the Catholic sector.

Also important as mentioned above was the Second Vatican Council and the papacy of John XXIII. The ferocious anti-clericalism of the Latin European Left had always been matched by the anti-communism of the Catholic Church. The Vatican Council marked an important shift in this regard. Not only did some bishops talk openly about dialogue with Marxists, but in the encyclical *Pacem in Terris* issued in 1963 while the Council was in session, John XXIII distinguished between a theory that is false and in contradiction with Catholic doctrine (i.e. Marxism) and a practice which, although flowing from such theory, has elements which are 'good and worthy of approbation'.[19]

Two books by Carrillo published in 1965 and 1967—*Después de Franco, Qué?* and *Nuevos Enfoques a Problemas de Hoy* respectively—give us a sense of the substance and the limits (whether these resulted from his personal beliefs, from constraints imposed on him by the party he led, or some combination of the two) of the PCE's evolution on the Catholic question. In the first work,[20] the Secretary-General of the PCE presented what was by now the rather traditional Communist analysis of the Church in Spain. He noted, on the one hand, that the Church no longer identified itself with the regime, but warned that this did not mean it 'had passed, in its entirety, to democratic positions'. The Communists, he went on, had much in common with *un catolicismo democrático y progresista* and there was no reason why, despite the obvious differences in ideology, Marxists and Catholics could not collaborate in the construction of a more just society.

Carrillo focused in *Después de Franco, Qué?* on the various Christian Democratic movements then developing in Spain, both within and outside the confines of the regime. Most interestingly, Carrillo noted the presence in Spain of left-wing Christian Democrats and urged them not to participate in efforts to create an Italian-style Christian Democratic party. Such a party would inevitably become, Carrillo stressed, 'the organisation of the Spanish neo-Right and an instrument of the financial land-owning oligarchies'. This argument was significant because from it developed the Spanish variant of the *compromesso storico* formula. Carrillo subsequently became convinced that preventing the emergence of a Christian Democratic party was one of the keys to securing the *ruptura* from Francoism, with success in that venture meaning that only the PCE of the major Western European Communist parties had succeeded in leading Spain into the anti-monopolist phase of *democracia política y social*.

In *Nuevos Enfoques a Problemas de Hoy*[21], by contrast, Carrillo had to explain why the general strike predicted by the PCE had failed to materialise and perhaps because of this, his analyses were more detailed and emphasised the complexity of bringing about radical change. His assessment of the prospects for change in the Catholic world, for example, were more guarded, and his criticism of the Spanish hierarchy was stronger. Time had demonstrated that the bishops had no independence 'in the face of the fascist temporal power', he said. They allowed the Church to be little more than 'an instrument of state policy'. Against this Church that defended conservative political and social positions, there now stood another, the so-called *iglesia de los pobres*, Carrillo stressed. For the latter—and this represented a change in the Communist analysis—religion was no longer what Marx had called the opium of the people, having become, instead, a *factor de progreso*. This was, of course, not quite the same as calling religion a factor for revolution (as some radical Catholics or Catholic radicals would have liked) but it was a step in that direction. In any event, Carrillo insisted that the *superación de toda alienación* was an issue which could be put on the historical backburner, that differences between materialism and Christianity should not prevent collaboration against Franco and in the construction of socialism. Such an offer of alliance and cooperation in the phase of developing socialism had never before been extended by the PCE.

The ambiguities in Carrillo's formula made his defence of democracy less than satisfactory. Catholics could not have been reassured by his cryptic remarks that Communist parties had to find less 'primitive' ways for dealing with religion than had occurred in Eastern Europe.[22] The concessions that Carrillo appeared to make with one hand, he took back with the other, but we should not underestimate the significance of some positions implicitly or explicitly sketched out in *Nuevos Enfoques* which was important because it underscored a growing awareness on the part of Spanish Communist leaders about the complexities of leading a revolution in advanced industrial societies. This realisation led to the adoption of Gramscian notions about the importance of the struggle of ideas in those societies where a rapid thrust to power had been precluded. The Church would be a key battleground in the 'war of position' with the class enemy.

Despite its limits, the offer of a long-term perspective for collaboration to Catholics was also significant in that it meant that the PCE had moved beyond considering alliance with Catholics in the labour movement, the university or elsewhere, from an essentially defensive point of view whose principal objective was detaching the Catholic sector from the regime. That persisted, of course, but the PCE now went on record as expressing a belief in the possibility of an active presence by Catholics on the side of those who favoured socialism. Santiago Carrillo clearly articulated this view when he declared in an interview with *Le Monde* that socialism would come to Spain with a crucifix in one hand and a hammer and sickle in the other.[23] Implicit in that formulation was a change in the alliance patterns and strategies of the PCE: the party had begun to articulate a vision of the advance to socialism which tried to transcend the classical formula of polarisation.

Of the traditional organisations of the Left, it was the PCE which showed the greatest flexibility in dealing with Catholic radicals and devoted the most attention to the Catholic question. Except in the labour movement, however, this policy did not pay off as quickly as many Communist leaders had expected. Most radicalised Catholics rejected the Communist alternative as too moderate and struck out to find or found other groups which would live up to the ideal of revolutionary militance and action in which they had been inculcated by Francoist education and propaganda. Even as they lambasted the PCE, however, some of these individuals used the Communist party as their point of reference. When, in the late 1960s and early 1970s, the inevitable disillusion with Maoism, Castroism or Trotskyism set in, and the much-touted prospects for armed revolution did not materialise, some began to reconsider their position *vis-à-vis* the Communist party.

One such person was Alfonso Carlos Comín. A long-time radical political activist (who also happened to bear an uncanny resemblance to Jesus Christ as He is depicted in the West), Comín had been a member of the *Frente de Liberación Popular* and then in the early 1960s joined the Maoist Catalan splinter group known as *Bandera Roja*, finally joining the PCE in November 1974. From a numerical point of view, the fusion was only mildly significant (and, then, primarily in Cataluña where BR was active), but from a broader perspective it represented an important step for the Communist party, bolstering the credibility of the PCE with the Christian Marxist sector, many of whom now saw the Communists as ready to make important ideological and organisational concessions.

A first indication of this came in February 1975, less than three months after the fusion, when the Executive Committee issued a statement on the membership of Christians in the PCE.[24] Although the communique was short, there was no mistaking its thrust. Admitting that the evolution of the Church in Spain and the role Christians had played in the battles defending the interests of the working class 'had not always been valued and understood' by the party, the Executive Committee promised to 'assume and impel forward' the socialist option chosen by Christians. Turning to the more sensitive question of what the *cristiano comunista* could expect once he joined the party, it promised the 'believer' access to any and all positions of responsibility, 'without any type of discrimination, with the same rights and duties as any other militant'. With the support of Carrillo, Comín pushed for further explicit statements about the rights and duties of Catholic Communists. Nearly two years after his entry into the party, the Catalan party issued its own substantially stronger statement on the question.[25] Stressing that the party was 'confessionally neither atheist nor believer', the communique argued that those Catholics who joined the party had overcome 'the confusion between faith and politics'. The PSUC, said the statement, should accept these people *with* their faith, welcoming them because their participation in the organisation would reinforce its lay character. The identification of communism with atheism, it went on, was 'metaphysical' in nature and had supposed 'a reduction in the political-ideological horizon of Marxism'. Lest anyone miss the point, the penultimate paragraph in the declaration stated: 'What we have expressed here about the militance of Christians is the *policy of the entire party*, a new policy which in some aspects demands a greater knowledge of the evolution of the Church by the Party.'

The flexible activist posture the PCE adopted toward the Catholic world contrasted with the more rigid and passive position of the PSOE. The Socialists showed great hesitation when dealing with the Church, and often appeared in as much of a quandary as the Francoists and the Church hierarchy over how to respond to the radicalisation of Catholics. The PSOE did not begin to deal with the issue until the early 1970s when a group of new leaders, some of Catholic background, successfully challenged the exile leadership for control of the party. While the PSOE was by no means blind to the changes taking place in the Spanish Church during the 1960s or to the favourable (for the anti-Franco opposition) impact of Vatican II, only in 1967 did the party declare 'there was no contradiction between socialism and religion' and that socialism, although 'lay, . . . was not anti-religious'.[26] Indeed, the hesitation the PSOE betrayed toward Catholic activists, almost as much as its insensitivity to the regional problem, led many Catholics in Cataluña, Valencia, and the Basque country to join the numerous rival socialist groups springing up in the various regions.

So important was anti-clericalism to the Socialist party's identity that as late as 1974 an unseemly blast at 'deteriorated Catholic merchandise' (that is, Catholics wishing to join the PSOE) found its way into the pages of the weekly *El Socialista*.[27] The author insisted as to 'the versatility and ductility' of the

Church, responsible for 'centuries of oppression of our people' and whose change of heart indicated only 'the total disintegration' of the regime. Although articles so full of vitriol were exceptional, little real effort was made to conceal the fact that the Church was a target for the PSOE. 'Remember,' said an official statement on the Church and education, 'we heard the corporate voice of the Church asking for liberty only when *it* has been the object of persecution under some political system.'[28] The PSOE held, until a few months before the death of Franco, to the programme enunciated at the turn of the century to include 'the laicisation and nationalisation of (all) education'.[29] Even the Socialists' Transition Programme approved at the Suresnes Congress in September 1974, while accepting gradualism in this matter, insisted as to the ultimate need for an *escuela pública única* (compulsory public education).[30]

The reasons why the PSOE retained this anti-clerical dimension are varied. Its tradition of laicism was strong, dating from its founding in 1879. Prior to the Civil War, to be a Socialist (and more generally to be of the Left) was to be anti-clerical. Reinforced after 1939, this tradition remained an important part of the world-view of party activists decades later. Circumstances also made the Catholic question a historically less pressing problem for the Socialists than for the PCE. Despite its anti-clericalism, the party had done well in the pre-Civil War elections, garnering 117 out of 350 seats in the Chamber of Deputies in 1931 and 99 in the Popular Front elections of February 1936. While Socialist anti-clericalism helped attract a relatively broad electoral clientele, the PCE, by contrast, never developed either a mass electoral base or the self-confidence which flowed from that accomplishment. Prior to the Civil War, the PCE had been a marginal group whose influence derived from the fascination of some left-wing Socialists with the Russian Revolution; during that conflict, its weight grew, but primarily because the Soviet Union was the only major power supporting the Republic.[31] Unable to dislodge the Socialists and Anarchists from their position of pre-eminence among anti-clerical Spaniards, a category which included a significant proportion of the population, the Communists attracted popular antagonism not only because of their anti-clericalism but because of their anti-democratic traditions, and this rendered very difficult any effort to develop a mass appeal. How to convince the electorate of its democratic intentions was an issue whose impact the PSOE, as a member of that Socialist family which built the European democracies and welfare states after 1945, felt less and less as time went by. For the PSOE, then, the power of the Catholic Church represented a challenge to popular sovereignty, but Catholicism was not an obstacle to Socialist vote-getting. In many ways, then, they did not need to articulate a new approach toward Catholicism.

Contributing to the Socialist anti-clerical posture was the control the exiled leadership of Rodolfo Llopis exercised over the party. Unwilling to cede power to those Socialists living in Spain but unable (and perhaps unwilling) to develop a feel for changes in Spanish society, the Llopis leadership remained anchored to the cleavages and the postures of the past. These factors constrained a more active PSOE effort *vis-à-vis* the Catholic Church and subculture. And yet, since the party retained some organisational presence in

Spain (and in the mid-1960s when nuclei of the activists were present primarily in Asturias and the Basque country), it did experience the effects of changes in Spanish society. Particularly important in this respect was the growth of socialist ideas and the proliferation of socialist groups in the country. Many who joined these groups had developed their ideas after initial exposure to and a reaction against the dominant conservative strain of Spanish Catholic thought. The present PSOE Secretary General, Felipe González, is typical in this respect of many university students who came to 'social awareness' through an earlier exposure to Christianity. But the convergence between Catholics and socialists did not occur simply because of the support the Church gave Franco. There was also an anti-capitalist strain in Catholicism which began to re-emerge with force in the mid-twentieth century, especially after Vatican II. This radical version of Christianity had a strong anti-industrial, romantic and utopian component, and led its adherents in Spain to support a variety of extreme Left groups ranging from the FLP and its curious blend of primitive Christianity and Communism, through the *Alianza Sindical de Trabajadores* (AST), later to become the Maoist *Organización Revolucionaria de Trabajadores*, to the Catholic syndicalist *Unión Sindical Obrera* (USO).

While some in these movements joined the PCE, others eventually drew closer to the PSOE, especially when that party, re-invigorated under the leadership of González and benefiting from the continued uneasiness many leftists felt toward the Communists, expanded and consolidated its structures. It was easier for a Catholic to reconcile his religious beliefs with membership of the PSOE than of the PCE. The PSOE adhered to Marxist doctrine, but it had far fewer totalitarian pretensions and was much more tolerant of internal dissent than the Communist party. There were certainly important differences between Christians and Marxists on such issues as the causes and nature of human alienation and how to overcome it, but by the late 1960s a growing number of Marxist-inspired socialists had qualified their adherence to that ideology, seeing it primarily as a method of analysis. Arguably, for them, Marxism did not represent 'an unappealable negation of faith in Christ' and atheism was not a fundamental element in Marxism.[32] One might, then, accept the Marxist critique of the Church as an historical institution, of Christianity as a specific religion, and of magical religion, but reject the notion that Marxism could make any definitive judgement here and now about the essence and future of religion. A Marxist who considered himself a Christian would have one view on that problem, and a Marxist with no religious commitment, another.

By contrast, a chasm separated Christianity from Leninism and its view (inherited from Friedrich Engels) of Marxism as science, of physical matter as the only reality. The PCE could claim to have dropped many of its fundamental tenets, but a question remained as to the depth of that conversion, particularly in the lower levels of the party and among labour activists. This, as well as the political culture and internal life of the PCE, was a cause for reflection among left-wing Catholics, even when they refused to break their contacts with the Communists.

As occurred with the French Socialists after 1969, the integration of Leftist Catholics contributed to the consolidation and renewal of the PSOE. Those who had been active in Catholic Action and related apostolic organisations entered the PSOE in a staggered fashion. A first group, of whom Jerónimo Saavedra is an example, joined the PSOE and UGT (its trade union affiliate) in the late 1960s. Others, like former JOC leader Eugenio Royo, Enrique Barón and Eduardo Martín Toval, among many others, came from the USO in the mid-1970s, when it became apparent that neither the USO nor the various regional socialist groups in the FPS could challenge the resurgent PSOE. The consolidation of the PSOE and the growing awareness that a left-wing Christian Democratic party would not materialise, also led many of the younger Catholics grouped around *Cuadernos para el Diálogo*—like Gregorio Peces Barba, Leopoldo Torres and Pedro Altares—to join the ranks of the PSOE. The last group of former Catholic activists came from Enrique Tierno Galván's *Partido Socialista Popular* (PSP), when it fused with the PSOE in April 1978.

What was critical was the emergence of the PSOE. Then it was the entry of leftist Catholics into the party—like the development of groups such as *Cristianos por el Socialismo*, or the role played by priests and other religious in the anti-Franco opposition—that encouraged a reduction in the anti-clerical temper of the PSOE, even as the party continued to defend many aspects of its traditional, 'lay' programme.

THE CHURCH AND THE LEFT UP TO THE PRESENT

By the end of the Franco era, neither the Left nor the Church was eager for a confrontation but both were anxiously manoeuvring to limit the other's margin for influence. For its part, the Church had moved from a position as principal ideological pillar of the regime to a sometimes critical neutrality. The success the Church had in overcoming its crisis of identity in the 1960s caught the Communists and others on the Left off guard, for they had underestimated the adaptability of the hierarchy and the chances that it would extricate itself from the embrace of the State, while remaining an influential participant in the affairs of the country.

The Vatican was instrumental in compelling the Spanish Church to shift its orientation, judiciously using procedures adopted at the Second Vatican Council to help loosen Church-State ties and shift the balance of power within the hierarchy in favour of 'conciliar' bishops. The shift in the composition and attitude of the Spanish hierarchy did not come overnight—the process was complicated not only by the bickering among bishops in Spain but by the split which developed at the Vatican over the implementation of conciliar directives—but eventually a new episcopal majority gained ground, a majority much less overtly political than its predecessors and with more pastoral concerns.

The individual who best personified this reformist wing of the hierarchy was Cardinal Enrique y Tarancón. Elected president of the episcopal conference in March 1972, Tarancón was often accused by his right-wing critics of temporalism, a catchword implying that he did not consider regime structures eternal and was willing to voice criticism of specific social and economic policies. Nevertheless, Tarancón could hardly be described as a radical or as a person whose sympathies lay with the Left. He simply concluded (as had Paul

VI) that Spanish society had not remained frozen and that as a result Church-State relations could not either. Convinced that the Francoist political model would not long outlive its creator, Tarancón worked to protect the interests of the Church in the post-Franco era.[33] If he and other prelates turned a blind eye to meetings of organisations like the *Assemblea de Catalunya* or the *Comisiones Obreras* held on church properties and often refused to authorise government entry into those premises, it was not because they agreed with the objectives or programmes of those groups. Rather, in the words of Martín Patiño who as vicar-general of Madrid was principal assistant to Tarancón, it was because '[The Church] felt obliged to allow them under our roof, if [it] did not wish to lose touch with the people'.[34]

The shift in the episcopal balance of power led to greater tension between Church and State in Spain. Cries of 'Tarancón, al paredón!' (Tarancón, to the firing squad!) became commonplace at rallies organised by the extreme Right in support of the Franco government. But, while the Church did not shirk from confrontation when its fundamental interests were at stake—as in March 1974 when the Arias Navarro government arrested the bishop of Bilbao after he delivered a homily asking for greater autonomy and liberties for the Basque region—neither did it seek out issues over which to break with the regime. This might have served the purposes of the opposition, but it was not what church leaders had in mind. They accepted political change primarily because church interests could best be protected under those circumstances. There were after all privileges like the government subsidy to the clergy (80 per cent of the priests in the country received a salary of 180,000 pesetas yearly), the virtual monopoly in the field of primary and secondary education, and the moneys granted for repair and construction of ecclesiastical buildings, all of which came from the state treasury.[35] By early 1977, a broad consensus had developed among the Spanish bishops that the Church should refrain from taking sides in the forthcoming parliamentary elections. Nevertheless, as suggested by the various statements reminding Catholics not to vote for those parties 'whose programmes are incompatible with the faith' or warning them against the possibility that behind apparently acceptable programmes lay 'an ideology or interests . . . [which] might be incompatible with Christian thought', this decision did not and could not result in neutrality.[36] Rather, it obeyed imperatives of realism and shrewd judgement. Various polls taken in late 1976 and early 1977 indicated that Spaniards were by and large quite conservative politically (on a Left-Right scale, they compared to the West Germans). With the general political situation apparently under control, the bishops did not wish to endanger the image, carefully cultivated since the early 1970s, that they too desired political democracy. A more vocal stance against the Left might endanger that credibility. Moreover, the episcopate was itself divided as to which party to support and hesitated in any case to tie the Church's fate to one party.

One notable consequence of this episcopal inhibition was the decision not to sponsor a Christian Democratic party. At one level, this outcome, which had been a major Communist party objective in the preceding decade, encouraged the Left. It indicated how much things had changed in Spain and in Western Europe more generally since the end of World War II when the

Church had not hesitated to put its prestige behind the Christian Democratic parties in an anti-Communist campaign. But, in the ensuing decades, the international climate had changed. The Cold War had declined and détente was still alive. Domestically, the Catholic Church had been embarrassed by its close ties to the Franco regime, and the radicalisation of religious and lay people in working-class areas, in Cataluña and in the Basque country, made discipline difficult to enforce. In this respect, Spain in the 1970s presented a contrast to Italy in the immediate post-war period. There, the Catholic Church had a cohesive Catholic Action movement and parish structure to put at the disposal of the Christian Democratic party. In Spain, however, the apostolic organisations underwent a radicalisation during the 1960s which led to their disintegration. When, in April 1968, most Catholic Action leaders resigned, the episcopate elaborated new statutes placing the HOAC under direct episcopal control and supervision. Catholic Action subsequently atrophied. The diminution in popular religiosity,[37] as well as the proliferation of regional groups, made the task of creating a cohesive Christian Democratic party very difficult. The ideological diversity was very evident among the various Christian Democratic groups—ranging from the pro-regime *Unión Democrática Española* headed by former Minister of Education Federico Silva Muñoz in José María Gil Robles' *Federación Popular Democrática*, Right-of-Centre but in the moderate opposition, to the *Izquierda Demócratica Cristiana* of Fernando Alvarez de Miranda which refused to make the legalisation of the PCE the linchpin of negotiations with the government, and extending on the Left to Ruíz Giménez and his *Izquierda Democrática*. In addition, the personal differences separating the most prominent of these individuals complicated the situation, confirming the perspicacity of the wag who remarked: 'With all due respect, these, not even God can unite.'

And yet, the absence of a viable Christian Democratic party in post-Franco Spain did not redound entirely to the advantage of the Left. Christian Democracy was not the only possible claimant to the political and social Centre. Adolfo Suárez and the UCD, capitalising on his success as architect of the transition, occupied that space in June 1977, and those Christian Democrats (with the exception of the PNV in the Basque country) who ran against the UCD suffered a devastating defeat at the polls, receiving less than 2 per cent of the national vote and not electing a single deputy. The UCD thus emerged as the functional equivalent of Christian Democracy in Spain. Whereas the post-World War II Italian pattern showed the DC relying initially for its support on the organisational structure provided by the Church and only later 'colonising' the bureaucracy, the UCD reversed the pattern. Because it did not have official Church backing and with the apostolic organisations in disarray, the *Unión de Centro* built itself first around the bureaucracy and the state apparatus. In some respects, its voters resembled those of the *Democrazia Cristiana*. Nearly 62 per cent were 'very good' or 'practising' Catholics, (compared to some 55 per cent 'regular practising' in Italy), while 34 per cent had 'irregular' attendance or were 'non-practising'.[38] Surprisingly, UCD voters were more likely, by a 63-58 per cent margin, than those of the *Coalición Democrática* (the major right-wing party headed by former Minister of the Interior, Manuel Fraga Iribarne) to view the role of the

Catholic Church in Spain as 'beneficial,' an anomaly probably reflecting conservative displeasure with the changes in the Church.[39] Despite these similarities with Christian Democracy, the UCD is a variant of a Centrist, catch-all party. A coalition of some fourteen groups and smaller parties, the UCD has been described as 'consociational'.[40] The religious cleavage, then, passes through the UCD, and this explains the tensions within that party over divorce and educational legislation. A resurgence in conflict over religious issues might lead not only to a realignment of and polarisation of the party system but to the demise of the UCD itself.

The tempering of the religious cleavage has contributed to the peaceful transition from authoritarianism and to the still-fragile consolidation of democracy in Spain, but there remains significant disruptive potential. One study shows the Spanish electorate as polarised between those who consider themselves 'very good' or 'practising' Catholics (some 42 per cent of the total) and the 17 per cent who view themselves as 'indifferent' or 'atheist'.[41] After the December referendum approving the Constitution, the Church moved toward a more active role in politics. It intervened in the March 1979 parliamentary elections and later increased pressure on Suárez (whose resignation in January 1981 some blamed on machinations by church officials in league with the *sector crítico* of the UCD) over divorce and other issues.[42]

Nevertheless, the salience of religion as an issue remains low, or at least, overshadowed by the regional cleavage. Some students of Spanish politics have found that religiosity today, rather than exacerbating conflicts, 'contributes to the torpor of political conflict'.[43] The effect may be temporary, but the results of the survey they carried out suggest that the devout have not been 'disposed to activism . . . tend[ing] to be quiescent instead of fanatical'. 'The religious cleavage' then, 'involves not so much an across-the-board pitting of the Right against the Left . . . as it does a continuum of political involvement versus lethargy.' Today, in contrast to the pre-1936 situation, religiosity is linked to apathy, not mobilisation. This finding is not so surprising, if we remember the lingering effects of the de-mobilisation caused by the Franco regime and the diminished capacity and will of the Church to mobilise its supporters. It does indicate, however, that a conservative reservoir exists in Spain.

Religion, then, has moved from the centre stage of political conflict, but its influence remains important for both the Right and the Left. At the elite level, the emergence of *Cristianos por el Socialismo*, the participation of prominent Catholics such as Francisco García Salve and (the recently deceased) Alfonso Carlos Comín in the highest policy-making bodies of the PCE, and the entry of former Catholic activists into the PSOE, were evidence of a fragmentation in the Catholic world. But the controlled transition to democracy and the consolidation, with all its vicissitudes, of Spanish 'centrism', were important in preventing this disaggregation from dramatically altering mass perceptions. There remains, moreover, an important relationship between religion and political participation or choice. Although there are competing interpretations of this relationship,[44] few dispute its existence. A cursory glance at survey data confirms its relevance. There is a linear progression between level of religiosity and self-ranking on a Left-Right, one-to-ten scale:

those who stand outside the Church place themselves at 3.5; the 'non-practising' at 4.0; the 'rarely' practising at 4.4; the 'sometimes' practising at 5.2; and the 'often' practising at 5.6.[45] Religiosity with a correlation of 0.34 is a better predictor of political orientations than class identification which correlates at 0.22.[46]

The Left still has difficulty attracting Catholic votes. Among those Spaniards indicating a party preference, only 24 and 11.8 per cent of the PSOE and PCE identifiers described themselves as 'very good' or 'practising' Catholics.[47] Among voters in the March 1979 parliamentary elections, only 36.1 per cent of those voting for the PSOE and 18.4 per cent of Communist voters described themselves as 'practising'.[48] This represented a setback not only for the Communists—who had expected a much quicker payoff for their overtures to Catholics—but also for the PSOE. The Socialists did surprisingly well in the June 1977 elections and are the principal opposition party in the country. But, despite the relatively slim margin separating them from the UCD (the PSOE received 30 per cent of the vote in 1979 compared to 34 per cent for the *Centro*), the electoral system over-represents rural, conservative and Catholic Spain, putting the Socialists at a decided disadvantage. Socialist efforts to project a moderate image have met with some success thus far, as is evidenced by the nearly 20 per cent of individuals who voted for the UCD in 1979 indicating the PSOE as a second choice.[49] Moreover, reflecting the Socialist ability to attract a rather heterogeneous audience, those who express a preference for the PSOE are almost evenly divided in their opinions as to the role of the Church in Spanish society: 27.5 per cent see that influence as 'beneficial'; 33.5 per cent see 'no influence'; and 35.3 per cent see it as 'harmful'.[50] But the PSOE still runs up against an obstacle in the Catholic voter. Nearly 9 per cent of those who would have voted for the PSOE as a second choice in the 1979 elections decided against this course because they perceived the Socialist programme to be at variance with their religious ideas.[51] Of those potential PSOE voters who described themselves as 'practising' Catholics, 12.7 per cent did not vote for the PSOE for reasons relating to religion.[52]

The PSOE has been careful not to press too far on the Catholic issue, but its adamant insistence on Church-State separation, an end to the state subsidy for schools run by religious orders, a liberal divorce law, and a statute legalising abortion have alienated numerous devout Catholics. This reflects the broader problem the Socialists face: how to reconcile their historical antagonism to the Franco regime and its social-religious values with an acceptance of (and, indeed, active collaboration in) the reformist transformation of its structures. One manifestation of this ambivalence (ultimately resolved by a vote in favour of the Constitution as a whole) was in the Socialist call for a republic. Church-State questions have also brought this problem to the fore as when the PSOE, seizing on a UCD decision to amend an agreed-upon constitutional text by explicitly referring to the Catholic Church, walked out of the Constitutional Commission deliberations. This may have been mere posturing on the part of the PSOE, and it is true that on the educational question, the party has moderated its demands considerably when compared to those sketched out in its 1976 programme.[53] But this neither earns the PSOE the support of Catholic parents' groups (like the *Confederación Española de Asociaciones de Padres de Familia y Padres de Alumnos*) nor eases the worry of those who see the PSOE as favouring the nationalisation of all schools.

The Communists were notably less successful than the Socialists in attracting Catholic voters, and this suggests one of the reasons why the PCE has not done well in the two elections of the post-Franco era. Blinded perhaps by the audacity (in the Spanish context) of their efforts during the preceding two decades, the PCE leadership underestimated the room for manoeuvre at the disposal of the reformist faction in the Church hierarchy. Moreover, perhaps because they had their eyes too fixed on the Italian experience, and because they believed too long that no reform of the Franco regime was possible from within, the Communists made the mistake of thinking that if only a Christian Democratic party could be prevented from occupying the Centre in Spain, the PCE could easily assume a dominant position on the Left and in the country as a whole.

After its legalisation in April 1977 and during the debates on the new Constitution, the PCE maintained a low profile on the religious question. In contrast to the PSOE, which withdrew from the Constitutional Commission over the wording of Article 16, the Communists voted with the UCD, the Popular Alliance, the Basque and Catalan nationalists, in favour of the revised text. As Santiago Carrillo aptly put it, 'We have been present during this vote as spectators, but (we are) not indifferent.' The PCE, he went on, 'did not deduce any discrimination in favour of the Catholic Church from [its] mention in the Constitution'.[54] Be that as it may, the Communist posture during the constitutional debate aimed at defusing the Catholic issue and strengthening the democratic credentials of the PCE. Although the Communists behaved in a statesmanlike manner on this issue and may reap dividends from this policy in the longer run, the immediate payoff was slim. As we have seen, only 18.4 per cent of those who voted for the Communists in March 1979 described themselves as 'practising,' a proportion nevertheless higher than that of the PCI in 1976 when 13.4 per cent of its voters attended church 'at least once a week' or 'often during the year'.[55] Given the relationship between religion and party choice, as well as the probably slow transformation in the religious cleavage, the Communists have a difficult road ahead before assuaging the fears of Spanish Catholics. One measure of the PCE's progress in that direction is the number of people who see no incompatibility between Catholicism and Communism. In 1977, Spaniards were asked the question 'Can one be a good Communist and a good Catholic at the same time?' and 32 per cent answered in the affirmative and 56 per cent in the negative, a distribution which approximates to that of Italy in 1963.[56]

CONCLUSION

This essay has explored the evolution in the relationship between the Left and Catholicism in Spain. Although Catholicism remains an important conditioning factor in national politics, the virulence of the cleavage associated with it has been tempered in the last four decades. Changes in the domestic and international Church, in Spanish society, and within the Left have all contributed to this transformation. In the post-Franco era, anxious to prevent a replay of the 1930s when disputes over religion contributed decisively to the Civil War, the Church and the Left have sought to keep these divisions from breaking a still-fragile democratic order. Still capable of arousing strong passions, as the recent tensions over divorce legislation indicate, the religious question will demand careful handling by church and party elites in the years to come. For a Left eager to assume the reins of government, Catholicism remains an important obstacle; a major condition for its victory at the polls will be continued accommodation and adaptation to the sociological realities of Spanish Catholicism.

NOTES

Parts of this essay will appear in 1982 in a book entitled *Communism and Political Change in Spain* to be published by Indiana University Press.

1. The phrase may be found in David Martin's 'The Religious Condition of Europe', in Salvador Giner and Margaret Scotford Archer (eds.), *Contemporary Europe, Social Structures and Cultural Patterns*. London: Routledge and Kegan Paul, 1978, pp. 228-87.
2. Spain had 50 per cent of its active population in 1939 engaged in agriculture; by 1977 that proportion had dropped to 20.7 per cent. José Félix Tezanos, *Estructura de Clases y Conflictos de Poder en la España Postfranquista*. Madrid: Cuadernos para el Diálogo, 1978, p. 233.
3. Juan Linz, 'Europe's Southern Frontier; Evolving Trends Toward What?', *Daedalus*, Vol.108, No. 1, (Winter 1979), p. 180.
4. Gerald Brenan, *The Spanish Labyrinth*. New York and London: Cambridge University Press, 1943, pp. 37-56, presents a brilliant analysis of the Church in Spanish society.
5. Reyes Mate Rupérez and J.M. Arbeloa, 'La Crítica de la Religión en el Socialismo Español', *Sistema*, No. 31, (July 1979), pp. 85-104.
6. See, for example, José Díaz, *Tres Años de Lucha*. Paris: Colección Ebro, 1970, p. 313; on the question of expropriation, see pp. 163-4.
7. The text, entitled, 'Episcopado Español a los Obispos de Todo el Mundo: Sobre la Guerra de España', may be found in Jesús Iribarren (ed.), *Documentos Colectivos del Episcopado Español, 1870-1974*. Madrid: Editorial Católica, 1974, pp. 220-42.
8. Max Gallo, *Historia de la España Franquista*. Paris: Ediciones Ruedo Ibérico, 1972, p. 137 for the phrase and Juan José Ruíz Rico, *El Papel Política de la Iglesia Católica en la España de Franco*. Madrid: Editorial Tecnos, 1977.
9. See José Chao, *Después de Franco, España*, Madrid: Ediciones Fellmar, 1976, pp. 69-72 for an exhaustive list of those measures. Popularisation of the term 'National Catholic' is attributed to José María González Ruíz by Fernando Urbina in 'Formas de Vida de la Iglesia en España: 1939-1975', in Rafael Belda *et al.*, *Iglesia y Sociedad en España, 1939-1975*. Madrid: Editorial Popular, 1977, p.85. Use of it goes back to the 1940s, but without the later connotations.
10. Ramón Chao, *La Iglesia en el Franquismo*. Madrid: Ediciones Fellmar, 1976, p. 83.
11. José Castaño Colomer, *La JOC en España (1946-1970)*. Salamanca: Ediciones Sígueme, 1978, pp. 77-81.
12. William P. Ebenstein, *Church and State under Franco*. Research Monograph No. 8, Center of International Studies, Woodrow Wilson School of Public and International Affairs, Princeton University, 1960.
13. The point is developed by Guy Hermet in 'Les Fonctions Politiques des organisations religieuses dans les régimes à pluralisme limité', *Revue Française de Science Politique* Vol.XXIII, June 1973, pp.439-73.
14. See Carlo Felice Casula, *Cattolici-Comunisti e sinistra cristiana, 1938-45*. Bologna: Il Mulino, 1976.
15. Félix Montiel in *Nuestra Bandera*, No.15, (February 1947), pp. 127-38.

16. *Programa del Partido Comunista de España (V Congreso)* (1954), p.13.
17. Dolores Ibárrui, *Informe del CC al Quinto Congreso del PCE.* (1954). pp. 98, 152.
18. He used the phrase in the book/interview *Demain l'Espagne.* Paris: Editions du Seuil, 1974, p. 166.
19. John XXIII, *Pacem in Terris.* New York: Paulist Press, 1963, paragraphs 159-60 (edited by William J. Gibbons, S.J.).
20. Santiago Carrillo, *Después de Franco, Qué?.* Paris: Editions Sociales, 1965, pp. 75-83.
21. Santiago Carrillo, *Nuevos Enfoques a Problemas de Hoy.* Paris: Editions Sociales, 1967, pp. 116-39.
22. Ibid., pp. 121-2.
23. *Le Monde*, 4 November, 1970. Carrillo had made a similar formulation in late 1963, at a PCE Central Committee plenum. See *Los Marxistas Españoles y la Religión.* Madrid: Editorial Cuadernos para el Diálogo, 1977, p. 84.
24. *Mundo Obrero*, 19 March, 1975.
25. 'Declaración del Comité Central del Partit Socialista Unificat de Catalunya' dated September 1976. Also to be found in the Appendix, pp. 201-11, of Alfonso Carlos Comín, *Cristianos en el Partido, Comunistas en la Iglesia.* Barcelona: Editorial Laia, 1977.
26. The quotes are from Victor Manuel Arbeloa, 'Posiciones políticas ante el cristianismo y la Iglesia', *Pastoral Misionera*, Vol.XI, No. 8, (November-December 1975), p. 729.
27. See the article by Anibal in *El Socialista*, second half January 1974. It was in answer to an earlier one by J. Borrás in *El Socialista*, second half November 1973 and elicited a response from B. Alonso in the same paper, issue of second half February 1974.
28. *El Socialista*, second half January 1975.
29. *El Socialista*, first half June 1975.
30. *Programa de Transición: La Enseñanza* (27th PSOE Congress, 1974), p.6.
31. See the chapter 'The Past as Prelude' in Eusebio Mujal-León, *Communism and Political Change in Spain.* Bloomington, Indiana: Indiana University Press, forthcoming.
32. Reyes Mate, *El Desafío Socialista.* Salamanca: Ediciones Sígueme, 1975, p. 148.
33. This theme is evident in the letters he issued in the Madrid diocese and collected under the title *Los Cristianos y la Política.* Madrid: Servicio Editorial del Arzobispado de Madrid-Alcalá, 1977. Also of interest is the Tarancón interview with *Mundo* (Barcelona), 28 February, 1976.
34. Cited in Edouard Bailby, *España Hacia la Democracia?* Barcelona: Editorial Argos, 1977, p. 97.
35. The estimate of priests' salaries is made in *Cambio 16* (Madrid), 18 September 1977. During the period 1939-74, the state spent 4.5 billion pesetas on ecclesiastical buildings. *El Europeo* (Madrid), 26 July, 1975.
36. The text of this statement by the Permanent Commission of the Episcopal Conference is in *El País*, 23 April 1977.
37. For example, the *Síntesis Actualizada del III Informe FOESSA 1978.* Madrid: Euramérica, 1978, p. 306, reported that the proportion of believers had dropped from 80 per cent in 1970 to 63 per cent in 1975. Of interest too is the discussion in Chapters 3-5 in Paulina Almerich *et al.*, *Cambio Social y Religión en España.* Barcelona: Editorial Fontanella, 1975.
38. Richard Gunther, Giacomo Sani, and Goldie Shabad, 'Party Strategies and Mass Cleavages in the 1979 Spanish Election', a paper presented at the 1980 Annual Meeting of the American Political Science Association, p. 9. In a manuscript entitled, 'Religion and Politics in Spain' (n.p., n.d.), p. 26, Juan Linz has noted that the sizeable 'non-practising contingent of UCD voters probably inhibits the *Centro* from adopting too pro-Church a position on many issues'.
39. On the proportions, see Gunther *et al.*, p. 11.
40. See the excellent article by Carlos Huneuus of Heidelberg University entitled 'La Unión de Centro Democrático, un partido consocional', *Revista de Política Comparada*, No. 3, (Winter 1980-81), pp. 163-92.
41. Gunther *et al.*, p. 8.
42. *El País*, January 1981, p. 31.
43. Peter McDonough and Antonio López Pina, 'Democracy and Disenchantment in Spanish Politics', in Paul Allen Beck *et al.* (eds.), *Mass Politics in Industrial Societies.* Princeton: Princeton University Press, forthcoming, pp. 15 and 37.

44. One form of the argument is made by Linz in the *Daedalus* article cited earlier; a variation, by Antonio López Pina and Peter McDonough in 'Religiosity and Ideology in Spain', a paper presented at the Conference of Europeanists, March 1979, pp. 3-4. The reader is also referred to Guy Michelat and Michel Simon, 'Religion, Class, and Politics', *Comparative Politics*, Vol. X, No. 1, (October 1977), pp. 159-86, and to Arend Lijphart, 'Religious vs. Linguistic vs. Class Voting: The "Crucial Experiment" of Comparing Belgium, Canada, South Africa, and Switzerland', *American Political Science Review*, Vol.73, No. 2 (June 1979), pp. 442-58.
45. Samuel Barnes, Antonio López Pina, and Peter McDonough, 'The Spanish Public in Transition', *British Journal of Political Science*, Vol. 11, No. 1, (January 1981), p. 57.
46. Ibid.
47. Gunther *et al.*, p. 9.
48. José Félix Tezanos, 'El Espacio político y sociológico del socialismo español', *Sistema*, No. 32, (September 1979), p. 60.
49. Ibid., p. 69.
50. Gunther *et al.*, p. 11.
51. Tezanos, 'El Espacio político', p. 70.
52. Ibid., p. 71.
53. Contrast the 1976 programme and the essay 'Enseñanza y Socialismo' by Luis Gómez Llorente in Equipo Jaime Vera (eds.), *La Alternativa Socialista del PSOE*. Madrid: Cuadernos para el Diálogo, 1777, pp. 107-36, with the statement in Felipe González, *Socialismo es Libertad*. Barcelona: Galbá Ediciones, 1978, pp. 133-47.

Christian Militants in the French Left

Renaud Dulong

'And no man putteth new wine into old bottles; else the new wine will burst the bottles, and be spilled, and the bottles shall perish.'

The Gospel according to St. Luke, 5:37

POLITICAL CLEAVAGES

From the events of May-June 1968 to the 1978 legislative elections, the possibility of the Left's accession to power transformed both the issues at stake and the behaviour of parties on the French political scene. As often noted, one of the features of this change has been the appearance of Christians in the ranks of a traditionally anti-clerical Left. This has not been due to a major re-orientation of Catholic opinion—indeed, the phenomenon hardly shows up at all in voting patterns, even in the election to the presidency of François Mitterrand. Rather it reflects a change restricted to Catholic activists. Political debates in both major left-wing parties—the Communist party and the Socialist party—clearly indicate the penetration of Christians in their respective camps and the reservations this has provoked among their secular militants. As for the *Parti socialiste unifié* and groups of the far-Left, they both owe their political influence and rank and file strength largely to the support provided by Christian militancy.

The arrival of Christians on the Left in France has been far from uniform. Not only have they spread out among existing organisations—in numbers difficult to assess[1]—but their specific approach and influence have significantly altered the profile of the Left itself in certain places. The integration of Christians into the French Left can be depicted in terms of its three traditional cleavages:

(a) Entry into the French Communist Party, which had in the past occurred via CGT militancy, was increasingly involving other trade unionists—from the CFDT in particular—as well as the non-unionised. Furthermore, Christian militants began to retain and assert a religious identity that previous generations of Christians who had moved into the PCF had virtually abandoned.[2]

(b) Within the PS, Christian militants rallied around two of the factions that emerged after the 1974 presidential election: the Rocard tendency from the PSU and Chevènement's CERES. These Christians came principally from the CFDT—some having made a transition through the PSU and the far-Left—but also from the civic movements and sometimes directly from Christian organisations.[3]

(c) Finally, there has been an important Christian contribution to the political ferment outside these major parties, on a far-Left where political instability has been the rule and organised elements difficult to isolate.

It might be thought that this dispersal of Christians among groups on the Left has been the result of ideological or strategic choices. The fact that other Catholic militants have become active on the Right might seem to justify such an explanation.[4] The crisis of the Church would thus have freed Christians to a point where they have become open to the entire range of political options. This notion conveys rather well the impression given by the militants themselves when they describe their political trajectories. However, it is not supported by the fact—recognised by all observers of French politics—that the politicisation of Christians to the Left has entailed a significant transformation of the Left's mobilising themes, because of the impact of the specific Christian sensibilities. I intend to argue, therefore, the opposite thesis—that the distribution of Christians in various political camps, far from reflecting the contours of the French political scene in general, results from the ways in which specific types of militants made the transition from religious commitment to political activity.

The politicisation of young Christians, I will argue, has been determined more by changes in the Church between the end of World War II and 1968—in particular in the Catholic Action movements—than by changes in the sphere of politics. Changes in the Catholic world took place in ways that conferred different meanings on membership in various Catholic organisations and gave rise to different forms of militancy. These contrasts are ultimately accounted for by the role of the Church in different socio-political settings. This causal link worked through processes internal to the religious sphere which this analysis will attempt to elucidate. In so doing we will confront the paradox that an organisation operating in a working-class Marxist milieu has remained loyal to traditional faith and to the Catholic hierarchy, while the organisation operating in a rural, traditionally Catholic setting has developed a critique of religion.

First, I will compare two extreme types of militant—those who joined the Communists and those who tended towards the far-Left—a cleavage due less to ideological issues than to a particular attitude towards institutions. The division between pro- and anti-Communist Christians has been based not so much on the question of Marxism as such—whether they are Communist, Socialist or on the far-Left, all left-wing Christians are Marxists—but on a cleavage that is implicit in the interaction of political groups with the French institutional system. A Communist respects established institutions even when he is struggling to transform them. The rationale of the far-Left, in contrast, is a wide-ranging critique of all institutions: State, School, Church, Family, etc. Of course, the ideological cleavage has marked political practices in the sense that the PCF apparatus itself constitutes one of these institutions; to steer clear of this apparatus, and, more generally, to avoid any institutionalised activity, Christians of the far-Left have scattered themselves among small and changing groups. Rather than classifying Christian militants as Left or far-Left, it is more salient to consider them in terms of a distinction between organisational and anti-institutional activists.

There is yet another type of militant—by far the most important group of individuals to have emerged from Catholic militancy—those now in the Socialist Party. This analysis will account for the intermediary position of this group, which vacillates both ideologically and in political practice between the organisational and anti-institutional poles. In the third part, I will discuss the demands which have made the presence of Christians felt in the Socialist camp and show that the movement for *autogestion* (self-management) has its roots in the institutional crisis experienced by the Catholic community. *Autogestion* provides perhaps the best example of the transfer of an issue from the religious to the political sphere.

First, it is essential to note that what is at stake is not so much the Church as such, as its position in a rural society experiencing social differentiation. My argument will be based on a comparison of two Catholic Action movements. These differ in terms of recruitment and their wider social settings: the first, a local branch of the JAC—*Jeunesse Agricole Chrétienne*[5]—draws its members from rural youth in Brittany; the second, a local branch of the JOC—*Jeunesse Ouvrière Catholique*—from the working-class youth of a Parisian suburb.[6] Since the characteristics of both localities described are common to many other areas—the evolution of agricultural Brittany has been shared by much of rural France, and the Parisian suburbs have not been the only working-class conurbation with powerful Marxist organisations—the analysis might be generalised for French society as a whole. But this would require a more complex explanation, for the Church does not have the same position of power in the whole of rural France as it has in Brittany, and in other working-class areas the weight of the CGT and the Communist Party can be counterbalanced by that of less radical organisations, even sometimes by that of the Church.

A brief word about the approach. The reader may consider with some justification that the study oversimplifies reality, since I have controlled both the number of contextual variables under analysis and the angle of enquiry. This has excluded perhaps a number of explanations that the inclusion of other variables might have suggested, and left unexplored other hypotheses suggested by the data at hand. But my concern has not been to describe the recent evolution of the relationship between Catholicism and the Left in France—a subject on which a great deal of ink has flowed already—but to formulate ideal types of the transition from religion to politics.[7]

THE JAC: A PRACTICAL CRITICISM OF RELIGION

The JAC in Brittany evolved in the context of a society experiencing major upheavals. These primarily concerned the structures of the agricultural economy and, in consequence, the entire rural social system. From an economic point of view, this evolution has involved the transition from a system of regional production based on dispersed and autonomous units of mixed-farming and animal-raising to one of organised and intensive production—specialising in animal-raising—of market-oriented commodities. The integration of the Breton economy into that of the rest of France and Europe has involved the substitution of the capitalist logic for one of family self-sufficiency. From the social point of view, it is this change of logic that in turn has determined a closer integration of Breton society with the wider system of norms and values of France. The impact of this process has varied according to the social group concerned. What for some has meant the disintegration of a way of life, a loss of regional identity and subservience to the capitalist system, has represented for others an access to modernity. The main feature of this society has been its subjection to a process of differentiation: what had appeared previously as a homogeneous collection of interrelated communities has broken up into a series of economically competing groups. The traditional political cleavage between Left and Right based on the religious school question has been replaced in part by the new issues of the national scene and by the problems posed by the evolution of the region.

The peasantry has constituted the major group affected by this change. Three phases can be distinguished. In the first, from the end of World War II until 1958-9, only production methods were concerned. It was a question of modernising agriculture, and that implied the specialisation of farming activities, the mechanisation of labour and production for the market. This revolution of productive structures produced a boost in output that outpaced the capacities of the commercial network. At that point a second period began in which technical questions receded before a new preoccupation with issues concerning agricultural organisations, the central question no longer being modernity but the need to control the economy; and the means required had had to be secured from the State. This period was characterised by impressive peasant demonstrations in 1961 and 1962 against the State. It was also a period of revival of agricultural syndicalism and saw the transition from a purely 'professional' to a politically active unionism. Furthermore, contacts developed with regional working-class organisations which, on the 8 May 1968, produced a common day of action bringing the period to a close. What emerged was the division of a peasantry until then apparently united. This occurred for two reasons: on the one hand, the productive system no longer seemed to be evolving to the equal benefit of all; the 'large' peasants were accused of building their fortunes on the backs of the 'small'. At the same time, new political cleavages were appearing on the basis of this division, a fringe group of militants denouncing more and more stridently the capitalist system, the power of the State and the forms these were taking at the local level.[8]

In fact, this sequence spans a confrontation of three generations. The generation of the 1950s imposed technical change and trade union revival on its predecessor. In turn, it found itself in conflict with the next generation—economically less secure and thus ideologically more radical. The structural transformation favouring the development of the first had rendered more difficult the circumstances in which the second had to establish itself. These conflicts gradually became set in well-defined union and political cleavages. Confronting the professional unionism that remained strong in the Chambers of Agriculture, the new unionism of the FDSEA and CDJA[9] became the terrain first of organisation, then of confrontation, of the two new generations. The latter would finally found the 'peasant-workers' movement; and the political cleavages emerged with the involvement of the first generation in the MRP and with Gaullism, of the second in the Socialist Party—with a fringe group in the Giscardian *Parti Républicain*—and the third in the PSU and on the far-Left.

The JAC clearly played a decisive role in this evolution. The young farmers who became the prime movers in the peasant movement had been members of the JAC, and peasant problems were taken up by the Catholic organisations long before they became union slogans and rallying calls. It was the Catholic militants who originally encouraged technical innovation, who became the driving force behind the large peasant movements of the 1960s, who politicised union activity and denounced the 'nouveaux riches' of the older generation, state power and the institutions of rural society. Each new theme for action seemed to come more from the training provided by the Catholic organisation than from direct union experience. The JAC appears to have provided the breeding ground for peasant unionism, the point at which the wider social movement crystallised and the crucible for the transformation of ideologies and political practice.

The ecclesiastical context in which the JAC emerged and evolved was directly opposed to the role it performed. The Church in Brittany was distinguished by its traditional religious practices, conservative political role and authoritarian clergy. With a strong regional base, a monopoly of school education, and a wide-ranging societal influence achieved through a variety of institutions, the Church was the foundation of the social structure and a cohesive force among the local communities. Not even the mayor or large landlord enjoyed the power of the parish priest. Moreover, the JAC had been created explicitly to reinforce this power by organising rural youth from the moment it left school.[10] Before it became a force for progress, training radical militants, it had to undergo a considerable internal transformation. The next step will be to examine how this occurred.

I intend to describe as the practical criticism of religion that process through which militants, under the pressure of socio-economic difficulties, moved from a position of subservience to religious authority to one of autonomy in thought and social and political activity. This expression signifies that the process unfolded on two related levels: ideologically, it involved a critique of official doctrine and, at the level of group practices, the independence of the JAC with respect to the Church. Two essential aspects of the process were its collective character and the fact that it took place entirely within the religious sphere. Neither philosophical considerations nor explicit political motives led to the critique of religion which proceeded, rather, from demands and references internal to the religious system.

(a) The ideological shift did not involve an explicit criticism of religious faith, but rather a progressive change in the reference points of militant thought. From the movement's beginnings until the 1950s, its reference points were official theology and, in particular, the social doctrine of the Church. This dogmatism steadily receded in favour of a direct consultation of the gospel, read by the militants in the light of their own experience. This ideological change was to open militant thought to the influence of the political and union ideas that evidently could not be entertained within the social doctrine of the Church.

(b) This change of concerns indicated a modification in the relationship between the JAC and the hierarchy, revealing the distance the organisation was gradually taking from the ecclesiastical authorities. This was to appear most clearly in relations between the local group and the parish. At the beginning, the parish priest had initiated and led group activities but it soon became more common for a young curate to assume this responsibility.

Little by little, JAC activities were escaping the confines of the parish: they now had their own premises, and young people were celebrating mass independently of the Sunday service, etc. At the regional level, the leaders, too, started to affirm their autonomy from the Church hierarchy. Only the national leadership maintained a link—and a reduced one—with the episcopal authorities.

(c) The impact of this change on the JAC itself was to alter the status of the chaplaincy. Although its role throughout this process remained one of initiating change, and legitimating and articulating new demands, its priestly powers, paradoxically, were diminished. This paradox was expressed in the ambiguous behaviour of the chaplains for, while endeavouring to step aside in favour of the militants themselves, they continued to exercise the authority that came with age and experience. They were progressively to become the experts of the movement, their competence no longer confined to the spiritual domain but extending to social, economic and political questions. In adopting this role they were to be the first to experience the identity crisis that afflicted their colleagues elsewhere in the Church at a much later date.[11]

At this point it is useful to make a theoretical digression. The phrase 'practical criticism of religion' refers not just to a process, but on a larger scale, to a more general ideological transformation. This expression conveys two aspects of the transition from religion to politics. It has consisted of a critique of the official interpretation of the Christian message within the religious sphere as well as an anti-institutional change at the level of political practices. Behind this conception of the transition lies a theoretical position based on a particular reading of the facts: the evolution of the militants was determined less by individual choice with regard to ideology and political practice than by the constraints of socio-economic change. They have been the bearers of structural transformation rather than autonomous actors. Faced with the upheaval of agricultural structures in a context characterised by the traditionalism of the parish clergy and the inertia of rural society, the farmers have been forced to perform a critique of their religion. This has been achieved not with philosophical concepts but by an important and collective shift in religious ideology and, above all, by maintaining a distance from establishment institutions. This interpretation of the evolution of the Christians is consistent with the perspective which first appeared in works on the sociology of Catholicism which emphasises change at the base rather than the summit and is interested more in the changing mentality of the faithful than in the theological trends and positions of the hierarchy which concern it only very partially.

To illustrate the connection between changes internal to the JAC and those it has initiated in the wider social environment, it is necessary to examine specific instances of this articulation in the activities of the organisation. Three factors have contributed to this change: the first concerns the function of the JAC as a meeting place for rural youth; the second its attitudes to religion, politics and society; and the third, the absence of any political or union alternative, will be revealed by a comparison with the JOC.

In the first place, the evolution of the JAC has been due to the nature of its activities: simply by bringing together young people and providing them with a terrain for the comparison of different experiences, the JAC made itself vulnerable to all the change it was to experience, especially that concerning its political and union orientations. This no doubt is true of all Catholic Action movements, but applies particularly to those enrolling young farmers; their youth makes them especially open to the influence of change and their occupation tends to isolate them in their conditions of work. In bringing together the children of the peasantry, the Church encouraged the formation of a group consciousness.

In the second place, the principles taught to these young people for influencing their social milieu implicitly required them to define their position with regard to change. These guidelines are summed up by the Catholic Action slogan 'look-evaluate-act' (voir-juger-agir): look at reality, evaluate as a Christian and act accordingly. This tenet aimed principally at upholding a mode of behaviour, inspired by the Christian ethic, fast disappearing from the world. It became an ideological stimulus for internal change in the JAC, since the definition of action in accordance with reality required an adequate theory for conceiving that reality. The official canons of the Church soon appeared outmoded in the light of the new imperatives of peasant Breton society. If the objectives of modernisation characterising the first period were still compatible with the social doctrine of the Church, the ambition of controlling the economy, requiring the mobilisation of farmers against the State, hardly squared with official instruction which, after the second period, no longer provided a theoretical reference point. The role of the tenet 'look-evaluate-act' as ideological stimulus suggests that it functioned by establishing a relationship between theory and practice like that of the Marxist dialectic: if the practice recommended by the theory fails to produce the expected results, then it is the theory that must change. The adjustment of the young farmers to the realities of a radically changing Breton economy implied, therefore, a critique of the principles for social action proposed to them in the past. The change initiated by the JAC in the peasant world required, in turn, that the organisation rethink its ideology.

This task could not be treated simply as the replacement of the social doctrine of the Church with more modern, and therefore more profane, concepts for comprehending reality without neglecting the specific nature of the JAC as a Catholic organisation and the Christian identity of its members. The hold of religious ideology on the militants was such that a radical critique of religion was required before a non-religious interpretation of the world could become possible. And such a critique, like all the critiques performed within Christian thought, had no recourse other than an appeal to the gospel, this time wrested from the hold of religious authority. At the same time, the place of doctrine in the Catholic edifice required the critique to be performed outside the walls of the institution. The practical consequence was that ideological change meant putting distance between the JAC and Church authorities.

This process, described as a task of ideological deliberation, might also be characterised as a struggle, in spite of the fact that there has been little open conflict between the JAC and the Church hierarchy.[12] An institution like the Church possesses considerable resources for absorbing conflict, healing rifts, or reducing them to disputes of personality. In this case, the institutional form taken by the crisis has been a division of the clergy. The leadership of the movement has been removed gradually from the hands of the parish clergy and entrusted to younger priests with a more favourable view of the evolution of the militants. The conflict has crystallised between these two fractions of the clergy, sometimes producing quite sharp divisions.[13]

The critique of the Church and its hierarchy has been mainly effected in the most recent period of the peasant movement's evolution with the radicalisation of demands and the politicisation of union debate by the new generation. Among the enemies of the 'peasant-workers' movement, on the side of capitalism and the wealthy farmers, were the Church and the social order it was endeavouring to maintain in the countryside. If the 'peasant-workers'—due to numerical weakness—appear rather marginal in the peasant world, their activities, notably during the 'milk strike' of 1972, have demonstrated a capacity to mobilise. Above all they have rendered explicit the crisis of rural social organisation and brought into the open conflicts that had been latent from the beginning. For the theme of modernisation was raised by the young militants against all the forms of backwardness of the society they wanted to reform. Although their protest led only to a reform of production methods, they had to confront all the traditionalist forces of Breton society during this phase. They received support from the agricultural extension and education services and from certain notables, but at the same time they had to strike out against the patriarchal system of farm management and the absolute power of the priests over the life of local communities. Interviews with militants from this period bear witness to the struggle they waged to impose a new mode of production, and they refer to it as being as much a struggle for influence against the parish clergy as a conflict of generations.[14]

However, it was the subsequent generation which was to carry to completion the critical process in which these militants had become involved. This can be explained by the economic situation described above, namely the militants of the first generation being able to establish themselves socially because of their economic success. The next generation, in less secure economic circumstances, was to carry the critique to its logical conclusion, and, moreover, to use it against its predecessor, now accused of having become the 'new notables' of rural society. In fact, union positions continued to provide a springboard for access to power in local society[15], and former JAC militants soon found themselves heading town councils, professional bodies or associations. This militant fringe provided numerous personnel for the Socialist Party when it turned to the conquest of Brittany after the 1971 Congress of Epinay, and it also provided militants for the Republican party of Giscard d'Estaing.

Those who followed them in the Catholic organisation were no longer partners in the same success. Economic change meant that professional success had become more difficult to achieve for the young farmers; a number of JAC militants were to leave agriculture for factory or office work[16] and those who stayed remained in debt for many years. The worsening economic horizon explains why this generation intensified its critique of a society which no longer seemed to have room for them, why they recognised the damaging consequences of capitalism, concealed from their elders by the ideals of ability and progress, and why they did this from within a JAC even more marginalised from the parishes.

When they began to formulate their demands in political terms, the militants who had passed through the JAC expressed them in much the same way as they had done within the movement. There are numerous traces of their interpretation of the gospel—an appeal for a more fraternal world, a concern for the poor, etc.—but, above all, a strident anti-institutional stance which made them as suspicious of political institutions as of others. Instead of joining the parties of the Left, they were to develop a form of militant prophetism. This brought the Christian militants to the ranks of the far-Left where they figured more as protesters than as strategists.

THE JOC: POLITICAL AND TRADE UNION ALTERNATIVES

Operating in an urban environment with a strong working-class presence, recruiting its members from among young wage earners, the JOC—during the same phase in the evolution of the Church—had to come to terms with the organisations that shaped the contours of the Parisian suburbs: the CGT and the Communist party. That meant that all the problems facing the members of the Catholic organisation in their working life were directly expressed in terms of the class struggle. Furthermore, the explicit intention of the Church hierarchy in creating this organisation was to counter the influence of Marxism in the working-class milieu by inviting young people to reflect upon the problems of work from a perspective inspired by the social doctrine of the Church. What before World War II might have been a struggle for influence became in the period concerned a situation of peaceful coexistence. The CGT and the PCF were so powerful in the Parisian suburbs that a Catholic organisation like the JOC presented no threat. The episcopal hierarchy and the leaders of Catholic Action in the region accommodated to the circumstances. From an objective of reconverting the worker to Christianity, a more modest role amongst the working class was defined, the militants no longer inspired by proselytism but becoming more deeply concerned with their personal condition as Christian workers.

To clarify further the nature of the network of relationships surrounding the JOC, one should consider the dual influence exercised upon the organisation by the Communist party and the episcopal hierarchy. Since the Popular Front and the Resistance, the French Communists have sought a certain collaboration with Catholics as a means of extending their influence. This can be seen in the discourse of the Communist leaders and in the corresponding efforts of local militants to engage non-communists known to be Christians in the management of town councils, trade unions and other organisations over which the PCF exercised a dominant influence. Catholic Action became a movement predisposed towards providing this type of militant, who would assume real responsibility but also keep a certain distance from party-political involvement. Such prudence was the result of individual decision; the organisation, as will be seen, gives a great deal of freedom to its members in political and trade union choice. In contrast, it was clearly as a movement set in a working-class environment that the JOC constituted, along with its adult branch, a 'token' working class for the Catholic hierarchy. With such organisations the Church once again had a right to speak on the condition of the working class and take a stand on social conflict, and to behave as if the whole working-class world was still within reach of its influence.

This dual set of relationships has provided the social and institutional context of the JOC. On the social side, there was an urgent call to union action and political involvement by an organisation whose members experienced capitalist exploitation every day and who were therefore highly susceptible to Communist arguments. On the ecclesiastical side, there has been a large margin for manoeuvre tied both to the hierarchy's acknowledged incompetence with regard to the working class, and the bad conscience that the feeling of being completely foreign to it could not fail to provide.[17]

In contrast to the JAC, the JOC evolved in a context polarised sharply by class conflict, where struggle was a visible reality. Also, the JOC was autonomous from the beginning, accountable in only a minimal sense to a hierarchy favourable to any initiative which would lead to a greater involvement of the Church on the side of the workers. The experience of the JOC can in no way be described in terms of the practical criticism of religion we defined previously. The local organisation remained for a long time an integral part of working-class parishes and its ideological evolution can hardly be described as avant-garde either in religious practice or in its relation to doctrine. And if the slogans of trade unionism ended up on congress banners after the 1970s, they remained alongside contradictory proclamations of brotherly love.

However, like the JAC, the JOC continued to provide a part of its personnel to trade union organisations. In the 1950s, the CFTC, which had not yet become the CFDT[18], even considered that the role of the JOC lay essentially in the training of future trade union leaders. If one looks at the militant trajectory, the CFTC-CFDT seems to have benefited positively from an influx from the JOC, but this concerned mainly those areas where the union's base was strong. This was not the case in the Parisian suburbs.

There, the dominance of the CGT imposed a choice on the Christians—to join the trade union at the risk of conflict between their ideology and Marxism, or to remain on the margins of the working-class movement.

The question of the relationship with Marxism greatly exercised the Church during this period. It involved a good deal of theological deliberation and provoked numerous adjustments on the part of the hierarchy. A direct consequence was the 1954 decision to halt the 'worker-priests' experience. Although the JOC was the major organisation concerned, it did not become involved in what appeared to be a rather abstract debate. Its militants responded according to their own concrete circumstances and avoided any debate that might have threatened their unity. This concern with unity was also reflected in the project of reconstructing the unity of the working-class movement, defined in relation to trade unionism. In consequence, an important fraction of JOC militants joined the CGT, a number of them taking Communist party cards. Others became involved in the CFTC-CFDT in order to preserve a degree of consistency between trade union involvement and their religious position.

One can, therefore, distinguish two directions taken by young Christian workers on the path to political action, the respective importance of which is difficult to judge: one leading to the CGT and the PCF; the other involving them for a long time in the CFDT from where they would later move on to the Socialist party. These two paths had coexisted institutionally in the adult branch of the JOC founded before the War—the *Ligue Ouvrière Chrétienne*— which had changed its name to the *Mouvement Populaire des Familles* in 1941 without losing its status as a Catholic Action movement; in 1950, having become more politically oriented and having moved closer to the Communist party, it became the *Mouvement de Libération du Peuple*, this time breaking away from Catholic Action. The succession of titles is a good indication of the gradual transition to political action, but alignment with the Communist position conceals the fact that another group of militants made a different choice. After the split in 1953, a small but important fraction joined the Communist party while the remainder created the *Union de la Gauche Socialiste*, one of the elements of the future *Parti Socialiste Unifié*[19].

Thus, although Christian militants moved towards political action as much as the peasants, there was no corresponding organisational transformation. As we suggested at the beginning, there have been two ways of moving from religion to politics, one proceeding by the critique of the religious system, the other proceeding in continuity with it. In the second case, as far as internal ideology was concerned, the growing importance of problems associated with the workplace was articulated within the framework of Catholic thought. At the level of relations with the Church, the JOC remained an organisation of Catholic Action, more obedient and less restive than the others—in particular, than the JAC. In comparison with what was previously said on the subject of rural organisation, the JOC's position appears paradoxical, since young Catholics were more strongly provoked to challenge religious ideology in the environment of the factory than in the context of a rural society still heavily imbued with the Christian ethos. Furthermore, political and trade union involvement entailing a direct confrontation with Marxist ideology should have been even more likely to have induced the Catholic organisation to modify its relationship with the Church, if not to retrace a process similar to the JAC's.

This apparent paradox can be resolved by an analysis of the internal functioning of the JOC similar to that used to explain the transformation of the JAC. In both cases, the ideological stimulus has been the same: 'look-evaluate-act'. The Catholic worker activist was necessarily led, like the militant farmer, to consider his situation and find answers conforming with the teaching of the Church. The requirement of consistency with doctrine clashed immediately—in places like the Parisian suburbs where the power of the CGT and Communist party relegated other organisations to marginal roles—with the ways in which these two organisations posed the problems of the workplace: in terms, that is, of class conflict. The power of the CGT imposed this definition with such success that it discouraged from the beginning any attempt to provide an alternative interpretation of the world inspired by the social doctrine of the Church. In this situation, the tenet 'look-evaluate-act' would lead less to a particular type of involvement in trade unionism than to a consolidation of the members' religious commitment, to protect it against destruction by the realities of daily struggle. Prevented from playing a specific role on a terrain totally dominated by the Marxist organisations, the JOC retreated to the religious domain, leaving its members free as to their political and trade union involvement. The function of the JOC rested, therefore, on a division of activities between the religious and union-political domains, a distinction legitimised by the separation of the temporal from the spiritual, characteristic of the theology of the Church at the time. When members reported back to meetings of the organisation about the problems of their working lives, the dimension of collective action was carefully distinguished from personal positions, the first being the concern of the trade union, the latter demanding a response in Christian terms. In the same way, a division of labour was instituted between the CGT and the JOC so that both could avoid any criticism of doctrine.

Of course, the same individuals being active in both organisations, the separation could not be complete: while the CGT had to take account of the specific profile of militants from the JOC, the latter had to deal with the religious implications of trade union struggle.

The testimonies I have gathered from former JOC militants lay great emphasis on the extraordinary confidence they placed in the organisations of the working-class movement—trade unions and political parties, but also in the JOC itself—a quasi-religious confidence which might suggest that their respect for the Church was transferred to other organisations. On the contrary, it was the Leninist tradition of the French working-class movement that prevented the possibility of an anti-institutional critique occurring within the JOC. Each time favourable circumstances arose for such a critique— notably during the crisis of the JEC in 1965 and in May 1968,[20] the JOC revealed its reservations about protest over the ecclesiastical system by stressing its solidarity with the traditions of the working-class movement.[21] This dual loyalty to the Church and the working-class movement has thus had contradictory effects on the JOC. While these dual loyalties put militants who engaged in trade union activities from religious motives in difficult positions, at the same time it endowed the organisation with sufficient prestige to ensure it a large degree of autonomy from the religious hierarchy. If liturgical innovation and a more direct appeal to the gospel appeared within the JOC, they did not result, as in the JAC, from a struggle against the Church as an institution but, on the contrary, reflected the autonomy the organisation had already acquired.

There are, therefore, several reasons for the absence of a critical process.

Our analysis of this phenomenon in the case of the JAC suggests the importance of the fact that the socio-economic problems of the working-class remained outside the purview of the Catholic organisation, which could therefore avoid considering how these problems related to the Church. One can deduce from this comparative analysis that the determining factor has been the existence of a political-union alternative. Essentially, it was the presence of a class trade union which freed the JOC from having to deal with the questions which, in the case of the JAC, had led to dispute with the church authorities. The trade union alternative allowed militants to make the transition from religious reflection to political action via another organisation without involving an operational transformation of the JOC itself. At the same time, this transfer from one organisation to another has been facilitated by a similarity of structures in the JOC and the unions, and has not required the militants to alter their behaviour. The absence of an active farmers' union forced the militants of the JAC to mobilise through their own movement entailing, in turn, its radical ideological and institutional transformation. Secondly, the nature of the Church's presence in the socio-economic context explains the difference between the JOC and the JAC. Whereas in one case the Church did not oppose the militant activities of the young Christians, in the other the power of the Church over rural social life constituted one of the major obstacles to its transformation.

For both factors, the social context in which the organisations operated was critical. In the case of the JOC the context is that of an industrial social class with its own organisations and traditions: an adversary active in a domain different from that of the Catholic organisation; and, moreover, the occurrence of conflict in a situation of relative autonomy from the Church. It should be noted also at this point, that urban segregation has eased the task of the Church by preventing workers and bosses from finding themselves on the pews of the same churches. In contrast, the context of the JAC was that of a socially and economically homogeneous society whose operating principles were defined by a Church with absolute authority. The Breton Church had fashioned rural society into a totalitarian community, in the sense that no aspect of life in those communities was free from the hold of religion and open to a new type of unionism. This was so much the case that the process of social differentiation in the communities induced by economic change has necessarily entailed a crisis of the Church, the cleavages between social groups emerging along religious as much as along political or economic lines. The JAC has been the locus of transition from a homogeneous society to a network of confrontations, to the extent that it was able to formulate the principle of this differentiation in keeping with the religious approach and therefore at a level meaningful to the community.

PREHISTORY OF AUTOGESTION

An analysis of the crisis of the Church in which Christian militancy was forged, illuminates in part the renewal of the themes preoccupying the French Left, in particular the appearance of new demands, proposals and projects in the ideologies of the political parties. Without claiming a role as avant-garde of the French Left for the Christian militants, it is a question of showing how certain themes have emerged on the political scene stemming from the crisis of the Church. The issue of *autogestion*, which has been at the centre of ideological debate since 1968, will be taken as an example of this phenomenon.

Autogestion became current in French left-wing circles during the period 1968-78. The popularity of the expression has been such that even technocrats and centrist politicians were to adopt it as their own. Because of its widespread use the word took on a wide variety of meanings.[22] During the decade following May 1968, the *autogestion* movement crystallised a large number of issues concerning the transformation of society without having to define them explicitly. From this point of view, the first dimension of the *autogestion* movement was its critical dimension.

Critical of what? In asking this question about the wide variety of uses to which the concept of *autogestion* has been put, one can gain a better understanding of its diversity. The appearance of the expression in the last two Communist party congresses shows that it has come to represent a critique of Stalinism as a model for socialism. A distance with regard to Eastern European societies is evident in the meaning given to the term by the non-Communist Left. But for them, the principal meaning lies in other critical dimensions concerning the functioning of French society. In newer Socialist party factions (*tendances*) *autogestion* is mainly a criticism of the concentration of power; for PSU militants, *autogestion* is a denunciation of the destruction of the social fabric due to state authoritarianism; for the CFDT it refers rather to the arbitrary use of employers' power in firms . . .

These shifts in meaning suggest that the history of *autogestion* can be found in the documents of different factions of the Left. It is indeed striking that the path to political involvement followed by one Christian militant faction has paralleled the trajectory of this theme. Throughout the whole period, *autogestion* has remained the reference point for the definition of CFDT political projects. It became an integral part of PS ideology in the autumn of 1974 when, at the *Assises du socialisme*, the party of François Mitterand was joined by the fraction of the PSU led by Michel Rocard; the latter had centered his electoral campaign for the presidential election of 1969 wholly around the theme of *autogestion*. At the same time, a part of the PSU, with numerous militants of Christian origin, went over to the ranks of the PS. They came in particular from the ranks of the CFDT, the local civic movements and even more directly from Catholic movements such as *Vie Nouvelle* and *Témoignage Chrétien*. These new arrivals were to organise themselves in two PS *tendances*, CERES and the faction of Michel Rocard, and the concept of *autogestion* became the means by which the Christians maintained their identity in the face of the ex-SFIO secular elements.[23]

The expression *autogestion* appeared on the French political horizon during the explosion of May 1968, but it is difficult to locate before that. It has been suggested that French trade unions have used the theme to revive the libertarian spirit of Proudhonian anarcho-syndicalism that had so deeply influenced the beginnings of unionism in France. This notion is based on the role played by the metallurgy workers of the region of Nantes in triggering the strikes of May 1968, and on the fact that this region represents the most solid bastion of the anarcho-syndicalist tradition. However, the link we have been able to establish between the history of *autogestion* and the trajectory of Christian militants suggests another hypothesis—equally difficult to confirm with documentary evidence but more plausible with regard to the evolution of French society as a whole—which attributes its origins to the transformation of Christian militancy.

My argument is based in part on the enquiry into Breton regionalism on which the analysis of the JAC was grounded. Analysing the evolution of CFDT personnel, I have shown that the expansion of the CFDT in this region paralleled the formation of a new proletariat, rural in origin, in the new firms established in Brittany under the aegis of the decentralisation policy.[24] In emphasising these rural origins, I would suggest an interpretation of the ideological differences between this proletariat and the working-class proletariat organised by the CGT, less in terms of the absence of a tradition of struggle than as the effect of the other struggles through which rural society has evolved, and for which the institution of the Church has provided the focal point. This analysis suggests a relationship between the crisis of the Catholic Church and the evolution of the CFDT. This relationship is obviously not the same for the union as a whole, even if the same phenomenon is observed in other regions where the effects of industrial decentralisation are taking place in a rural society experiencing differentiation.

In locating the origins of *autogestion* in the French Left, it is necessary to stress its anti-institutional character which, moreover, provides the common link between the different uses to which the term has been put during its history. These differences stem above all from the type of institution to which the critique of *autogestion* has been applied: the school or the family; parties and trade unions; the system of representation; the state bureaucracy; and so forth.

Although the Church is evidently different from these other institutions, it is, in a sense, the institution *par excellence* that, historically, has provided a model for all the others, and in which the stakes of power and knowledge have been defined in terms of the Absolute. But the origins of the institutional critique within the Church owe more to its position in rural society. I showed in the first part of this article how the social transformation experienced by the peasantry has been closely linked to the practical critique of religion made by the militants of the JAC. This has meant an attack on the Church as the foundation of rural society, the point at which the various elements of local power converge, and as the nerve centre for all changes in the agricultural world. But the Church is not an institution like the Rotary Club. It is unique in its ability to unify all internal relationships around the interpretation of God's message, in other words, to base its legitimacy and the social order which it defends on a metasocial principle.

Emerging from the ferment of Catholic Action, the anti-institutional critique is linked to an original position which continues to characterise the behaviour of Christians in the political arena. It stresses rank and file activity rather than the decisions of leaders, limited struggles rather than large-scale strategies, and the transformation of society as opposed to the seizure of state power. The best evidence of this new orientation is the flourishing of voluntary associations during this period. These associations—to which Christians from Catholic organisations have contributed a great deal—have established a new relationship between local society and political forces. In articulating concrete issues—the improvement of housing, the construction of local amenities, the redirection of a road, etc.—the associations have brought new questions concerning urban life into the political arena. This new political concern with the issues of ordinary life indicates a shift in the orientation of militant action from political to civil society. This seems clearly to result from experience in Catholic Action and from the lack of response of the Church to the problems encountered by militants. In this sense it is the direct descendant of the forms of charitable action at the end of the nineteenth century which constituted social welfare. Thus Catholicism has produced a form of militancy whose logic leads it to deny the relevance of political action in favour of action specifically aimed at society from a perspective of popular control and participation. Although *autogestion* only subsequently provided an ideological basis for this political practice, its origins can nonetheless be located in the ferment experienced by the Catholic Church before 1968. The importance of the 'General Assemblies' of May 1968 in the formulation of the *autogestion* movement was central, but they functioned above all to permit militants from Catholic organisations to legitimise in the political arena a mode of action already defined in their earlier involvements. The Christians were finally in their element during the May 1968 movement.

An identification of *autogestion* in terms of the political practices through which it has evolved, suggests that its ultimate target was the political parties, or rather, the party bureaucracies. *Autogestion* explicitly criticises the delegation of authority on which political life has traditionally been based. It has produced the sharpest cleavages precisely on the French Left itself where it challenges the Leninist and the Republican traditions. It appears that militants wanted to legitimise a new orientation of political activity within these organisations prior to a conquest of the State, and, indeed, to encourage the leadership of left-wing parties to renounce this project in favour of a transformation of society 'from below'. Without denying the importance of the critique of Stalinism as formulated by various far-Left movements in the changes that have occurred on the Left, I suggest simply that this theoretical challenge would not have had the same impact in the absence of widespread anti-institutional sentiment. The origins of this sentiment lie beyond the context of Christian militancy in the disintegration of rural society. But the specific forms it took, prior or parallel to Marxist formulations, reveal the particular contribution to political ideology made by Christian militants. Returning to the point made in the conclusion to the analysis of the JAC, there was a kind of political prophetism, outside the traditional themes of the French Left, denouncing political practice rather than formulating political strategy. It has often been noted that the role performed by Christians on the Left has been to protest, rather than to contribute positive proposals. The preceding analyses suggest a reformulation of this observation: the political criticism of religion has evolved into a religious critique of political practice.

Christian militants arrived on the political scene with the elements of an anti-institutional critique they had been forced to make on the path to political consciousness. This ideological deliberation had not been informed by a particular philosophy but was based on a reappropriation of the religious message from its official interpretation. The anti-hierarchical critique and, more generally, the challenge to the delegation of power and knowledge, were inspired by an unfettered rediscovery of the gospel. The reference to political prophetism is not, therefore, merely metaphorical, but a way of emphasising the religious dimension of the political critique and its origins in a new interpretation of the Christian message which defines Christ as the prophet *par excellence*, in such a way as indeed to challenge his role as founder of the Church. This ultimate reference point for Christian political involvement explains why they have preferred communitarian utopias to plans for social transformation and the critique of social structures to the formulation of political strategy.

NOTES

This article was translated from the French by Martin Rhodes.

1. The difficulties are compounded by the fact that when joining political parties Christians leave or have already left the Catholic organisations, sometimes even abandoning all reference to their religious past.
2. This was recognised officially for the first time in the documents of the 22nd Congress in February 1976.
3. Cf. Hugues Portelli, 'Au rendez-vous du Parti Socialiste', *Esprit*, (April-May 1977).
4. A perfect example of this other type of militant, Michel Debatisse headed the *Jeunesse Agricole Chrétienne* before becoming President of the *Fédération Nationale des Syndicats d'Exploitants Agricoles*. He came out in the 1974 presidential campaign for Valéry Giscard d'Estaing and became Secretary of State for the Food Industry in the second government of Raymond Barre.
5. In 1963 the JAC became the *Mouvement Rural de la Jeunesse Chrétienne*.
6. The JAC study was undertaken in 1972 as part of research into the regional question in Brittany (Renaud Dulong, *La Question bretonne*. Cahiers de la Fondation Nationale des Sciences Politiques, Paris: Armand Colin, 1975.) The research on the JOC was based on interviews with former militants.
7. The first part of the analysis appeared in 'L'Eglise de l'Ouest et les luttes de classes dans la paysannerie', *La Pensée*, No. 175, (June 1974).
8. Cf. Claude Servolin, 'L'absorption de l'agriculture dans le mode de production capitaliste', in *L'Univers politique des paysans*. Cahiers de la Fondation Nationale des Sciences Politiques, Paris: Armand Colin, 1972.
9. FDSEA: *Fédération Départementale des Syndicats d'Exploitants Agricoles*.
   CDJA: *Centre Départemental des Jeunes Agriculteurs*.
10. The creation of the JAC in Brittany was actually more complex. On the point, cf. Suzanne Berger, *Peasants Against Politics*. Cambridge, Mass.: Harvard University Press, 1972.
11. The chaplains of rural Catholic Action were the first of the clergy to show signs of an identity crisis. In 1964 they met to discuss the question 'Why be a priest?' Cf. André Rousseau, in *Histoire des Catholiques en France*. Toulouse: Privat, 1980.
12. The conflicts between the Catholic organisations and the episcopacy appeared after 1968. They became especially acute in 1973 and 1974 when the central issue at stake became quite clearly the Marxist analysis of society by the Christian militants.
13. This specialisation of the clergy has been assessed. A 1976 study shows that 90 per cent of the supervision of rural parishes was in the hands of priests over the age of 45, while 66 per cent

of the clergy involved in the movements with laymen were under 45. Cf. André Rousseau, op. cit.

14. Cf. Bernard Lambert, *Les paysans dans la lutte des classes*. Paris: Editions du Seuil, 1970.

15. In 1953, Michel Debatisse, the head of the JAC, declared, 'We can be proud when something like a third of the mayors of rural communes have come from the JAC.' Cited by André Rousseau, op. cit.

16. The change of name mentioned in note 5 accompanied a reorientation of the movement. The MRJC has three branches: a farming branch; an education branch; and an industrial branch. In this latter period, the organisation experienced an important decline in numbers.

17. The fact that at a gathering of the JOC held in 1974 the General Secretary of the PCF found himself several yards away from the Archbishop of Paris, attests to the peculiarity of this situation.

18. In 1964, the CFTC, *Confédération Française des Travailleurs Chrétiens*, became the CFDT, *Confédération Française Démocratique du Travail*.

19. Cf. J.M. Donegani, in *Autrement*, No. 8, (1977).

20. JEC: *Jeunesse Etudiante Chrétienne*. The evolution of this movement could equally have provided a point of comparison for this analysis. Cf. Danielle Hervieu-Léger, *De la mission à la protestation*. Paris: Edition du Cerf, 1973.

21. Cf. André Rousseau, in *Social Compass*, Vol. 25, No. 1, (1978).

22. Daniel Vidal in analysing May 1968 showed that this demand substituted for a whole series of others. Starting from CGT leader Georges Séguy's well-known phrase, '*Autogestion* is an empty slogan', Vidal shows how this formula overcame the inertia of the social movement's system of protest—and allowed the maximum development of its capacity for mobilisation—by the absence of a 'signified' for the 'signifier'. [Translator's note: Dulong is referring to the semiotic concepts of 'signifié' and 'signifiant' used originally by Saussure to characterise the relationship between the two aspects of the linguistic sign.] Daniel Vidal, 'Les conditions du politique dans le mouvement de mai-juin 1968', in *Grèves revendicatives ou grèves politiques*. Paris: Anthropos, 1971.

23. Cf. Hugues Portelli, op. cit.

24. Cf. Dulong (1975), pp. 91-2.

The Political Cultures of French Catholicism

Jean-Marie Donegani

Opinion surveys and electoral geography over the past twenty years in France have demonstrated the link between Catholicism and political conservatism. There has been, first, a long-standing historical tradition of close association between the Right and the Catholic Church as an institution. When in 1893, Leo XIII urged the French Catholics to rally to the republican regime, and Pius XI in 1926 condemned *Action Française* and told Catholics to leave this extremist group which fed their nostalgia for the *ancien régime*, there were major tensions and splits.[1] But between their religious and political loyalties, the majority chose the former even though they did not personally accept the political values of the Republic. Catholics continued *en masse* to support the parties closest to the old reactionary Right. When the papacy allowed the Catholics to re-integrate into national political life, after being 'internal exiles', it totally condemned socialism, and then communism, both heirs to the French Revolution and the Republic. The result was that under the Third and Fourth Republics, one of the fundamental cleavages of French political life cut between the Church and the conservative or reactionary Right on one side, and the republican State and the left-wing parties on the other.[2] This split emerged not only in matters concerning the institutional interests of the Church (legislation on Church-State separation, or fights over the schools) but also on social and economic questions. Here the connection with religion did not involve political stakes defined in terms of conflicts of interest or power, but, more profoundly, entailed different conceptions of the world and philosophies of life.

Since the beginning of the Fifth Republic, the clergy—and Catholics in general—no longer intervene in politics as they once did to express hostility to the socialist and communist Left.[3] In the past twenty years, moreover, the teachings and positions of the Catholic hierarchy have become more flexible about links between the Faith and political choices. The encyclical *Mater et Magistra* of 1961 stated that Christianity and Communism are fundamentally opposed and that Catholics could not support even apparently moderate socialist theories, for their only objective was material well-being and their only perspective for the social order, a limited, worldly horizon.[4] Ten years later, Paul VI's *Octogesima Adveniens* letter carefully distinguished between ideologies and the concrete historical movements that embody them. While the same disapproval was expressed about Marxist ideologies in accordance with church tradition, the judgement about socialist movements was more moderate than that of 1961. Paul VI simply warned Christians against the kind of theoretical ambiguities and idealism that allowed any aspirations to justice and equality to be called socialist, regardless of the historical record and concrete functioning of actual socialist experiences; there was an essential link between Marxist analysis, the practice of class struggle, and the type of totalitarian and violent society to which such a process leads.[5]

In 1972, the French bishops' Commission on the Workers' World issued a statement intended to be responsive to those Catholic working-class activists who had become socialists.[6] The document restated the historic opposition between the Christian faith and the materialist philosophy of Marxism, but did not condemn the socialist aspirations of the working-class world, recognising in them the contemporary form of the workers' long-standing solidarity and desire for more justice. Finally, in the same year the full Assembly of the Episcopate,[7] and then in 1974 the pastoral session of the Permanent Council of the Episcopate,[8] while still arguing that Marxist analysis was flawed in reducing man to his class membership, nonetheless recognised the structural character of the injustices in French society and reaffirmed the necessity of political pluralism for Christians. The Episcopate refused to link, as some had wanted, Christian faith to a socialist choice. But it did accept the full implications of political pluralism and affirm that the faithful might, without violating their faith or the vision of man it entailed, choose to be socialists.

But although the Catholic hierarchy no longer directly indicates its position in favour of the Right, and although it has greatly reduced the doctrinal obstacles to Catholics opting for the Left, nonetheless, the links between being a Catholic and voting for the Right remain very tight. In the 1965 presidential election only 7 per cent of regularly practising Catholics voted for Mitterrand and 90 per cent chose de Gaulle, Lecanuet or Tixier-Vignancour.[9] In 1974, Chaban-Delmas, Giscard d'Estaing and Royer received only 29 per cent of the non-Catholic vote, but 90 per cent of the vote of regular church-goers, only 8 per cent of whom voted for Mitterrand.[10] In the 1973 legislative elections, 56 per cent of regular church-goers voted for the Reformers or the Majority, 10 per cent for the Socialist party, 2 per cent for the PSU, and 1 per cent for the Communist party; 31 per cent of the non-practising electorate voted for the Reformers or the Majority and 67 per cent for the Left.[11]

The geographical distribution of the Socialist gains in 1973 led some to speculate that Catholics had shifted their voting patterns, for the Socialist party had progressed considerably in areas of past weakness, zones, for the most part, of strong religious practice.[12] In fact, the Socialist advance in Catholic departments where the old Socialist party (SFIO) had been weakly implanted, was made in districts where religious practice was the weakest. As Peyrefitte has noted, 'Whenever on the second round a Communist faced a candidate of the Majority, practising Catholics voted massively for the Majority. ... When the Socialist party stood against the Majority, the latter had a considerable advantage among regular practising Catholics, in all regions. . . As for the behaviour of church-goers in the [Catholic] west of France, their traditional loyalty to the Majority parties was no less staunch than elsewhere.'[13] These conclusions are confirmed by the analysis of the results of elections in Brittany in March 1978. 'Left gains were most difficult where Catholicism remains strongest. Contrary to a popular notion, the Socialist party advance in Brittany took place essentially—as much evidence proves—not because regular practising Catholics slipped to the Left, but because of the growing detachment of Catholics from regular practice.'[14]

The Breton case undoubtedly reveals the evolution of political behaviour of the French Catholics in general. If the Left has benefited over the past few years from the Catholic electorate, it is because the religious behaviour of this electorate has greatly changed. Regular practice has declined from 23 per cent in 1966 to 15 per cent today, a fall all the more important in view of the fact that the criteria defining 'regular practice' have over this period been modified by the polling organisations to take into account the evolution of religious mores.[15] In other words, to the extent that the political behaviour of Catholics is homogeneous today, it is apparently due as much to religious decline and to spreading secularisation in French society, as to changes in the clergy and hierarchy who no longer openly support the Right.

As for those Catholics who still regularly attend mass, their conservative political orientation remains steadfast. This strong and stable link between regular religious practice and a Right vote has been thoroughly studied, notably by Michelat and Simon.[16] Their typological analyses show that degrees of religious practice are linked to coherent systems of political opinions and attitudes. The greater the degree of religious integration, measured by the frequency of practice, the greater the right-wing vote, no matter what the other characteristics of individuals or what the socio-economic and regional context. This relation 'is not simply an external relationship between religious practice and vote. Everything suggests, rather, that it takes place on a deeper level: that of beliefs, convictions, and emotions, of the conception of society, of the systems of norms and values with which cultural and electoral behaviours are strongly associated.'[17]

These considerations suggest two problems, the first relating to a long-standing tradition within French Catholicism that favours socialism, even communism, in the name of the very same religious principles that underlie the Church's attachment to the Right. What are the components of this current, and how has it found expression? What are the political or religious interests at stake? Next, the very nature of French Catholicism as a cultural system raises questions. Is it a closed and homogeneous system or, given its diversity and fluidity, should it be treated, rather, as a set of profoundly different subcultures, each the expression of different and even antagonistic social groups?

FRENCH CATHOLICISM AND THE LEFT

In the last presidential election (May 1981) 19 per cent of regularly practising Catholics, 30 per cent of occasional church-goers, and 59 per cent of non-practising Catholics did not vote on the first round for any of the candidates of the Right (Giscard d'Estaing, Chirac, Debré, Garaud).[18] While there have always been some Catholics (rather few) who have voted Left, the Left Catholics that have been significant until now have been not so much the dissident electors as a certain number of the faithful who, in their participation in groups within the Church, have displayed alternative conceptions of the role of faith in making political choices, and alternative conceptions of the

Church's mission in society. These 'Left Catholics' are primarily activists in social movements, or gathered around special publications, and their influence and audience greatly exceed that which their numbers would suggest.

The trends within left-wing Catholicism are quite diverse. *Témoignage Chrétien*[19] and *Vie Nouvelle*[20] are groups which have no institutional links with the Church but explicitly position themselves within it in order to persuade its members of the links, both in theory and in experience, between Christian faith and socialism. The objective is both religious and political. The groups use religious references to convince members of the need for socialism. What is at stake is the rediscovery and proclamation of the real Church underneath the Church that has betrayed the cause of the gospel message to the oppressed. These groups seek also to constitute within socialism a specifically Christian group that will be able to attract the Catholic masses away from the Right.[21] These organisations are dominated by the socially-mobile salaried middle class, who have more educational than economic capital. The ideology they acquire in these organisations allows them to break with the orthodoxy and the devotionalism of the traditional middle classes, or of the working class,[22] and to distinguish themselves by their politico-religious non-conformity from the upper classes to which they do not yet belong.[23]

Another trend is the 'anti-institutional' tendency represented by *La Lettre*[24] and the *Chrétiens-Marxistes*.[25] For these groups the issue is no longer one of leading Catholics to socialism by patient education; it is to fight against the 'dominant religious ideology' and to propose other expressions of Christian faith, mainly based on a Marxist interpretation of social relationships and change. The main objective here is, paradoxically, basically anti-religious. The 'Marxist Christians' want to engage battle on religious grounds against the Church, but they do not propose ecclesiastical alternatives. Rather, starting from their politics, they seek 'possible new expressions of faith'. They distrust the Communist party, for them, just another Church. Similarly, *La Lettre* sees itself as a Christian avant garde, denounces the bourgeois appropriation of the gospel, and tries to define how religious faith might be brought to bear on life, first of all, in politics. In the struggle against Catholic religious ideology these groups were joined by *Echanges et Dialogues*, an even smaller and more ephemeral group with, nonetheless, a certain impact on French Catholicism between 1968 and 1975. As a movement of priests fighting to obtain the right to work, to marry and to participate in politics, *Echanges et Dialogues*, like *La Lettre* and *Chrétiens-Marxistes*, brought together Left Christians who had been mobilised by a struggle against the Church in the name of its own religious message.[26]

Finally, Left Catholicism has found expression in Catholic Action movements, created in the 1930s, first with youth movements for workers (*Jeunesse Ouvrière Chrétienne*), farmers and self-employed, then with adult groups for these categories.[27] This form of organisation mirrors the transition that began in France before the war and culminated in the 1960s—from a Christian to a secularised society. The parish, based on a geographically defined territory, was not adequate in a society where social particularisms came to prevail over local particularisms. Christianity, if it did not want simply to retreat, had to occupy the social terrain in a more aggressive, dynamic fashion and to root itself in the very divisions of society. But this new form of religious organisation—Catholic Action—quickly gave rise to political problems unknown in the parish. Thus, for example, in 1950, the *Mouvement Populaire des Familles* (MPF), an adult working-class movement, became involved in politics after having long rejected and excluded political considerations from its doctrine and its action. When the Assembly of Cardinals and Archbishops withdrew its support and founded another organisation in its place, the *Action Catholique Ouvrière* (ACO), the MPF transformed itself into a political party (*Mouvement de Libération du Peuple*, MLP).

This collective trajectory reveals the cross-pressures experienced by Catholic Action in working-class milieux, especially during the Cold War. The desire to be loyal to the working class, a legacy of the JOC, led to the discovery of politics and to crypto-communism. At this point, conflict arose between class loyalties and religious loyalties: the reason given by numerous MLP militants for refusing to work with the Communist party was its atheistic materialism. The conflict was resolved by the movement's plunge into politics as a party—but at a double price: abandoning the Catholic connection and giving up the link to the working class.[28] The trajectory of these workers was very different from that followed by the middle-class members of *Vie Nouvelle* and *Témoignage Chrétien*. The latter started from their Christian faith and moved to the discovery of politics and to a struggle for an alliance of Christianity with the socialist conceptions of justice and liberation. In the former, the point of departure was that of the JOC: to be both totally Christian and totally worker. When the third component—politics—arose, none of the three was possible.

The first crises thus arose in the working class where the strength of political solidarity was particularly important. But the same problems raised by the intrusion of politics in the activities and doctrine of Catholic Action movements would be posed in ever sharper ways in the 1950s and 1960s in the student movement and in the peasant movement.

Even if, originally, the task of the Catholic Action movements was a missionary one, the specialisation by social milieu inevitably led the leaders of these movements to absorb, or at least to express, the social, syndical, and political problems which these social groups confronted. From the moment a church movement identifies with a specific social milieu, a kind of commitment rapidly follows that makes it difficult to disentangle the temporal from the spiritual. This was all the more problematic because the doctrine of the Catholic Action movements expressed a theology of incarnation that essentially eliminated the distinction between temporal and spiritual life, a distinction already ambiguous in the traditional social doctrine of the Church.[29]

From this point of view, 1965 and 1975 were milestones in the transformation of Catholic Action, as the result of which the very principles that had presided at its birth disappeared. In 1965, Mgr. Veuillot, then Archbishop of Paris, asked the student movement *Jeunesse Etudiante Chretienne* (JEC) to recognise that their only aim as a lay movement was the supernatural end of all missionary effort. But the leaders of the student organisation refused. Their new orientations eroded the distinctions among temporal, syndical, political, and missionary action. At this point the bishops withdrew the movement's mandate and organised it with other leaders.[30] In 1975, the Assembly of Bishops specified that in the future when Catholic Action movements made temporal choices, they would do so on their own responsibility and in no way commit the Church.[31] Thus the theory of Catholic Action as the agent of the hierarchy, the theory of the mandate, is dead, like the society in which it had emerged.

Since then, Catholic Action movements have become increasingly politicised. The university movement, *Action Catholique Universitaire* (ACU), born in 1966 out of the crisis of the JEC, was, by 1970, asking the same question: should one give priority to political commitment or to evangelisation? The activists chose political involvement and the movement defined itself as following a revolutionary, anti-capitalistic line. It identified itself as a movement of the Church but refused to represent the Church in the student world. The JEC also explicitly moved into radical politics. The new peasant movement (*Mouvement Rural de la Jeunesse Chrétienne*, MRJC), that replaced the *Jeunesse Agricole Chrétienne* (JAC) in 1961, also became radicalised and defined its task as leading young country-dwellers in a 'broad struggle for a new society'.

The JOC and the ACO, in contrast, have not experienced in recent years the same kinds of conflict with the Church as the other movements, undoubtedly because these movements have a longer experience of politics. The working-class Catholic Action movements do not define their role as a political one, for the mystique of working-class solidarity leads them to believe that the unions and Left parties are the only legitimate political incarnations of working-class interests. Also, most of their members are union or party activists. The JOC and ACO define themselves as organisations where the temporal commitments of their members are considered in Christian perspective.

Left-wing Catholicism in France is thus, above all, a Catholicism of movements and an activist Catholicism. Born out of the desire to re-conquer society for religion by a strategy of identification with, and penetration of, various social groups, this Catholicism cannot by definition be measured by specific forms of religious practice or by the usual criteria of religious participation. As Michelat and Simon have shown, the links between politics and religion can be illuminated by examining the degree of practice of Catholics.[32] This remains significant, even as rate of practice declines. But there is another Catholicism in which religiosity expresses itself on other registers, by other channels, and which cannot therefore be grasped through the traditional surveys of religious practice. For this Catholicism, the strength of commitment and participation in social movements and the extent to which these are oriented by faith, are as significant as signs of religious membership as attending mass is for other Catholics.[33]

Left-wing Catholicism is, as we have said, a Catholicism of movement and activists. In its objectives, it takes up the old struggle of the Catholic Church against the modern world and against liberalism, as Emile Poulat has pointed out.[34] For the Church, modernity meant that religion no longer enveloped all of society and all of individual existence; it meant specialisation, a division of classes, and social competition. Twentieth-century Catholicism has above all been intransigent in its rejection of such a modern world, seen as deformed and disorderly. Christian social doctrine has identified a 'third way,' not as a centrist alternative or as a tactic for reconciling liberal capitalism and socialism, or workers and bourgeois, or Left and Right. Rather this 'third way' expressed an integralist rejection of all of these terms, seen as the common creations of modern society. Integralist Catholicism sought to restore the role of religion as the organising agency in all society and not simply as one of the specialised spheres of society. Thus integralism and today's Left Catholicism have common origins. The latter is *not* a liberal Catholicism that has shifted to the Left but, like integralism, is a project that from the outset has had a totalistic vision of restoring the reign of religious values in all society.

René Rémond has accounted for the ease with which Marxism was able to graft itself on to religious faith for Left Catholics: 'Taking a long view of the politics of French Catholicism over the past century, it apparently has never really accepted or completely assimilated democratic postulates and behaviours. These imply the relativity of political choices, accepting differences, paying attention to other points of view, a pragmatic search for compromise: all things that Christians do not easily conceive or practise.'[35] Intransigent Catholicism lies at the origins of Catholic Action and of the other currents of Left Catholicism that we have surveyed. In the most politicised groups, those that are most critical of church institutions (*Chrétiens Marxistes, La Quinzaine, La Lettre*, etc.) as with those groups focused on militant pedagogy and socialist struggle (*Témoignage Chrétien, Vie Nouvelle*, etc.), the issue is always the same: linking faith to politics, justifying political struggles in the name of the gospel, forging theologies that transform earthly activities into sacred, transcendent causes.

French Catholics have constantly oscillated between two extreme positions, one strictly subordinating political decisions to ethical norms and to the doctrine of the Church, the other affirming the specificity of political action and claiming its complete independence of religious and moral imperatives.[36] It is obvious that Left Catholicism is entirely associated with the first position. In recent years, Catholic Action movements have been emancipated from the control of the hierarchy and this is a sign that secularisation is overcoming Catholic intransigence by setting loose the instruments it had forged to re-Christianise society. But viewed in another way, the doctrines of most of these groups show that the intransigent mentality is not dead. For Left Christians organised as such, the issue remains one of legitimising their political choices by religious references and therefore of incarnating their total faith in a new social project.

THE NATURE OF FRENCH CATHOLICISM

Having considered the origins and principal components of Left Catholicism, we move to the issue of the homogeneity of Catholic culture. If Catholics are defined by degrees of practice, two conclusions follow: that there are fewer and fewer Catholics strongly integrated into their Church since there are fewer and fewer regular church-goers; and that these Catholics belong, in the overwhelming majority, to the traditional Right. Concluding an analysis of non-directive interviews of Catholics, Michelat and Simon write: 'The culture of declared Catholics is at root that of a traditional France, predominantly rural and land-owning, and with a conservative orientation.'[37] However indisputable the conclusion, the question arises of whether Catholicism might not be linked to cultures other than that of the traditional Right. If so, from which specific religious values might other political linkages proceed?

A first approach to this question is provided by a set of non-directive interviews with a sample of French people aged 20-40 years.[38] The study sought to identify the main patterns of self-perception and of conceptions of the world underlying the behaviour and attitudes of French adults. The respondents were told the following: 'I would like us to discuss what it means or what it could mean today for you to be happy.' This very general suggestion, understood by everybody, was intended to elicit the conceptions of the respondents in the most varied domains: family, work, society, politics, religion, etc. Of the seven broad world-views that emerged in the analysis of the interviews, three explicitly derive their coherence and inspiration from Catholicism. Indeed, although the question in no way directly prompted such a response, the answers explicitly referred to religious faith. But the differences among these three models are so fundamental that we can in no sense treat Catholics as an homogeneous population characterised by a set of common behaviours. Broadly speaking, the three models differ in the ways in which the respondents affirm their faith, in their ways of life, and in the aspects of life that they consider most important.

Three affirmations of faith

The respondents of model A see themselves as men and women of conviction. They act according to a certain conception of themselves and of the world, knowing that it is a choice, a risk, and hardly certain. Truth in religious matters, as in politics, does not come from above or from an explicit reference to divine transcendence; rather it must be sought in the heart of historical events, in a life in which the concrete and the 'experienced' are preferred to rational and conceptual constructions. It is not easy to believe, these respondents say, and yet it is the strength of their political and religious conceptions that lies at the basis of their behaviour and gives them added meaning.

For the respondents grouped in model B, the issue is not choosing one's side, taking a position amidst uncertainty, but on the contrary, sticking to a certain number of certainties. To believe and to hope is to affirm a basic truth that comes from above; faith is responding to a gift received at birth. Religious truth is primary and implies many consequences on ethical, social and political levels. It follows that what is at stake is not so much changing the world as 'standing up' to it and to its possible perversions.

Finally, the respondents of model C, leaving aside convictions and certainties, search above all for simplicity in the expression of faith. They wish to show that a return to the spirit, a communion with nature and humanity, is possible in the simplicity of everyday life. They see themselves as different from the others, from the majority that has not yet left the traditional forms of political and religious expression. For them, the concern is to give witness by their lives, more than by what they say or do, to the reality of 'another way', possible here and now.

Three ways of being, three ways of acting

'One must fight, things must change, nothing is inevitable.' To be an activist on social or political issues is, for the respondents of model A, the fundamental way of living one's faith and expressing it. In opposition to the values of normality and stability that they consider as invasive in our society, they see themselves as the defenders of sacrifice and selflessness. In so doing, they refuse to act as individual heroes or isolated witnesses, but try to persuade others that all participate in a collective history, the meaning of which derives from its objectives. For these Christians, as activists in political parties, in unions or associations of the Left, their basic conviction is of belonging to humanity in such a way that nothing that affects the lives of others can be indifferent to them. Life means 'acting with' others to bring about the reign of their ends.

For the Catholics classified in model B, the issue is not one of becoming an activist but rather of being exemplary, and remaining exemplary. Having no doubts about the values they hold as the result of the initial act of grace, they treasure their moral ideal more than all else, even when they have the feeling of being in the minority. They place a high value on the individual; they fear collective action and political ideologies, seeing in them threats to the individual personality and to faith itself. Valuing order and concerned about moral collapse in society, they strive to remain exemplary, to 'stand up' to a troubled world by serving the cause of 'human beings'.

Refusing to be exemplary, let alone activists, the respondents of model C see themselves as witnesses. It is not a question of involvement in a collective struggle ('act with') or of disinterested service for people ('do for'), but rather of transforming oneself, of returning to an original simplicity (to 'remake oneself'). Demonstrating that another life is possible is, as far as they are concerned, a symbolic matter of living in accord with a religious faith rather than an issue of political action which they decry.

Three contexts of life

Finally, we can identify different patterns of life favoured by the respondents clustered around each model. These preferences mirror their religious and political attitudes. Thus, if 'community' recurs often in the language of the respondents of model C, it is not only because it is a concrete reality for them, but also because it is a symbol invested with deep emotional significance. Community signifies the rejection of both the anonymous urban crowd and the ambiguity of collective action. This reflects the previously-discussed desire to distinguish themselves from the majority and also the kind of religious socialisation that marked the childhood of all the respondents of this model.

The respondents of model B focus not on the new community, but on the traditional family. The family is really perceived here as the basic unit of society, as its very heart, protecting its members against the aggressions of the outside world and allowing them to forge strong personalities to confront society and stand up against it.

The sense of belonging to a collectivity far larger than the compass of people directly known, the desire to see one's life as part of history—all this makes it difficult for the respondents of model A to specify the real or symbolic context in which they choose to live. Some speak of social class, others describe themselves as belonging to the world of humble folk or the poor. What is certain is that this context and the conception of self is less circumscribed than in the two other models: it is a vision of a world much wider in time and space, on the religious level as well as on the political level.

These three models are fundamentally different and represent different populations, but are all expressions of diverse values drawn out of Catholic culture. These results should encourage us to identify in the sociology and history of Catholicism the possible existence of different subcultures and to focus more on the cross-currents and sub-themes that run through Christianity. One approach that appears fruitful in this regard, is to examine the tensions in Catholic spirituality and theology between an emphasis on the figure of God, 'all-powerful Father, creator of heaven and earth', and an emphasis on the figure of Christ, God made man, who by his death and resurrection has sanctified and made divine all humanity and its history. Only Christianity has organised, from the very beginning, the faith of men around two poles: faith in God, the Supreme Being and ultimate reference for human action; and faith in Jesus Christ, a historical person and the incarnate word of God. The first pole is usually called theocentrism and the second Christocentrism.[39] The tension between these two references has been a constant in the Church's history. One or the other has probably been dominant in different periods and has provided a framework of reference for different world-views. These poles may have been selectively identified with by different social groups, given the contradictory implication that each has for politics and society, as well as for religion.

Thus the primary religious attitude attached to the theocentric vision is confidence in a God who is all-powerful, fundamentally unknowable, but whose will is accessible by the intermediary of grace. This attitude inspires a spiritual outlook whence all existence derives meaning by the contrast between the infinite greatness of the deity and the infinite smallness of the creature. Here, all comes from above and therefore the worshipper can only be conscious of his own weakness and of his want. It is the authority of the Father and not that of the Hero that is stressed. This authority, based on the family unit, assumes the form of a protective tutelage to which one accords confidence and respect. In the evolution of Christianity, the reinforcement of the theocentric pole should be seen in relation to the stability of a society based on natural order and strongly organised around paternal images.

The family here is not only the refuge of each of its members but also the witness of a divine order, the pillar of society. This is because the family embodies a benevolent authority and reconciles the principle of authority with a basic, diffuse warmth. The family thus provides the model of what all society and all social history should be: an order without violence. The translation of such an attitude to politics and society can easily be surmised. This type of believer prefers regimes based on a figure of benevolent authority. He is attracted to forms of social organisation based on a system of hierarchical responsibility in which everyone has a specified place and contributes to the same task and to the same social order without tension or conflict.

The Christocentric faith opens on to a totally different world. Here, what matters first is not the order of things and the omnipotence of the Father, but history and the history of men. When divinity is at stake, it is first and foremost that of Christ, that is, of a God incarnated in history and thus of men reconciled with time. A moment in history is rendered sacred: the one in which, two thousand years ago, God was born to men. But more important, all human history becomes holy, since it is inscribed between this first Epiphany and the final *parousia*. In this perspective all life and everything in life takes on a meaning defined by the two historical points. Individual life is invested with meaning by a sense of all mankind moving forward; the family and natural community appear static marks, here and now, of the eternity of the Father and of the force of his order, but without the same central position as in the theocentric vision. On the strictly religious level, the reference to God the master of all things, is replaced by the reference to the Christ of love; religious expression emphasises the emotional, even an identification with the emotional states of Christ, rather than adoration and submission before the Creator. The fundamental attitude to the divine is no longer marked by deference, devotion, and respect, but by enthusiasm and fervour, possible because of the human face of divinity.

Many of the themes and attitudes that characterise each of these two versions of Christianity are, aside from their purely religious aspect, usually considered as characteristic of the political worlds of Right and Left in France. Recall what Slama has recently written of the Right and Left: 'The principle of the Right is the natural hierarchy, the principle of the Left is fraternity.' The Right, according to Slama, 'demands a harmony between man and his environment that roots the individual in the determinism of the natural order: to each his place, his job, his status . . . Whereas the Left conscience is inspired by a Promethean vision of man in nature, dominating and taming it, the Right has characteristically distrusted man's power in the world and had a basic respect for the world as it is.'[40] The affinities are striking between the attitudes associated with the Left and the ones that we have just qualified as deriving from Christocentrism, and between the attitudes of the Right and the ones that we have found in the theocentric vision.

Thus we consider it certain that at least two subcultures coexist within Catholicism, subcultures with opposing views of the relations between the self and others, of the divine, and of history.[41] Given this double polarity in Christianity, the long-term existence of two theological, spiritual, and social currents, we may hypothesise that Catholicism offers, in its theocentric version, ideological support to dominant or declining social groups. It might offer non-dominant social groups, those that hope to change their position, another kind of support in its Christocentric version.

The respondents of the third Catholic model are more difficult to characterise. They speak sometimes of God, rarely of Jesus Christ. This suggests theocentrism, but their insistence on being witnesses, on the brotherly spirit of community life, and on the freedom of each person concerning his vocation, makes it more plausible to treat this vision as closer to Christocentrism. In fact, this new set of conceptions is becoming common. Over the past ten years, this model type, often of Catholic upbringing, in pursuit of a dream of communion with nature and community with his fellow men, has become as familiar as that of the activists of model A or of the church-goers of model B.

Perhaps we should then modify somewhat the dual opposition that we have proposed to explain the religious attitudes involved in our models. Indeed the Christian faith has not been so much bipolar over the past twenty centuries as tripolar. Alongside God the Father and Christ the Brother, there has been a third pole, symbolised by the image of the Holy Spirit. Let us call this 'spiritualocentrism'. In Christian thought, the Holy Ghost is most often associated with the themes of love, liberty, and presence. Like Nature, it is fertility. It recalls origins, the roots of being. It negates the opposition between ideas and matter. The spirit, inspiration, envelops both body and soul, thus escaping any dual opposition. It is life, the well-spring of life. The believer is expected to be able to recognise it in the depth of his being, in his heart. In Christian myths the spirit gives birth to all community, starting with the first one: at Pentecost the spirit is supposed to inspire the Church, the community of believers that it continues to inhabit. In sum, it is the spirit that accompanies man in his most intimate solitude as well as in the life of any community.

In Christian thought, and in the life of the Catholic Church, the image of the Spirit is associated with a range of symbols that express specific values and attitudes, not only sacred ones involving the relations between the individual and the divinity, but also social and psychological ones involving the relations of the individual with himself and with others. The striking affinity between the themes that theology has elaborated around the third person of the Trinity and those developed by the respondents of model C, suggests the hypothesis that there exists a third Christian pole from which arise values and attitudes, hardly or not at all expressed by the first two poles.

In our view theocentrism and Christocentrism genuinely correspond to two opposing and coexisting systems of values and attitudes within Catholicism. They probably both have specific histories—if still largely unexplored—and both are embodied in subcultures corresponding to different and antagonistic social groups. The existence of a 'spiritualocentric' trend in Catholicism is less certain. But considering this pole might, if we carefully examine its implications for values and attitudes, enable us to account for some of the changes within the Church, especially over the past ten years. Thus the flourishing of spiritual movements, of prayer groups like the charismatic revival, or the appeal of contemplative convents, might be the signs of the emergence of a current reflecting this third religious pole. The development of small communities and perhaps some of the ecology sentiment might draw on the same trends.

This exploratory survey by non-directive interviews has forced us to recognise the diversity within Catholicism and, consequently, has led us to question theories about *the* political culture of Catholics. The political culture characteristic of regular church-goers, built on respect of natural hierarchies and social conservatism, is undoubtedly the dominant culture within French Catholicism. But other systems of behaviour and attitudes clearly can find in the Catholic religion the symbolic resources necessary for their organisation. Thus, French Left Catholicism, the principal trends of which we have surveyed, is not an aberration or an accident in French political and religious history. It is one of the constituent elements in Catholic culture, undoubtedly a minority and hence often invisible in surveys. But on this current many people with no apparent religious connections draw the values that organise their behaviour and world-views.

NOTES

1. A. Latreille and R. Rémond, *Histoire du catholicisme en France*, Vol. III. Paris: Spes, 1962.
2. R. Rémond, *La droite en France*. Paris: Aubier, 1969, pp. 268-73.
3. A. Coutrot and F. Dreyfus, *Les forces religieuses dans la société française*. Paris: A. Colin, 1965, p. 212.
4. Jean XXIII, *Encyclique Mater et Magistra*. Paris: Spes, 1962.
5. *Lettre apostolique de SS. le pape Paul VI à Monsieur le Cardinal Roy à l'occasion du 80ème anniversaire de l'encyclique Rerum novarum*. Paris: Ed. Le Centurion, 1971.
6. *Foi et marxisme en monde ouvrier*. Note de la commission épiscopale française du monde ouvrier, July 1977.
7. *Politique, Eglise et foi. Pour une pratique chrétienne de la politique*. (Rapports présentés à l'Assemblée plénière de l'episcopat français, Lourdes 1972), Paris: Ed. Le Centurion, 1972.
8. *Libération des hommes et salut en Jésus-Christ*. (Réflexions proposés par le Conseil permanent de l'episcopat suite à la session pastorale de 1974), Paris: Ed. Le Centurion, 1975.
9. M. Brulé, 'L'appartenance religieuse et le vote du 5 décembre 1965', *Sondages*, No. 1, (1966).
10. *Sondages*, Nos. 1 and 2, (1974).
11. *Sondages*, No. 1, (1973).
12. A. Lancelot, 'La France de M. Bourgeois-République', *Projet*, No. 76, (June 1973), pp. 670-85.
13. C. Peyrefitte, 'Religion et politique', *L'Opinion française en 1977*. Paris: Presses de la Fondation Nationale des Sciences Politiques, 1978, pp. 117-34.
14. P. Braud, 'Les élections legislatives de mars 1978 en Bretagne', *Revue Française de Science Politique*, Vol. 28, No. 6, (December 1978), p. 1028.
15. In 1966, French people who attended mass every Sunday were considered regular church-goers. Today, both those who declare they practise every Sunday and those who go once or twice a month are considered regular church-goers.
16. See G. Michelat and M. Simon, *Classe, religion et comportement politique*. Paris: Presses de la Fondation nationale des sciences politiques et Editions Sociales, 1977; and G. Michelat and M. Simon, 'Religion, class and politics', *Comparative Politics*, Vol. 10, No. 1, (October 1977), pp. 152-86.
17. G. Michelat and M. Simon, 'Niveau d'intégration religieuse et comportements politiques', *Actes de la 15ème conférence internationale de sociologie religieuse*. Venise: Lille, Secretariat de la CISR, 1979, p. 126.
18. SOFRES survey in *Le Nouvel Observateur*, 1 June 1981.
19. *Témoignage Chrétien* began in 1941 as an underground publication in which Catholics opposed Nazism, collaboration, and the Vichy regime in the name of Christian faith. Later,

TC led a fight against colonialism and imperialism. Today they print 70,000 copies each week.
See R. Bedarida, *Les armes de l'Esprit. Témoignage Chrétien* (1941-44). Paris: Ed. Ouvrières, 1977; and J.P. Gault, *Histoire d'une fidélité*. Paris: Ed. *Témoignage Chrétien*, 1963.

20. In 1947, *Vie Nouvelle* brought together former Scouts who wished to live according to evangelic ideals and to find forms of communal life. Inspired by Emmanuel Mounier's personalism, members of *Vie Nouvelle* progressively discovered politics, especially during the Algerian War. Today, *Vie Nouvelle* has 3,500 members. See J. Lestavel, 'La *Vie Nouvelle* et ses militants', *Esprit*, Nos. 4 and 5, (April-May 1977), pp. 153-69.

21. *Témoignage Chrétien* and *Vie Nouvelle* are among the principal organisations backing *Chrétiens pour le socialisme* (Christians for Socialism) in France.

22. H. Lasserre, 'Religion et ascension sociale: l'exemple des ouvriers chrétiens', *Revue française de sociologie*, Vol. 13, (1972), pp. 392-8; 'Ethique chrétienne et esprit de classe', *Archives de sociologie des religions*, No. 34, (1972), pp. 25-7.

23. A. Rousseau, 'Mais ces chrétiens de gauche d'où viennent-ils?' *Autrement*, No. 8, (1977), pp. 23-30.

24. *La Lettre* prints 3,000 copies a month. It took over the *Quinzaine*, a *progressiste* publication condemned by the Vatican in 1955. The *Quinzaine* had 6-7,000 subscribers and united Christian militants against anti-communism.

25. The 'Christian-Marxist' movement was started in 1975 by Catholics who used Marxist references to distinguish themselves from the 'traditional Left' of *Témoignage Chrétien* and *Vie Nouvelle*. Its publication, *Cité Nouvelle*, prints 3,000 copies.

26. See P. Baligand *et al.*, *Echanges et dialogue ou la mort du clerc*. Paris: IDOC France, 1975.

27. See A. Dansette, *Destin du catholicisme français: 1926-1956*. Paris: Flammarion, 1975.

28. J.M. Donegani, 'De MPF en PSU: un mouvement entre en socialisme', *Autrement*, No.8, (1977), pp. 116-25.

29. B. Besret, *Incarnation ou Eschatologie? Contribution à l'histoire du vocabulaire religieux contemporain*. Paris: Cerf, 1964.

30. J.P. Ciret and J.P. Sueur, *Les étudiants, la politique et l'Eglise*. Paris: Fayard, 1971.

31. *Chercheurs et témoins de Dieu. Annoncer Jésus-Christ dans le temps qui vient.* (Assemblée plénière de l'épiscopat français, Lourdes 1975), Paris: Ed. Le Centurion, 1975.

32. G. Michelat and M. Simon, (1977).

33. On the psychological and social dimensions of religious identification and modes of individual expression of the sacred, see J.M. Donegani, 'Itinéraire politique et cheminement religieux: l'exemple des catholiques militants au Parti Socialiste', *Revue Française de Science Politique*, Vol. 29, Nos. 4-5, (August-October 1979), pp. 693-738.

34. See E. Poulat, *Eglise contre bourgeoisie. Introduction au devenir du catholicisme actuel*. Paris: Casterman, 1977; and S. Bonnet, 'Politique et religion dans l'oeuvre d'Emile Poulat', *Revue Française de Science Politique*, Vol. 30, No. 3, (June 1980), pp. 599-607.

35. R. Rémond, 'La greffe du marxisme et ses fruits', *Autrement*, No. 8, (1979).

36. R. Rémond, 'La politique des chrétiens', *Christus* Vol. 13, No. 52, (October 1966).

37. G. Michelat and M. Simon (1977), p. 75.

38. J.M. Donegani, G. Lescanne, *Les raisons de vivre des Français*. (1982).

39. H. Bremond, *Histoire littéraire du sentiment religieux en France*. Paris: Bloud et Gay, pp. 23-59; and J. Milet, *Dieu ou le Christ*. Paris: Ed. de Trévise, 1980.

40. A.G. Slama, *Les chasseurs d'absolu. Genèse de la gauche et de la droite*. Paris: Grasset, 1980; pp. 31-2.

41. See for an earlier statement of this hypothesis, R. Rémond, 'Droite et gauche dans le catholicisme français contemporain', *Revue Française de Science Politique*, Vol. 8, No. 3, (1958), p. 259 and Vol. 8, No. 4, (1958), p. 803. See also, J. Laponce, 'Dieu à droite ou à gauche?', *Canadian Journal of Political Science*, III, No. 2 (June, 1970), pp. 257-74.

The Catholic Church and Italian Politics: The Impact of Secularisation

Douglas A. Wertman

Much has been written about the impact of the Catholic Church and the religious factor on the post-war Italian political system. This article will discuss first how the Church's role in Italian politics has changed and will then examine the Church's audience by analysing the religious behaviour and attitudes of the Italian public in recent years and in the perspective of the past several decades. Finally it considers how these changes may affect the electoral base of the Italian Christian Democratic Party.[1]

THE CHURCH AND ITALIAN POLITICS: 1945-81

This section will review changes in the Church's role in Italian politics since 1945, in particular, in its willingness to intervene for the Christian Democratic party (DC) and in referendum campaigns against divorce and abortion, and especially during the 1970s and 1980s. Any analysis of the Church's role in Italian politics must start from an identification of the actors. These include the Pope, the CEI (Italian Bishops' Conference), individual bishops, parish priests, and the organisations of the Catholic subcultural network, including Catholic Action, the Confederation of Small Farmers (Coldiretti), and the Italian Christian Workers' Association (ACLI).

Under Pope Pius XII (from 1939 until 1958), the Catholic Church fully mobilised its resources in support of the DC. In 1946, and even more so in the confrontation election of 1948, the Church made an all-out effort in support of the DC against the Communists and presented the elections as conflicts between good and evil. This strategy was termed by Poggi as one of 'maximum involvement'.[2] There were public pronouncements by the Pope and the bishops and the Pope actively intervened during these early election campaigns: for example, before the 1946 Constituent Assembly elections, Pius XII told Italian voters that they had a choice between 'the champions and the destroyers of Christian civilisations'.[3] There were also direct appeals by the parish priests on election day itself—Italian elections are held all-day Sunday and Monday morning. The Church's direct intervention was all the more significant because its infrastructure had remained intact during Fascism, and it was the only organisation able to match, or better, the Communist network. In addition, the level of weekly church attendance was quite high—possibly as much as two-thirds of the population—so that a broad range of Italians could be reached directly, each Sunday, by the Church's messages. The Christian Democratic party had a weak infrastructure (as it still does) and was heavily dependent on the Church. Thirdly, the Catholic organisational network was quite strong and also intervened directly in support of the Christian

Democratic party. Catholic Action, whose structure was intact at the end of World War II, had three million members and, together with the affiliated Civic Committees set up to work during election campaigns, was ready and willing to be mobilised by the Church. In 1976, the headline of a magazine article pointed to the weakness of the Catholic network by asking: 'General Montini, how many divisions do you have?'[4] In the 1940s and 1950s, however, when 'General' Pacelli (Pope Pius XII) openly supported the DC and attacked communism, he had a strong, united organisational network at his disposal.

When Amintore Fanfani became DC party secretary in 1954 he began a major effort to build up the party organisation and to reduce the DC's reliance on the Church. Four years later John XXIII became Pope, and, during his papacy, there was a substantial shift towards taking the Church out of politics. At the same time, through Vatican Council II and encyclicals such as *Mater et Magistra* and *Pacem in Terris*, Pope John changed the tone and style of the Church's messages.[5] His policies were an important factor in two ways: in making possible the 'opening to the Left', which brought the Italian Socialist party into the governing coalition in the early 1960s; and by decreasing the stridency and the extent of the electoral involvement of the Italian bishops. Already by the 1963 election, and even more in the 1968 election, the statements of the Italian Bishops' Conference (CEI) reflected Pope John's de-emphasis of direct church intervention in politics. Pope Paul VI, elected in mid-1963, for much of his papacy continued the same policy, avoiding direct public involvement in Italian politics.

In the 1970s and 1980s, however, there has been a return to more open and active church intervention in Italian political life, though in a sporadic and more selective fashion. Divorce, the Communist party's success in the 1975 regional elections, the selection of some dissident Catholics to run as independents on the Communist party ticket in the 1976 elections, and abortion have been the major reasons for this.

The Church now faces three major objective limitations:

(1) only about one-third of Italians attend mass weekly (half the number of the late 1940s and early 1950s);
(2) the Catholic organisational network is much weaker and also less willing to support the Church, particularly by direct political intervention;
(3) the Church is not as monolithic as it once was.

Any decision for direct intervention against divorce, abortion, or communism will find some bishops and probably many priests unwilling to join in actively. The Pope's direct involvement becomes ever more crucial as the stretch of the Catholic Church and related organisations becomes shorter; there are many Italians who hear church messages only through the Pope's pronouncements.

By the 1970s, the Catholic organisational network had greatly altered. Catholic Action has approximately 700,000 members (about a quarter of the membership of the late 1940s) and it is more divided in its view of its role in Italian politics, as the events of the 1970s have shown. The Confederation of Small Farmers (Coldiretti) still represents well over a million farm families, but it has a considerably smaller membership than twenty or thirty years ago as a result of the tremendous decline in the agricultural population. The

Coldiretti continue to be an important influence in many rural areas in Italy, remain closely intertwined with the DC, and have more than twenty national, regional, or local officials in the DC parliamentary delegation.

Especially since 1969, both the Italian Christian Workers' Association, ACLI, organised by the Church shortly after World War II for working-class Catholics, and CISL, the Catholic trade union confederation formed in the late 1940s, have taken positions more independent of the DC as well as of the Church. Thus, the commitment to the DC—especially in the case of CISL and ACLI, and Catholic Action to a lesser degree—and the strength of particularly, Catholic Action and the Civic Committees, but also the Coldiretti, have declined when compared with the 1940s or 1950s, or even the 1960s.

The Divorce Referendum

In December 1970, after years of debate over the issue, a divorce bill became law in Italy.[6] Under pressure from the Church, the Christian Democrats had tried to block this and succeeded in getting Parliament to pass a law implementing the referendum provisions of the 1948 Constitution, at last making a referendum possible. While the threat of a Catholic-backed referendum did not prevent the passage of the divorce law, it did make possible the Catholic-sponsored effort, supported by the Italian Bishops Conference and which resulted four years later in the referendum to repeal the divorce law.

The May 1974 referendum, which defeated the repeal by a substantial 59 to 41 per cent margin, was a watershed event, for it showed the extent of secularisation in Italian society, the declining influence of the Church over the Italian public, and the divisions within, and weakness of, the Catholic subculture. It undoubtedly accelerated the growth of dissent within this subculture. Religious influence was clearly no longer the dominant force in Italian culture. Also, of course, the divorce referendum marked the beginning of the first major threat to DC dominance of the Italian political system, for the DC had fought an all-out campaign for repeal.

The Italian Bishops' Conference (CEI), on 22 February 1974, issued a document on the referendum which many observers compared to pre-Vatican II statements. It argued that every Christian ought to defend the 'unity of the family and the indissolubility of marriage by making use of the constitutional instrument of the referendum'.[7] To support divorce would be an act of disobedience for Catholics, the bishops stated. But among the Italian public there was widespread feeling that one could at the same time 'be a good Catholic and be in favour of the divorce law'. Seventy-three per cent indicated support for this view in an April 1974 survey. Even a majority of those attending church weekly (by 60 to 38 per cent) thought that a good Catholic did not have to favour a repeal.[8]

The Pope's position throughout the campaign was somewhat more restrained than that of the CEI. Though he made clear his opposition to the divorce law, as he had when he expressed his 'deep grief' at its passage, he did not take the hard line of the bishops. Some bishops and lower clergymen disagreed with the CEI statement. Many of the bishops *did* reiterate the hard line of the CEI in their pastoral messages, but others, who also opposed divorce, did not want the Church so committed in politics. Cardinal Pellegrino, then Archbishop of Turin and a leading progressive among Italian bishops, stated that 'the institutions of the Church should refuse all direct responsibility in the conduct of the referendum'.[9]

There were also many cases of individual priests who openly opposed the CEI's position on divorce and/or on the divorce referendum—or who at least refused to give it their full support. Some were disciplined. One indication that many priests apparently made no effort to win support for repeal comes from the same April 1974 survey reported above. When Italians were asked from which interpersonal sources they had heard directly about the divorce issue, only 13 per cent named their parish priest—compared to 54 per cent mentioning family and 50 per cent friends and colleagues. Even among those attending church weekly, only 23 per cent had heard their priest speak on the divorce issue.[10] Though this figure undoubtedly would have been somewhat higher if the survey had been taken immediately after the Sunday of the referendum rather than shortly before, it is clear that many priests chose not to discuss the divorce referendum in their sermons. This strongly suggests that the Church's messages are less often transmitted by parish priests to practising Catholics than in the 1940s or 1950s.

Catholic Action formally supported the bishops against divorce, but a substantial group within Catholic Action rejected the idea of an anti-divorce crusade and instead argued for the free choice of each Catholic on the question.

The 1975 and 1976 elections

During the campaign for the June 1975 regional and provincial elections, the CEI failed to renew its call for the 'unity of Catholics'—the traditional endorsement of the DC. Amintore Fanfani, then party secretary for the second time, in his post-mortem on the election claimed that the absence of the CEI's traditional endorsement of the DC was a major reason for DC losses and PCI gains.[11] The reserve of the Church was clearly a victory for those in the Church who preferred less Church intervention in Italian politics. It also reflected the questions of some within the Church as to whether the DC, unless it reformed and revitalised itself, was really worth supporting.

Following the substantial gains by the Communist party in the June 1975 elections, the conservatives within the Italian episcopate won the day in December 1975, when the CEI issued a statement similar to the strongly anti-communist declarations made in the autumn of 1975 by Cardinal Ugo Poletti, the auxiliary Bishop of Rome. The CEI said: 'It is incompatible with the profession of the Christian faith to adhere to or support those movements, even if in diverse forms, which are based on Marxism, and which in our country have their fullest expression in Communism.'[12]

Within the episcopate there was substantial disagreement over the extent to which the church should involve itself in the 1976 elections, and over whether the CEI should endorse the DC and condemn the Communists, who at this point it seemed might overtake the DC as the largest party. A catalyst to church intervention was the decision of a number of well-known Catholic dissidents to run as 'independent' candidates on the Communist party ticket. On 21 May 1976, in a statement comparable in many ways with the pre-election speeches of Pius XII in the 1940s and 1950s, and a clear departure from John XXIII's efforts at depoliticisation, Pope Paul VI condemned Communism, called for Catholics to be 'united more than ever'—a clear endorsement of the DC—and strongly criticised the Catholics who had become candidates on the PCI lists, saying that the Catholic faith 'cannot be put together with a view totally and intrinsically opposed to its nature'.[13] After this papal statement to their assembly, the Italian bishops took a position which amounted to clear support of the DC and condemnation of communism.

While the Pope and the bishops clearly intervened more deeply in 1976 than in any election since the papacy of John XXIII, the total effort of the Catholic subculture certainly cannot be compared to the 'maximum involvement' of Catholics behind the DC during the late 1940s and the 1950s. The objective limitations discussed earlier, the smaller numbers attending church regularly, the weakness and/or lack of commitment to the DC of many organisations within the Catholic subculture, and the divisions within the Church and unwillingness of some bishops and many priests to follow the lead of the CEI, made an electoral effort like that of 1948 impossible.[14]

The papacy of John Paul II

In considering the role of John Paul II, elected in 1978, in Italian politics, it is important to remember that he is not Italian and is, therefore, less familiar with and less interested in Italian politics than his predecessors. Also of great significance is the fact that he comes from a combative Polish Church which is, in effect, an active cultural alternative to the official communist political culture. The hierarchy of the Polish Church has always played a direct role in Poland, one not dependent on intermediaries such as Catholic organisations or a Catholic political party like the DC. These factors help to explain the course which John Paul II has steered with the Italian church over the past three years—drawing back from direct involvement in elections or close linkage to the DC, but intervening forcefully on the question of abortion, a central moral concern of the Catholic Church. The 1979 election campaign clearly showed that Pope John Paul II was not prepared to intervene in support of the DC. In addressing the pre-election conference of the CEI, the Pope, in contrast to Pope Paul VI in 1976, chose not to involve himself directly in the 1979 Italian elections.

The Italian Bishops' Conference, following the Pope's lead, issued a 1979 pre-election statement very different in tone and message from its anti-communist declaration of December 1975 and its 1976 intervention. The May 1979 statement of the CEI omitted the traditional pro-DC phrase urging the 'unity of Catholics' in the elections.[15] The closest that the bishops came to supporting the DC, or mentioning communism or abortion, was in the statement that: 'Not every political choice is compatible with the gospel.

Coherence today excludes support for all political candidates and programmes which propose solutions in conflict with Christian principles on questions such as civil and religious freedom and the respect for human life and the family.'[16] There has been no evidence since the 1979 elections of any intention on the part of Pope John Paul II to involve the papacy or the Italian bishops actively again in support of the DC.[17]

While the Pope has not intervened in Italian elections, he was the leading (and active) spokesman for the Church in the 1981 abortion referendum campaign. In 1976, an effort to change the original abortion law, which was very restrictive and dated from the Fascist period, was defeated by the DC and MSI together. In 1978, however, the lay political forces were able to pass an abortion law which in effect permits women over the age of 18 to have a free abortion in any public hospital during the first trimester of the pregnancy. The Radicals wanted to broaden the right to abortion, for example, by allowing abortions in private clinics. The Catholics wanted to limit abortions only to cases when the physical health or the life of the pregnant woman is at risk.

Two separate referenda were proposed on the 1978 abortion law. An initiative of the Radical party called for further liberalisation, while the other, proposed by the Catholic *Movimento per la vita* (right-to-life movement) and eventually supported by the Christian Democrats and the neo-Fascist Italian Social Movement, called for a more restrictive abortion law. Though the Church did not at first fully support the efforts of the *Movimento per la vita*, it did eventually back the collection of signatures. Once the referendum was set, the Pope and the Italian Bishops' Conference both intervened in support of the initiative to restrict abortion. The Church's position is absolute: abortion is wrong under all circumstances. While continuing to state this moral position, the Pope and the CEI openly and forcefully backed the effort to restrict abortion to the limited circumstances permitted in the initiative of the *Movimento per la vita*.[18] The DC also endorsed the restriction of abortion, but without undertaking the kind of all-out campaign it had waged on divorce.

In the May 1981 referendum, 32 per cent voted for the Catholic-sponsored proposal (even fewer than had voted for the repeal of the right to divorce in 1974), and only 11.5 per cent chose the Radical party's proposal. Apparently more than half the voters (along with all the parties except the Radicals, Christian Democrats, and MSI) opposed changing the present abortion law.

Pope John Paul II clearly considers the question of abortion one of the most central for the Church. In the first two years of his papacy, he discussed abortion in seventy-six speeches or documents—averaging about one every ten days.[19] In the two months before the referendum, the Pope spoke out often against abortion, stating, for example, a week before the referendum: 'It is the duty of the Church to reaffirm that abortion is the murder of an innocent human creation. Therefore, the Church considers all legislation which permits abortion to be a serious offence to the basic rights of man and to the divine commandment "Thou shall not kill".'[20]

The result of this forceful intervention by the Pope in the abortion referendum campaign was a heated polemic among Italian political leaders over whether the Pope had the right to involve himself so directly in Italian affairs. Numerous magazine and newspaper headlines, and speeches by the leaders of lay political parties, used the word 'crusade' to describe the efforts of the Church in general and the Pope in particular. The assassination attempt on the Pope a few days before the referendum and the overwhelming defeat of the church-backed effort have calmed the debate about the Church's role for the moment, but the Pope's willingness to intervene on this occasion suggests that he would be ready to do so again if he considers it a moral issue central to the Church.

This section reviews mass attitudes towards religion and the links between religion and politics. It considers trends in and correlates of church attendance, attitudes toward divorce and abortion, and views on the clergy and on the critical question of whether one can be a good Communist and a good Catholic at the same time. The Church's audience is smaller and support for its positions has decreased, limiting the Church's ability to intervene effectively.

Church attendance: How many and who?

An individual's religious commitment has a number of facets, in particular, the 'ritualistic'—the specifically religious practices required of adherents—and the 'experimental', the feelings, emotions or sensations about religion.[21] The indicator of the ritualistic factor commonly used in survey research is frequency of church attendance. The level of church attendance has been viewed as a measure of the individual's insertion in the Catholic organisational network' and 'psychological identification with the Catholic subculture'.[22]

In Italy, many surveys of the past three decades have asked about the frequency of church attendance, using various measures. Some have asked whether the person has gone to mass or been in a church in the past seven days and others ask about habitual behaviour and measure weekly or regular church attendance. Comparison of the results of these two types of questions, at the same time and sometimes in the same survey, shows that 5-8 per cent more people attend church on any single Sunday than attend church weekly.[23]

The most recent results show that, in April 1980, 35 per cent reported attending church at least weekly, 44 per cent a few times a year, and 17 per cent never. In summer 1981, 39 per cent indicated that they had been in church within the past week, 18 per cent within the past month, 16 per cent within the past three months but not the past month, 13 per cent in the past year but not in the past three months, and 14 per cent not at all in the past year. In other words, while about a third of the Italians attend church weekly, about 38-40 per cent attend church on any given Sunday—except Easter, Christmas, or other special holidays, when attendance is much higher.

As Table 1 shows, those who attend church most frequently are women, older people, and residents of rural areas or very small towns. Looking at the combined impact of these characteristics, weekly church attendance is least common among young men (aged 20-34) and men living in large cities, and

TABLE 1

WHO ATTENDS CHURCH WEEKLY IN ITALY?
APRIL 1980*

Total (N̲)= 1,116; all proportions shown as percentages.

___

Sex

Men	26
Women	45

Age

20-34	22
35-54	33
55 and older	49

Sex and Age

	Men	Women
20-34	16	28
35-54	23	43
55 and older	32	64

Community Size

Up to 5,000 residents	44
5,000 to 20,000	34
20,001 to 50,000	35
50,001 to 250,000	34
More than 250,000	27

Community Size and Sex

	Men	Women
Up to 5,000 residents	31	57
5,000 to 20,000	22	45
20,001 to 50,000	26	43
50,001 to 250,000	30	37
More than 250,000	19	35

___

*Each percentage in the table represents the portion of each group which attends church at least weekly. The portion of the total sample attending church weekly is 35 per cent of the total.

Source: April 1980 Eurobarometer survey, conducted by DOXA in Italy.

most widespread among older women (aged 55 and older) and women living in rural areas or small towns. Interestingly, older men (55 and older) and younger women (aged 20-34), or men in rural areas or smaller towns and women in large cities, attend church to about the same degree. This suggests the importance of age (generational change will be discussed later) and size of community in intensifying the impact of sex differences. In particular, though women among all age groups of 20 and older are more likely to attend church weekly than men of the same age, these differences are less pronounced among the young.

Size of community makes a difference for a number of reasons. About half of the Italian parishes serve 12 per cent of the population; in other words, many parishes exist in sparsely populated rural areas or very small towns.[24] Conversely, the Church does not have a strong presence or network in cities, particularly large ones. Moreover, peer pressure toward church attendance is undoubtedly greater in small communities than in more anonymous large cities. Finally, farmers, possibly because of the kind of work they do and their dependence on and closeness to nature, attend church more regularly than other occupation groups.

Self-perceived religiosity

Data are also available on the experiential factor, that is, the feelings or emotions of the individual toward religion. Involvement in the rituals of the Church is only the outward manifestation of a religious experience that 'gets its value from the point of view of the believer',[25] expressing a sense of 'union' with the Divine.[26]

Religious experience has been measured in two ways in Italy during the 1970s: how religious the individual considers himself to be; and how much importance religion has in the person's life. Most recently, in April 1980, 22 per cent of Italians considered religion of great importance to their life and 36 per cent considered it of some importance; 39 per cent thought it of little importance or said they did not belong to any religion. In 1972 and 1975, respondents were asked how religious they considered themselves to be. Though these questions are somewhat different from those used in 1980, they are close enough for comparative analysis, particularly given the pattern and magnitude of the change reported below. Over the period 1972-80 the proportion of people considering religion of little or no importance to their lives (or seeing themselves as little or not at all religious) has almost doubled—from 21 per cent in 1972 to 31 per cent in 1975, to 39 per cent in 1980. At the same time, those considering religion of great importance (or seeing themselves as very religious) have changed very little and not in any consistent pattern over the past decade.

Sex and age are the two factors most closely correlated with self-perceived religiosity, and, as with church attendance, young men (9 per cent) and old women (41 per cent) are at the extremes in considering religion of great importance to their lives.

Attitudes on major religio-political issues

Divorce and abortion have been by far the most important religio-political issues of the 1970s and early 1980s. In both referenda, popular majorities supported ideas opposed by the Church; even fewer voted with the Church in 1981. Between 1947 and June 1970, DOXA asked Italians eleven times whether they would vote for a law instituting divorce. Over this period, support for divorce varied between 22-35 per cent, but there was always majority opposition (ranging from 56-71 per cent).[27] Changes clearly began to occur after the passage of the divorce law in late 1970, in part reflecting the event itself. Data reported by Luzzatto Fegiz suggest that a number of Italians would give up opposition to divorce once the law was passed.[28] While the opponents of divorce still outnumbered proponents in February 1971, it was by a more narrow (53 per cent to 41 per cent) margin than in June 1970 (57 per cent to 31 per cent).

Between February 1971 and March 1974, the attitude of a considerable number of Italians changed to support of the divorce law; the referendum ended with a 59 per cent to 41 per cent margin against repeal, confirming the findings of pre-referendum surveys. In a March-April 1981 survey, 69 per cent of those with an opinion (compared to 37 per cent in 1968 and 44 per cent in 1972 on a similar question) indicated support for 'maintaining the right of divorce'. This shows a further increase in support for divorce from 1974 and a substantial shift over eleven years away from the Church's position on this issue.[29] The most pronounced differences in attitudes are between those aged 21-35 (70 per cent against repeal of the divorce law) and those aged 55 and older (34 per cent against repeal); between men (58 per cent) and women (44 per cent); and between those with an elementary education or less (41 per cent) and those with high school or more (69 per cent).[30]

As would be expected, position on divorce is strongly related to the frequency of church attendance: those attending church weekly favoured repeal by a 46 per cent to 37 per cent margin, compared to opposition to repeal among those attending church at least once in the past three months (54 per cent to 33 per cent), and those never attending church (60 per cent to 29 per cent). Most interesting is the fact that, despite the efforts of the Church on this issue, 37 per cent of those who attend church weekly did not accept the Church's view. It should be noted that the strong opposition to divorce of the Bishop's Conference was not shared by all bishops or priests, and many (60 per cent) of the regular attenders rejected the view that one could not be a good Catholic *and* support the divorce laws.

Clearly, many practising Catholics (37 per cent) voted in opposition to the Church's position on divorce, and, as reported earlier in this paper, many (60 per cent) thought they could vote as they wished without violating their religious commitment; few had heard about divorce directly from a priest. Overall, this presents a picture of the Church with a limited influence over only a minority of the Italian voters.

Abortion was the second important religio-political issue by the mid-1970s, with the unsuccessful effort in 1976 to pass a revised abortion law (the Fascist code still being in effect then), the passage of a new law in 1978, and the two referenda on the issue in May 1981. Support for abortion appears to have increased substantially over the past decade. In October 1980, 32 per cent favoured abortion on demand, compared with 26 per cent in 1977 and 21 per cent in 1975.[31] Among women, support for abortion 'in all cases in which the woman wants it' increased from only 9 per cent in 1972 to 26 per cent in 1977. No 1980 breakdown is available, but in every survey where sex breakdowns on abortion can be examined, men and women do not differ in attitudes toward abortion—suggesting that the changes in attitudes on abortion apparent for women probably also occurred among men. Overwhelming majorities in October 1980, as in 1975 and 1977, thought abortion should be authorised if the pregnancy resulted from rape (78 per cent); if there was the risk of a malformed baby (86 per cent); when the woman's physical health is threatened (87 per cent); or when the woman's life is threatened (91 per cent).

In April 1979, 62 per cent agreed (42 per cent strongly) with the slightly more ambiguous statement 'women should be free to decide for themselves in matters concerning abortion'. A DOXA survey carried out in 1977 before the restrictive abortion law was changed, came up with a very similar division of opinion on abortion, though on a somewhat different question. In 1977, Italians, by a 55 per cent to 36 per cent margin, said that abortion is not a crime and that a woman should not be punished for undergoing an abortion.

Surveys showed virtually no male-female differences. Interestingly, this is in contrast to the other religiously-related behaviours and attitudes discussed thus far—with more women than men attending church weekly, considering religion of great importance, and opposing divorce. The largest differences were by age—again underlining the importance of this factor. In October 1980, abortion 'on demand' was supported by 36 per cent among those aged 18-34, 27 per cent among those aged 35-54, and 15 per cent among those aged 55 and over. In April 1979, 74 per cent among those aged 15-19 and 20-34, 62 per cent among those aged 35-54, and 48 per cent among those of 55 and older, agreed that women should be free to decide for themselves about abortion.

In the 1979 survey, the position on abortion was strongly related to degree of religiosity. Only 27 per cent of those who considered religion of little importance in their life, and 31 per cent of those for whom religion is of some importance, but 55 per cent of those calling it of great importance, disagreed with the woman's right to decide on abortion. As with divorce, however, many (42 per cent) even among the most religious agreed that women should be free to decide for themselves on abortion.

Views on the clergy and on the Church in politics

Sympathy toward the clergy has declined somewhat in the past thirteen years, with gradual secularisation. On a 0 to 100 scale, the mean sympathy score for the clergy dropped from 58 in 1968 to 47 in 1981. Data from two intermediate points (1972 and 1975) show that most of this decline took place between 1972 and 1975—the period of the divorce referendum. However, this decline over the 1968 to 1981 period should not be seen as specific to the clergy. Putnam, *et al.* report that 'strikingly, public approval of virtually every one of these groups [the three major parties, the unions, and the big industrialists] declines over this period, even though they symbolise very different elements in Italian society'. Interestingly, the clergy received a higher average sympathy score than any of the other institutions tested.[32]

Italians generally believe that the clergy have the right and even the duty 'to intervene in discussions, even with public pronouncements' on questions such as marriage (29 per cent say the Church has the right, and an additional 48 per cent that it has the duty) and abortion (25 per cent say that it has the right and 37 per cent that it has the duty), according to a 1976 DOXA survey.[33] A third think that the clergy should not be involved in this way with abortion. Though this question was asked five years before the referendum, it suggests that at least then, a majority was willing to see the Church involved in public discussions on abortion. We have no data for 1981 after the heated debates over the role of the Pope and the Church in the abortion referendum campaign.

On 'politics in general', however, there is overwhelming opposition (75 per cent) to church intervention; only 18 per cent approve such involvement. Though there were more not answering on the same question in 1958 (54 per cent disapproved and 25 per cent approved church intervention in politics), it appears that, at least for the past twenty years or so, there has been widespread opposition to church involvement. In related questions in the 1972 Sani-Barnes survey, 72 per cent thought that the Church should not involve itself in political life, and 70 per cent did not think that 'a good Catholic [should] follow the advice of the Church to vote for a political party'.

Good Catholic/good Communist?

The anti-Communism which has always been an important source of Christian Democratic electoral support, comes not only from political conservatism, but also from its religious base. The Church intervened in a massive way in the late 1940s and during the 1950s in support of the DC, but also against the Communist party. In the 1976 elections, there was also great concern expressed by the Church about communism, especially after a number of prominent Catholic dissidents agreed to run as 'independents' on the Communist party ticket.

DOXA, between 1953 and 1976, asked seven times whether one can 'at the same time be a good Catholic and a good Communist',[34] (see Table 2). Between 1953 and 1970, there was a substantial shift from a large majority saying no, to an even division. The same even split occurred in the 1974 and 1976 surveys. Christian Democratic voters have changed a little (from an overwhelming 87 per cent to 5 per cent margin of no over yes in 1953, to a, still large, 62 per cent to 28 per cent no in 1976). By contrast, most Communists have always said that it is possible to be both (in 1976, by a 75 per cent to 18 per cent margin). In 1976, while 54 per cent of those regularly attending church said that one could be both a good Catholic and a good Communist, fully 36 per cent differed from the Church's view on the issue at a time (November-December 1976), only six months after Pope Paul's intervention and criticism of the Catholics running on the Communist ticket in the June 1976 elections.

TABLE 2

CAN ONE BE A GOOD CATHOLIC AND GOOD COMMUNIST
AT THE SAME TIME?, 1953-76*

	1953	1961	1963	1968	1970	1974	1976
				percentages			
Yes	21	19	28	36	44	45	45
No	67	60	56	47	44	42	45
Don't Know	12	21	16	17	12	14	10
Total	100	100	100	100	100	101	100

*'Do you think that one can be a good Communist and a good Catholic at the same time?'

Source: Data provided by DOXA. Total may be more than 100 per cent due to rounding.

Trends in church attendance: The secularisation process

Secularisation has been defined in a variety of ways. It will be viewed here as a process of 'decline of the explicitly religious values throughout society' which results in 'religion occupying a diminishing part of consciousness'.[35] Earlier discussions of the divorce and abortion referenda, as well as the mass attitudes toward these two issues, have suggested the impact of secularisation in this sense in Italy. However, the most commonly used indicator of secularisation—in part, because it is the most available—is a longitudinal comparison of the level of church attendance. Secularisation in Italy, defined in this way, has been discussed and documented by a number of scholars. Factors of importance in creating this secularisation process include increased urbanisation (we have seen the impact of community size on church attendance), the decline in the Italian population working in agriculture, and the effects of the vast mass mobilisation of students and workers in the late 1960s and early 1970s which was accompanied by substantial changes in values within Italian society.[36]

Table 3 clearly shows the decline in church attendance over the past several decades—with the big drop in the level of weekly church attendance occurring between the mid-1950s and the early 1970s. In the past decade, however, the overall level of church attendance has been quite stable. Between autumn 1972 and summer 1981, DOXA, on ten occasions (though only a few are reported in Table 3), asked the same question to those aged 15 and older: 'Do you remember when you were in church the last time (even if only for a few minutes)?'[37] In these ten surveys, the proportion reporting that they had been in church within the past seven days varied only between 37-43 per cent, with the most recent in summer 1981 being 39 per cent. The secularisation process thus had occurred at a rapid rate before the 1970s and, therefore, before the 1974 divorce referendum. Italy has already been substantially secularised; the most dramatic change has already taken place, but the evidence suggests that this process is continuing. In addition to generational changes discussed below, evidence of a continuing secularisation of Italian society comes from changes during the 1970s in self-perceived religiosity and in attitudes toward divorce and abortion discussed earlier in this article.

TABLE 3

WEEKLY CHURCH ATTENDANCE IN ITALY, 1956-81

percentages*	
1956	69
1959	57
1961	53
1968	48
Spring 1972	40
Autumn 1972	36
1974	40
1975	35
April 1976	37
October 1976	31
1978	36
1980	35

*These percentages represent the proportion in each survey reporting weekly church attendance (or having been in church in the past seven days).

Source: The data come from surveys conducted by or for the following: DOXA (1956, 1961, Autumn 1972, October 1976, and 1978); Demoskopea (1974 and April 1976); The Civic Culture study (1959); Samuel Barnes (by CISER, 1968); Samuel Barnes and Giacomo Sani (by Fieldwork, Spring 1972); Giovanni Sartori and Alberto Marradi (by Fieldwork, 1975); and the April 1980 Eurobarometer survey (conducted in Italy by DOXA).

The large majority of Italians still maintain some link (even if only occasional and more limited than in the past) to the religious structure. There has been only a limited increase over the past decade in those who say that they never attend church (or that they have not attended church in the past year). Those reporting that they never attended church were in 1968, 6 per cent; in 1972, 7 per cent; in 1976, 20 per cent; and in 1980, 17 per cent. The DOXA trend data from 1972-81 show that the proportion saying they had not been in church in the past year varied little—between 14-19 per cent. More among the young, however, are in this group: 14 per cent of those aged 35-54 and those aged 55 and older report never attending church, but 26 per cent of those aged 20-34 do so.

While secularisation has occurred, it has been less a matter of the middle-aged and older turning away from religion, but rather more a case of generational change. The substantial age group differences in church attendance reported in Table 1 could, of course, result either from a 'generational' change, indicating a more permanent trend, or from a 'life-cycle' change, suggesting that many of these young will become more regular church attenders as they grow older.

It was argued earlier that the three characteristics most closely related to church attendance are age, sex, and size of community. The evidence suggests that this has been true for sex and size of community for the past twenty or twenty-five years, but not for age. In eight surveys done between 1956 and 1980 where church attendance by sex is available, weekly church attendance is lower now among both men and women than twenty or twenty-five years ago, indicating that secularisation is at work on the young of both sexes; male-female differences in weekly church attendance, however, have varied little—only between 16-25 per cent, with 19 per cent more women attending church weekly in April 1980. Though fewer data points are available, twenty years ago church attendance varied with the size of the community in a way fairly similar to the variation found in 1980.

But while church attendance varies substantially with age today, this was not true twenty or twenty-five years ago. Comparing the young and the old shows that in 1956 and 1961 there was virtually *no* difference by age in the proportion having been to church in the prior seven days (in 1961, 51 per cent of those aged 21-34 and 54 per cent of those aged 55 and older). By 1968, there was a 15 per cent difference in weekly church attendance between those aged 21-30 (45 per cent) and those aged 61 and older (60 per cent). In the 1970s, there have been quite large differences between the young and the old. In 1972, 30 per cent among those aged 21-30, but 57 per cent among those older than 60, attended church weekly; in 1980, 21 per cent among those aged 21-34, but 49 per cent among those aged 55 and older attended weekly). These age-group differences do not simply reflect a change from regular to occasional church attendance among the young; not only do fewer of the young attend church weekly, but more of the young never attend church. In April 1980, 26 per cent among those aged 20-34, compared with 14 per cent among those aged 35-54 and those aged 55 and older, reported that they never attend church.

Further examination of variation by age, including comparison of the same group as it aged across the twenty-year span from 1961 to 1980, suggests three patterns: those who were aged 35 or older in 1961 attend church today about as frequently as, or a little less than, they did in 1961, taking into account the somewhat greater life expectancy of women. Those who were aged 21-34 in 1961, attend church somewhat less today (36 per cent weekly) than in 1961 (51 per cent had been in church in the previous seven days). The big difference, however, is between the young of 1961 and the young of the 1970s. Weekly church attendance among those aged 21-34 in 1980 was 21 per cent, compared to 51 per cent in 1961.

We have, of course, seen throughout this article that there are fairly large young-old differences on most questions examined here, including religiosity, divorce, and abortion. The emphasis placed here on generational change rather than life-cycle change in the level of church attendance, is in agreement with similar emphases on generational change in studies on age differences among Italians in party preference[38] and in attitudes on foreign policy issues.[39]

Is there a revival in the religiosity of the young?

There has been recent speculation about a religious revival among those in their teens or early twenties. This speculation has been sparked in part by the development of *Comunione e Liberazione* (Communion and Liberation), which has approximately 100,000 members (mostly young), its own book stores, publishing company and communes, as well as several representatives among the Christian Democratic parliamentary delegation. It is a vital, active organisation which seeks to bring Christ and Christianity back into Italian society. Communion and Liberation has served, in some measure, to create a Catholic presence in many universities and among young people in many cities where such presence has long been weak or absent.

Data from the April 1980 Eurobarometer show that while among those aged 21-34, weekly church attendance is less common (21 per cent) than among those aged 35-54 (33 per cent) or those aged 55 and older (49 per cent), church attendance is more widespread among those aged 15-17 (44 per cent) and those aged 18-20 (34 per cent). However, this should not be interpreted as indicating a religious revival. First, the pattern suggests some role of parental influence, since those aged 15-17 are virtually all still living at home; some of those aged 18-20 have left the family, though many have not; but a substantial proportion of those aged 21-34 have left the home. Secondly, other data support the explanation that more people in the upper teens/lower twenties attend church regularly than those a little older. In the 1972 Sani-Barnes survey, 34 per cent of those aged 16-24 attended church weekly—more than the 25 per cent in the 25-34 age-group. However, by April 1980, only 21 per cent of this same group, now aged 24-32, attended church weekly. Thirdly, a major study on the religiosity of young people covering a survey of 5,000 people aged 18-25, has demonstrated, according to the principal researcher, Giancarlo Milanesi, that 'the process of secularisation, which has been occurring for years among the young people, has not stopped, as the oft-repeated hypothesis of the "return to the holy", of the "revival of religion" would lead one to believe.'[40]

Finally, as Table 4 shows, while more of those aged 15-19 than those aged 20-34, or even those aged 35-54, attend church weekly, it is clear that attitudinally (on self-perceived religiosity, divorce, and abortion) those aged 15-19 are very similar to those just a little older than them (20-34 age group). It is likely, therefore, that once the teenagers move into their twenties their patterns of church attendance will also approximate to those of the current 20-34 year olds. In sum, we conclude that there is no widespread religious revival among teenagers in Italy today.

TABLE 4

RELIGIOUS ATTITUDES AND BEHAVIOUR BY AGE
AMONG ITALIANS

Age	15-19	20-34	35-54	55 and older
		percentages		
Weekly church attendance (1980)	39	22	33	49
Religion of great importance (1979)	14	13	24	33
For the woman to be free to decide on abortion (1979)	74	74	62	48
Satisfied with result of divorce referendum* (1974)	67	70	53	34

Note: The percentage for each item represents the proportion of that age group attending church weekly, considering religion of great importance to their life, agreeing that women should be free to decide on abortion, or being satisfied with the result of the divorce referendum.

*The age groups available for this question were: up to 24, 25-39, 40-54, and 55 and older.

Source: The 1979 data are from the April 1979 Eurobarometer and the 1980 data are from the April 1980 Eurobarometer. The 1974 data are from Bollettino della DOXA, Vol. XXVIII, No. 15-16, (30 August, 1974), p. 120.

THE CHRISTIAN DEMOCRATIC PARTY AND RELIGIOUSLY-BASED SUPPORT

Many fewer Italians attend church weekly now than twenty years ago; many more support the right to divorce than ten or fifteen years ago; more support the right to abortion than a decade ago; and the younger generation is considerably less religious and more likely to differ with the Church on issues such as divorce and abortion. Italians generally oppose church intervention in politics. Even among those most likely to be influenced by the Church, that is, those attending church weekly or considering religion of great importance, a third or more hold views in opposition to the official Church position: 37 per cent favoured divorce in 1974; 60 per cent thought in 1974 that one could be a good Catholic and favour the divorce law; 42 per cent thought in 1979 that a woman should be free to decide for herself in matters concerning abortion; and 36 per cent said in 1976 that one could be a good Catholic and good Communist at the same time.

Given this secularisation, the public aversion to church intervention in politics, the apparent readiness of many regularly practising Catholics to differ with the Church, the decreased strength of the Catholic organisational network—and a disinclination of some within it to support the DC actively—and the diminished willingness of the Church to intervene for the Christian Democrats, what are the consequences for the religious base of the Christian Democratic electorate?

At such times as the divorce referendum, the 1976 elections, and the abortion referendum, religion is a highly salient force in Italian politics—and much more than in most other West European countries. While this appears to be slowly diminishing, religion also plays an important role in 'the passive relation to voting'.[41] The electorate of the Christian Democratic party remains very different from the electorates of other parties in terms of its church attendance and attitudes related to religious commitment. The Christian Democratic party has clearly not yet been significantly damaged by secularisation and declining support from the Church. The overall strength of the DC has been remarkably stable over the past five national elections since 1963 (varying only between 38.3 and 39.1 per cent)—though it must be kept in mind that this hides a shift toward increasing strength in the south and decreases in the north.

In the April 1980 Eurobarometer, 57 per cent of Christian Democratic voters claimed weekly church attendance. Thus the Christian Democratic electorate is very different from that of other parties in the portion reporting weekly church attendance among voters of small leftist parties—Proletarian Democracy and the Radical Party: 12 per cent; Communists: 14 per cent; among Socialists: 21 per cent; among voters of the three small lay parties—the Social Democrats, Republicans and Liberals: 34 per cent; and among MSI voters: 20 per cent. Religious adherence clearly remains an important basis of the Christian Democratic vote. Analysis of several surveys during the 1970s shows that the relationship between church attendance and support for the DC has changed little in the past decade, and the DC continues to receive the lion's share of the votes from those who attend church weekly. Among those declaring a party preference in April 1980, 70 per cent of those attending church weekly would vote for the DC, compared to 37 per cent of those attending occasionally, and 18 per cent of those who never attend church. Among those declaring their party preference in April 1979, the Christian Democratic Party gets 70 per cent of those considering religion of great importance in their lives, 44 per cent of those who feel it to be of some importance, but only 14 per cent considering it of little or no importance.

As with the population as a whole, there has been a considerable shift among Christian Democratic voters during the 1970s on the issue of divorce.

Looking at only those with an opinion, the right to divorce/opposition to the repeal of the divorce law among Christian Democrats was:

1968	1970	1974	1981
20%	24%	30%	47%

In 1981, by comparison among those with an opinion, the right to divorce was supported by 87 per cent of Communists, 83 per cent of the voters for other parties of the Left (PSI, PSDI, and DP), and by 70 per cent of the voters of parties of the Right (PRI, PLI, and MSI).[42]

On abortion, in a 1977 DOXA survey, abortion 'in all cases in which the woman wants it' was supported by only 12 per cent of Christian Democrats and 14 per cent of MSI supporters, but by 25 per cent of PSI voters, 37 per cent of the voters of the three small lay parties (PSDI, PRI, and PLI), and 41 per cent of the Communist supporters.

In sum, despite changes in the political role of the Catholic Church and a diminished willingness to support the DC, and despite changes in mass religious behaviour and attitudes as a result of continuing secularisation, we conclude that the Christian Democratic party still depends heavily on religiously-based support. The DC partisans are considerably more 'religious' overall, in terms of church attendance and in attitudes on issues such as divorce and abortion, than the supporters of other parties. As the pool of those who attend church weekly slowly declines because of continuing secularisation and the related generational shifts in attitudes, values, and party preference, new problems will arise for the DC in the 1980s. We can, however, expect religion to continue to weigh heavily as a 'passive' factor in Italian voting behaviour and as the single most important base of DC electoral support.

NOTES

The views expressed in this article are those of the author and not necessarily those of the International Communication Agency or the United States Government.

1. A more complete overview of the clerical issue in recent Italian political history would have to take account of Church-State relations and the interactions between Christian Democratic leaders and the Church. For lack of space, we must neglect these issues.
2. Gianfranco Poggi, 'The Church in Italian Politics, 1945-1950', in S.J. Woolf (ed.), *The Rebirth of Italy, 1943-1950*. London: Longman Group Ltd, 1972, pp. 135-55.
3. Giuseppe Mammarella, *L'Italia dopo il fascismo, 1943-1968*. Bologna: il Mulino, 1970, pp. 118-19.
4. Sandro Magister, 'Generale Montini, quante divisioni ha?', *L'Espresso*, 9 May 1976, pp. 11-12.
5. For a detailed discussion of the impact of John's papacy, see Alfonso Prandi, *Chiesa e politica: La gerarchia e l'impegno politico dei cattolici italiani*. Bologna: il Mulino, 1968.
6. For in-depth discussions of the divorce referendum, see Martin Clark, David Hine, and R.E.M. Irving, 'Divorce—Italian Style', *Parliamentary Affairs*, Vol. XXVII, (Autumn 1974), pp. 333-58; Arturo Parisi, *Questione cattolica e referendum: L'inizio di una fine.* (essay in the *Interventi* series), Bologna: il Mulino, 1974; and Alberto Marradi, 'Analisi del referendum sul divorzio', *Rivista Italiana di Scienza Politica*, Vol. IV, No. 3, (December 1974), pp. 589-644.
7. *Corriere della Sera*, 23 February 1974.

8.   This is a Demoskopea national survey reported in Giampaolo Fabris, *Il comportamento politico degli italiani*. Milan: Franco Angeli Editore, 1977, p. 68.
9.   *Corriere della Sera*, 19 April 1974.
10. This comes from a Demoskopea survey reported in Fabris, *Il comportamento politico degli italiani*, pp. 69-70.
11. See *Corriere della Sera*, 13 June 1975, and Antonio Caruso, 'I partiti italiani al'indomani delle elezioni', *La Civiltà Cattolica*, 2-16 August, pp. 282-91.
12. *Corriere della Sera*, 16 December 1975.
13. *Corriere della Sera*, 22 and 23 May 1976.
14. For a similar view, see Arturo Parisi, 'Il 20 giugno: resta aperta la questione democristiana', in Gualberto Gualerni (ed.), *I cattolici degli anni '70*. Milan: Gabriele Mazzotta editore, 1977, p. 207.
15. On the DC in the 1979 elections see Douglas A. Wertman, 'The Christian Democrats: Masters of Survival', in Howard R. Penniman (ed.), *Italy at the Polls, 1979*. Washington, DC: American Enterprise Institute, 1981, pp. 64-103.
16. *La Stampa*, 19 May 1979, p. 2.
17. In a March 1981 speech to some Catholic members of the French parliament from different parties, John Paul II spoke of what he called 'the legitimate autonomy of politics' with respect to the Catholic faith. Quoted in Sandro Magister, 'Convegni', *L'Espresso*, 12 April 1981, p. 20.
18. See the interview in the *Corriere della Sera*, 30 April 1981, pp. 1-2, with Father Bartolomeo Sorge, editor of the Italian Jesuits' journal, *Civiltà Cattolica*. See also the discussion in Sandro Magister, 'La crociata anti aborto', *L'Espresso*, 3 May 1981, pp. 6-9.
19. Magister, 'La crociata anti aborto', p. 9.
20. *Corriere della Sera*, 11 May 1981, p. 2.
21. Charles Y. Glock, 'On the Study of the Religious Commitment', Research Supplement to *Religious Education*, Vol. 42, (July-August 1962), pp. 98-110.
22. Samuel H. Barnes, 'Italy: Religion and Class in Electoral Behavior', in Richard Rose, (ed.), *Electoral Behavior: A Comparative Handbook*. New York: The Free Press, 1974, p. 213.
23. DOXA surveys done in autumn 1972, autumn 1976, and spring 1980, showed differences between those who had gone to church in the last seven days and those reporting weekly attendance of 8 per cent, 8 per cent and 5 per cent respectively. I would like to thank Dr Elio Brusati of DOXA for the data on church attendance reported here, as well as the summer 1981 data reported in the next paragraph.
24. See Parisi, *Questione cattolica e referendum* . . . (1974) pp. 13-14.
25. Herve Carrier, *The Sociology of Religious Belonging*. New York: Herder and Herder, 1965, p. 33.
26. Joseph E. Faulkner and Gordon F. DeJong, 'Religiosity in 5-D: An Empirical Analysis', *Social Forces*, Vol. 45, (December 1965), p. 253. The data in this section are from: 1972, Sani-Barnes survey; 1975, Sartori-Marradi survey; and 1980, April 1980 Eurobarometer.
27. Data are reported in *Bollettino della DOXA*, Vol. XXV, No. 8-9, (30 April 1971), p. 60.
28. Marradi reports the Luzzatto Fegiz findings and discusses the impact of the passage of the law on attitudes in Marradi, 'Analisi del referendum sul divorzio', (1974), p. 597.
29. These findings are reported in Robert D. Putnam, Robert Leonardi, and Raffaella Y. Nanetti, 'Polarization and Depolarization in Italian Politics, 1968-1981', (paper prepared for delivery at the 1981 Annual Meeting of the American Political Science Association, the New York Hilton, September 1981), pp. 37-8.
30. Data reported in this paragraph and the next come from *Bollettino della DOXA*, Vol. XXVIII, No. 9, (5 May 1974), pp. 79-81.
31. The 1972, 1975, 1977, and 1980 data come from DOXA surveys, while the 1979 data come from the April 1979 Eurobarometer.
32. Putnam, Leonardi, and Nanetti, 'Polarization and Depolarization . . . ', (1981), Figure 10 and p. 39.
33. The data from 1958 and 1976 reported in this paragraph and the next come from *Bollettino della DOXA*, Vol. XXXI, No. 3-4, (22 February 1977), pp. 12-13, 23.
34. The trend data in this section were provided by Dr Elio Brusati of DOXA.
35. Donald Eugene Smith, *Religion and Political Development*. Boston: Little, Brown, and Company, Inc. 1970, p. 114.

36. See especially Giacomo Sani, 'Ricambio elettorale, mutamenti sociali e preferenze politiche', in Luigi Graziano and Sidney Tarrow (eds.), *La Crisi Italiana*. Turin: Einaudi, 1979, pp. 303-28; and Gianfranco Pasquino, 'Italian Christian Democracy: A Party for All Seasons?', *West European Politics*, Vol. 2, No. 3, (October 1979), pp. 91-4.

37. I thank Dr Elio Brusati of DOXA for these trend data covering the past decade.

38. Sani, 'Ricambio elettorale, mutamenti sociali e preferenze politiche', (1979), pp. 303-28.

39. See Douglas A. Wertman, 'Italian Attitudes on Foreign Policy Issues: Are there Generational Differences?', in Stephen Szabo (ed.), forthcoming book on the 'successor generation' in Europe.

40. This new study is discussed in the *Corriere della Sera*, 12 September 1981, and 23 September 1981.

41. Gordon Smith, *Politics in Western Europe*. New York: Holmes and Meier Publishers, 1973, pp. 21-30.

42. The data reported above come from the following sources: 1968, Samuel Barnes survey; 1972, Samuel Barnes and Giacomo Sani survey; 1974, DOXA survey; and 1981, survey for Robert Putnam, Robert Leonardi, and Raffaella Nanetti.

Christians and Marxists in Allende's Chile: Lessons for Western Europe

Brian H. Smith

INTRODUCTION

In the late 1960s and early 1970s changes on the political Left and in the Catholic Church in Western Europe aroused interest in the possibilities for mutual rapprochement. Expectations of a more peaceful coexistence, and even the possibility of limited cooperation between the Left and the Church, were fuelled by electoral gains for communists and socialists; the distancing of some leftist parties from the Soviet line and their espousal of Euro-communism; the growth of movements within the Church favourable to socialism; and a more tolerant position by the Vatican and several national episcopal conferences towards new developments within Marxism.

The Left was primarily interested in diminishing Catholic support for conservative or confessional parties and reducing the hostility of clerical leaders to socialism. While some in the Church genuinely believed that the Left's socialist programme was more compatible with Christian principles than that of the capitalist Centre or Right, those in the hierarchy who expressed an openness to Marxism wanted to protect the Church if the Left should win an electoral majority or be invited into a governing coalition.

In the late 1970s interest in such a rapprochement waned as Euro-communism declined as a political force and the electoral prospects of the Left dimmed. The impressive 1981 victories of the French Socialists, and their subsequent incorporation of several Communists into the cabinet, however, renews the salience of the Christian-Marxist rapprochement question not only for France but also for Italy, Spain and Portugal, where the Left's electoral and/or executive chances could certainly be positively affected by French politics.

Such issues as the Church's official stance toward the implementation of a socialist programme (including education); Catholic cooperation with, or participation in, a leftist government; the political impact on practising Catholics' electoral behaviour of socialist rule; and the effect within the Church of expanded Catholic cooperation with the Left, are all once again critical questions facing Christians and leftist party leaders.

It would be premature to speculate about the prospects of resolving these challenges in ways acceptable to both sides. But on each of the points confronting the Church and the Left, the Chilean case during the Popular Unity government of Salvador Allende in the early 1970s offers some crucial lessons. Allende's coalition included Socialists, Communists and Radicals. It came to power without official Church opposition and maintained correct relations with the hierarchy throughout its term in office, including Catholics in cabinet positions, and steadily increasing its electoral support from practising Catholics while in power. The only issue which precipitated strong episcopal opposition was the school question, but intense conflict was avoided. Within the Church an activist minority strongly supported the objectives of the regime and acted as a catalyst in the founding of Christians for Socialism movements throughout Latin America, North America and Western Europe.

The Chilean developments offer a rich historical experience from which to explore how conflicts were or were not defused between the Left and the Church, testing the boundaries between coexistence and conflict, and estimating the costs for both sides in espousing such a rapprochement. This essay examines these issues in Chile and concludes by speculating on the relevance of this experience for Europe in the 1980s.

RELIGION AND POLITICS IN CHILE BEFORE ALLENDE

The patterns of religion and politics in Chile prior to 1960 were in some respects similar to those in much of Western Europe, but in others quite different. The similarities included: a nominally Catholic culture; multiparty electoral competition which included Conservative, Liberal, Radical, Christian Democratic, Socialist and Communist parties; and strong negative correlations between intensity of religious practice and vote for the Left. In Chile, however, religious issues in politics historically have not been as divisive as in Western Europe. Unlike France in 1905, for example, the separation of Church and State in Chile in 1925 occurred without major conflict between Catholics and the Left. Thereafter clerics ceased instructing Catholics how to vote. For the next thirty-five years, however, practising Catholics maintained their traditional allegiance to the Conservative party which, unlike the European Right, did not lose support after 1945 since it never aligned itself with fascism.

A Christian-inspired party, though in existence since 1938, did not, prior to 1960, attract large groups of practising Chilean Catholics as in many countries of Western Europe. This party, first known as the Falange Nacional (1938) and later the Christian Democratic party (1957), never developed a strong base among working-class groups since a significant Christian trade union movement had not emerged in Chile. Finally, the school issue never became as salient in Chile as in France, for, although Catholic schools began to receive public subsidies in the mid-1950s, this was not strongly contested by the Left, nor made an issue in electoral politics.

However, after the socialist Salvador Allende (with communist support) nearly won the presidential election in 1958, and votes for the Right declined in parliamentary and local elections in the early 1960s, significant numbers of Catholics shifted their support to the new Christian Democratic party. The hierarchy, while not officially endorsing a particular party, warned Catholics in 1962 that a Marxist electoral victory would cause 'persecution, tears and bloodshed' for Chilean Christians.[1] In 1964, when the Conservatives and Liberals backed the Christian Democratic (PDC) candidate out of fear of an impending victory by the united Left, Eduardo Frei of the PDC won the presidency with 55.7 per cent of the national vote. Allende received 38.6 per cent and Julio Durán, the Radical party candidate, 4.9 per cent with 0.8 per cent of the ballots null or void. Frei also received overwhelming Catholic backing, enjoying support from nearly three-quarters of the regularly practising Catholics in Santiago.[2]

By 1967, however, changes in Chilean Catholicism were leading the official Church to put distance between itself and the Christian Democratic party. Frei's reform programme frustrated many younger and idealistic party members, who desired a more aggressive attack on domestic and foreign capitalist interests. The reforms of Vatican II (1962-65), more openness on socialism by Pope Paul VI (*Populorum Progressio*, 1967), and the strong call for radical transformations in Latin America by 150 bishops at Medellín (1968), all gave legitimacy to Chilean Catholics wishing to see more rapid social changes than Frei's administration offered. Some left the PDC in 1969 and formed a new Christian-inspired party, the Movement for Unitary Popular Action (MAPU), calling for a unity among the working class behind the Left to work towards fundamental change in society. More conservative Catholics who had backed Frei in 1964 as a means of stopping Allende, found his reforms in agriculture, education and taxation threatening to their economic interests. They withdrew their support for the PDC in the late 1960s and backed the National Party (founded by Conservatives and Liberals in 1966). Sensing this disaffection among many Catholics with Christian Democracy, and the possibility of a leftist victory in the 1970 presidential elections, the bishops ceased making public statements against Marxism and emphasised the need for further structural changes benefiting the poor.[3]

Throughout this period the Left made overtures to the Church and to progressive Catholics in the hope of defusing religious issues in politics. In 1965 at the Thirteenth Congress of the Communist party, Senator Luis Corvalán, Secretary General, praised the progressive changes in the Church and promised that peaceful coexistence between the Church and a revolutionary government in Chile could be possible if the former refrained from 'interfering in party politics'. The *Programme of the Communist Party* adopted at its Fourteenth Congress in 1969, recognised that a growing number of Chilean Catholics 'are sympathetic to the revolution' and are 'seeking contact with popular organisations and with Communists'. The party welcomed such developments, stating that 'this experience constitutes the beginnings of dialogue' and enriches 'the revolutionary movement with new groups'.[4]

Moreover, in late 1969 when the Communist, Socialist and Radical parties formed a new electoral coalition—the Popular Unity (UP)—they announced a party platform for 1970 which on the whole did not threaten the Church. It ruled out as inapplicable to Chile, a strong centralised state, dictatorship of the proletariat, and single-party rule. It espoused complete nationalisation of basic resources and large critical industries. Most mining, agricultural, industrial, commercial and service enterprises were, however, of medium or small size and were to remain under private ownership, or involve the state only as a partner with private capital.[5]

The UP also committed itself to safeguard all liberties basic to Chile's democratic tradition, including freedom of speech, press, assembly, and worship. While the entire educational system was to be brought under more direct supervision by the state so as to inculcate socialist values (including private schools, most of which were Catholic), additional subsidies were to be given to both public and private institutions. The UP also guaranteed that all affected groups would be consulted and invited to participate in the planning and operation of this unified educational system.[6] Such promises, if kept, would give church officials and parents of children in Catholic schools a voice in designing and implementing the new programme.

In the face of these political realignments and promises by the Left to respect democratic freedoms and the interests of the Church, the hierarchy officially espoused a neutral position in the 1970 campaign, claiming Catholics could vote for candidates of their own choice. In turn, the new splinter party of young ex-Christian Democrats—MAPU—formally endorsed the Popular Unity candidate, Salvador Allende. In a close three-way election, Allende won a plurality of 36.2 per cent, followed by the National party candidate, Jorge Alessandri, with 34.9 per cent and the Christian Democrat, Radomiro Tomic, with 27.8 per cent; 1.1 per cent of the ballots were null or void.

Survey data collected in metropolitan Santiago one month before the 4 September election, indicate that shifts within the Church helped both the Right and Allende. While there was considerable Catholic fallout from Christian Democracy towards the resurging Right after 1964, significant numbers of Catholics moved to the Left. In fact, in 1970 Allende more than doubled his support among regularly practising Catholics in Santiago from his 1964 showing, and also substantially increased his appeal among those attending church occasionally. In a close, hard-fought campaign such gains among practising Catholics in the capital city where one-third of the nation lives were critical in the Left's national victory.[7]

RELATIONS BETWEEN THE CHURCH AND THE LEFT DURING THE TRANSITION PERIOD (SEPTEMBER-NOVEMBER 1970)

Since no candidate received a majority of the popular vote in the 1970 election (which is normal in Chilean multiparty competition), the Congress, controlled by Christian Democrats and the National party, was constitutionally mandated to choose the president by majority vote. Traditionally the Congress had selected the person with a popular plurality, but between the election in early September and the congressional vote in late October there was much domestic and international pressure to block Allende. The United States government and several US corporations provided substantial assistance to groups opposed to Allende's confirmation. A Chilean Right extremist group, having received support from the CIA, and hoping to provoke a military coup, attempted to kidnap army chief General René Schneider and mortally wounded him just prior to the plenary session of Congress.[8]

Amidst this climate of intrigue and fear, the Catholic bishops remained cautious but did not support those opposing Allende or attempting to undermine Chile's democratic process. In a private meeting with National

TABLE 1

CANDIDATE CHOICE AND RELIGIOUS PRACTICE AMONG CATHOLICS

(GREATER SANTIAGO, 1964 and 1970)

	Regularly Practising		Occasionally Practising		Non-practising	
	1964	1970	1964	1970	1964	1970
	%	%	%	%	%	%
Allende (Socialist-Communist)	9.8	22.2	18.1	30.5	25.2	35.3
Durán (Radical)	2.1		1.8		5.0	
PDC { Frei (1964)	74.9		62.9		52.4	
Tomic (1970)		28.7		25.2		27.7
Alessandri (National)		40.4		35.4		24.4
Undecided	13.2	8.7	17.2	8.9	17.4	12.6
Total Sample	N=235	N=171	N=337	N=246	N=361	N=119

Source: Centro de Opinión Pública, Santiago, Chile

party leaders during this interim period, Cardinal Raúl Silva Henríquez of Santiago refused their request to have the Church denounce the UP so as to secure Christian Democratic opposition to Allende in the coming congressional vote. The Episcopal Conference in late September urged citizens to overcome their fears of radical economic changes and to avoid resorting to violence as a way of preventing them.[9]

The bishops' refusal to play into the hands of the Right and the United States contributed to dialogue between the UP and the Christian Democrats. At the urging of the PDC, the UP parties agreed to support a constitutional amendment guaranteeing the strict observance of traditional freedoms by their government.[10] Once this was passed in Congress, the Christian Democrats agreed to vote for Allende and he was elected on 24 October.

Within hours of the congressional vote, a delegation of bishops led by Cardinal Silva paid the customary visit of church dignitaries to the president-elect. The conversation was cordial, and the Cardinal promised support for the incoming administration, declaring: 'We are at your disposal, Mr President, to help you carry out your major programme to promote the common good.' Allende reciprocated by attending with his new cabinet an Act of Thanksgiving (*Te Deum*) in the cathedral of Santiago which is traditional upon the inauguration of a new president. At Allende's request, leaders of other major religious denominations participated. The Cardinal prayed for the newly elected officials, who 'regardless of their personal ideologies or belief', deserve because of their 'legitimate authority' the 'respect and cooperation from all citizens in whatever promotes the common good'.[11] Thus, throughout the turbulent transition period official representatives of the Church and the Left maintained correct relations, and Allende began his presidency with significant ecclesiastical legitimation.

CHURCH-STATE COOPERATION (NOVEMBER 1970-APRIL 1972)

During his first year in office, primarily through the use of existing legislation and executive powers, Allende made significant strides towards socialising the economy. Congress unanimously approved total nationalisation of foreign-owned copper mines; the government gained control of two-thirds of the credit of banks and many key industries; agrarian reform was accelerated. Allende imposed price freezes on basic consumer goods, raised wages by 66.6 per cent and salaries by 35 per cent, expanded public works projects, and increased money circulation by 100 per cent. He, like Mitterrand in France in 1981, sought to provide immediate increases in services and employment. He also wanted to stimulate a sluggish economy (operating at less than 70 per cent industrial capacity) by raising consumer demand.

The economic and political successes of this strategy were rapid and dramatic in 1971. Unemployment in Santiago dropped from 7.1 per cent to 3.7 per cent; wage and salary earners' share of national income rose from 50 per cent to 59 per cent; gross domestic production increased 8.9 per cent and inflation decreased from 34.9 per cent to 22.1 per cent. The popularity of these measures was reflected in the national municipal elections of April 1971 when the parties in the Popular Unity coalition received 48.6 per cent of the vote—a substantial increase over Allende's 36.2 per cent plurality in 1970.

Groups within the Church also responded positively. A month after the local elections, the bishops issued a major pastoral letter, 'Gospel, Politics and Various Types of Socialism'. In it they acknowledged that many forms of socialism were 'compatible with the spirit of Christianity' when socialist systems did not turn the state into an 'uncontrollable and dictatorial force.' They claimed that in contrast to experience with Marxist-Leninist regimes, the 'Chilean case presents unique possibilities' if 'the good sense and democratic maturity of our people, the strength of Christians and the openness and critical spirit of Marxists themselves toward their own system' prevailed. The hierarchy offered support for all that was liberating in the transition to socialism and acknowledged that Catholics could participate in such programmes.[12]

The bishops, however, indicated they would oppose any policy that restricted freedom, and recognised 'significant incompatibilities between Marxism and Christianity' making a synthesis between the two ideologies impossible. In addition, they stressed that official representatives of the Church should not identify publicly with any party or use their moral authority to promote partisan positions. Such neutrality, they argued, enables the Church to perform its mission with integrity and to speak to the moral issues affecting the entire society.[13]

On several occasions in 1971 and 1972, Cardinal Silva followed up this cautious but generally positive position of the bishops with gestures of support for UP objectives. He participated in the 1971 May Day celebrations sponsored by the Central Workers' Confederation (CUT) and urged the unity of all workers, despite the fact that the CUT was dominated by the Communist and Socialist parties. On national television, after the UP administration refused compensation upon nationalising the copper mines of Kennecott and Anaconda, Cardinal Silva appealed to the people of the United States to respect Chile's efforts to gain control of its own natural resources, saying: 'I think the process of nationalisation of copper is constitutionally impeccable.' Later when the copper companies tried to get court-imposed embargoes on Chilean copper in Europe, Cardinal Silva obtained denunciations of such efforts from the Justice and Peace Commission of the Episcopal Conference of France.[14]

Groups at lower levels of the Church were also open to socialist goals. Several Catholic secondary schools run by religious congregations increased tuition fees to rich students to provide more scholarships for the poor, and some offered to turn over their facilities to the government for exclusive use for working-class pupils. Several meetings of clerical and lay leaders planning pastoral objectives for 1971 and 1972 praised socialist objectives and urged Christians to have a constructive attitude towards them.

The administration for its part manifested a corresponding openness toward church interests and to progressive Christians. Allende continued public subsidies to Catholic primary and secondary schools, and increased those to the Catholic university system to expand programmes for the poor. Throughout the entire three years such subsidies continued to grow, so that by 1973 they paid 80 per cent of the operating costs of the Catholic University of

Santiago, as compared to 60 per cent in 1970. When additional groups of Christian Democrats left the PDC in July 1971 out of impatience with the party's reluctance to support enthusiastically Allende's programme, he appointed to his cabinet representatives of this new Christian Left Party (MIC) to join those already there from MAPU. Thus, during the first year and a half, no significant tension emerged between Church and State; indeed each side contributed to furthering the other's interests.

MODERATING EFFORTS OF CHURCH LEADERS AS OPPOSITION GROWS (APRIL 1972-
MARCH 1973)

By early 1972 serious opposition to the UP's programme was emerging. The National and Christian Democratic parties (together a majority in Congress) passed a constitutional amendment in February 1972 requiring specific legislation for all past and future nationalisations. Allende vetoed the amendment. By this time, however, groups associated with the Movement of the Revolutionary Left (MIR), not in Allende's coalition, were taking over industries and farms at a faster pace than the administration wanted or was capable of managing.

At the same time black-market profiteering by merchants to avoid price controls, disruptions in agricultural production as land reform accelerated, and distribution policies favouring working-class areas, all combined to produce bottlenecks and consumer goods shortages in middle- and upper-income urban areas. Violent clashes between anti- and pro-government forces occurred in several cities.

As tension mounted, the hierarchy issued a statement in mid-April 1972 praising the accomplishments to date of the administration. They also emphasised that the change underway was the will of the vast majority, urged greater mutual respect and understanding and warned against sectarianism and violence.[15]

Economic disruptions and political polarisation continued, however. Domestic and foreign private investment declined dramatically, loans and credits from private and public banks dependent on US capital were drastically curtailed, and badly needed spare parts in nationalised industries (especially copper) were denied from the US. Inflation had climbed to over 30 per cent by July 1972 and would reach 163 per cent by December. In July the Christian Democrats broke off conversations with the UP over further nationalisations, and subsequently announced an electoral alliance with the National party for the 1973 parliamentary elections. By September there were rumours circulating about a rightist plot, abetted by foreign interests, to overthrow the government.

The official Church again spoke out. Cardinal Silva on television warned of the 'spectre of fratricidal war' and urged citizens to modify laws 'with the same processes by which they were made'. He also reaffirmed confidence in Chile's 'democratic traditions and its public leaders'.[16] While implicitly calling upon the administration to establish a clearer legal framework for nationalisations, his denunciation of violence and affirmation for public authority was an important sign of continued support by the official Church for Allende's government.

The Church continued along this line during the October strike. Truck drivers and owners, protesting the establishment of a state trucking agency in one province, were joined by shopkeepers, taxi drivers, construction workers, physicians and bank employees. The National and Christian Democratic parties supported the nationwide work stoppages, and the latter refused to confer with Allende to find a political solution to the impasse. The bishops accepted such an invitation, however, and ten of the thirty active prelates met with the president on 20 October. The Executive Committee of the Episcopal Conference subsequently issued a public statement calling upon all Christians to find a constructive solution to the crisis and urging that the March 1973 congressional elections take place in a 'democratic atmosphere'.[17]

Allende agreed to take into his cabinet three members of the military and promised no further state intervention in the trucking business. But the country by late 1972 was irreversibly polarised and each camp looked to the congressional elections for decisive victory.

CHURCH-STATE TENSION DURING THE FINAL SIX MONTHS (MARCH-SEPTEMBER, 1973)

The elections of March 1973 did not break the political stalemate. The Left failed to gain a majority, but the opposition did not gain the two-thirds necessary to override presidential vetoes. Urged on by Left-wing Socialists and sectors of the Communist party, Allende chose at this time to implement the educational programme outlined in his 1970 platform. Shortly after the elections the Minister of Education announced a reform, known as the National Unified School System (ENU), to expand opportunities for the poor and to introduce a single set of educational values—'socialist humanism'. To achieve this, the State would coordinate all levels of education, change curricula, and provide more adult and worker education. Private schools (25 per cent of the total, mostly church-related) would be required to implement this ideology and programme; ENU was to be introduced in all secondary schools within three months and be in full operation by 1976.[18]

The Catholic bishops for the first time in two and a half years, publicly opposed the government. Not only did they reject any government-imposed ideology in their school system but they argued that this violated the UP's 1970 promises to consult widely before educational reforms. They also complained that the project did not respect religious values and was based on the erroneous assumption that a majority of the country favoured the revolutionary ideology underlying ENU. While praising the aspects of ENU that would favour the poor, they urged more discussion of the proposal with those affected by it, including parents, teachers and students.[19]

Opposition parties, the military, the conservative media, and associations of parents and students in private schools also vigorously criticised ENU. Major demonstrations of Catholic students were orchestrated against it in the streets of Santiago. The church-controlled television station operated at the Catholic University of Santiago bitterly denounced ENU, with the very conservative director, Fr Raúl Hasbún, stating that a confrontation between Marxism and the Church was inevitable. He also attempted unsuccessfully to expand the station's transmission beyond Santiago without the necessary government permission.[20]

Faced with such strong united opposition, the administration capitulated. The Minister of Education sent a conciliatory letter to Cardinal Silva, insisting that ENU did respect pluralism and the values of Christian humanism but announcing a postponement 'to permit democratic and constructive debate'.[21]

In June the bishops issued a longer statement contending that, despite administration claims that ENU respected pluralism, in fact ENU was dominated by Marxist-Leninist ideology and disregarded parents' rights to determine their children's education. They also charged that it was unconstitutional, since the Statute of Democratic Guarantees, added to the constitution just before Allende's confirmation, stated that education should be democratic, pluralist and free of partisan orientation.[22]

By the time this second episcopal document on ENU appeared the issue was secondary as other more pressing matters took priority. The administration was moving ahead on the economic front with its nationalisation programme. The extreme Left MIR engineered another series of factory seizures without government approval. This resulted in violent clashes with the police. The right-wing Fatherland and Freedom movement called for a civil war to overthrow Allende. A party convention of Christian Democrats in May passed by narrow margin a resolution stating that Chile faced the prospect of dictatorship by the Left and that the PDC had to increase its opposition to the administration. Strikes for higher wages by copper miners broke out accompanied by violence.

As crisis mounted, nine bishops in the central region, in June criticised both government and opposition. The prelates expressed concern about what they felt was the tendency toward 'absolute statism'. They also condemned actions which opposition forces were abetting—black-market profiteering, the exodus of professionals from the country and violence in mining areas—and they appealed for greater mutual respect among contending groups despite ideological differences.[23]

Calls for moderation had little effect. Teachers and other professionals joined miners in demanding higher salaries; anti-government groups rallied on the campus of the Catholic University of Santiago; riots and shootings spread. Rebel troops attacked the presidential palace, but were repelled by loyalists. Fatherland and Freedom claimed responsibility for the abortive coup and called for a total armed offensive to overthrow the government. In mid-July the Episcopal Conference warned of imminent civil war if political leaders could not agree, and urged another attempt at negotiation between the administration and the opposition.

Groups on the Right (Fatherland and Freedom and the National party) flatly rejected the bishops' appeal as did their counterparts on the Left (the MIR, and Left-wing sectors of the Socialist party). The leadership of the PDC, and of the Communist party and moderate Socialists, all responded favourably to the Church's call for dialogue, and in late July the president of the PDC, Patricio Aylwin, conferred with Allende. He pressed for a clearer limitation on nationalisation policies, a new role in government for the military, and demanded that the armed forces immediately act against paramilitary groups on the Right and the Left. No response was forthcoming from the administration. Truckers began another nationwide strike, joined by shopkeepers and professionals, which was openly supported by the PDC. Fatherland and Freedom carried out sabotage of power stations and railroad lines, and the MIR claimed to have infiltrated military barracks.

On 17 August the Cardinal personally made a final effort at mediation. At his request Allende and Aylwin met in his home and the president promised to begin moving on PDC demands in the near future. No action was taken, however, and in late August the PDC introduced a bill in Congress accusing the government of illegalities and calling on the military to preserve constitutional order. On 9 September the Christian Democrats publicly asked Allende and all elected officials to resign and call new elections. Two days later the armed forces staged a successful and extremely repressive coup; Allende died and constitutional government in Chile came to an end.

In sum, despite the strains during the final six months of the Popular Unity's term, the top leadership of Church and State maintained open communications and adjusted their respective positions to avoid all-out confrontation. Allende relented on the education issue, and the bishops, while critical of certain policies, to the end supported constitutional government.

In a climate of fairly peaceful Church-State coexistence, the Left won more electoral support from practising Catholics. Table 2 shows that it doubled its support among regular church-goers between 1970 and 1973, and increased its base by two-thirds among those who attended Church occasionally, as well as among the non-practising. The PDC also gained among Catholics during this period but not proportionally as much as the Left. Moreover, the Right declined in popularity among Catholics after 1970, hovering around the 10 per cent level.

In comparing Catholic party preferences in Chile in 1973 with those in France, Italy and Spain at about the same time, it is clear that regularly practising Catholics in Chile were considerably further to the Left—twice as many people as in France and Italy, and two-thirds more than in Spain. Most devout Catholics in France still backed the Right in the 1970s and their Italian counterparts supported Christian Democrats. In Spain a plurality of regularly practising Catholics backed the ruling centrist party (UCD) in about the same proportion as the most devout Chileans favoured the PDC. Those with less contact with the Church in Western Europe (occasionals and non-practising), however, showed significantly more identification with the Left than such Catholics in Chile. The religious factor in Chilean electoral politics by the end of Allende's term in office did not weigh on partisan cleavages with the force that it has exerted in Western Europe.

CHRISTIAN-MARXIST SYNTHESIS WITHIN THE CHURCH

As the Chilean bishops were preparing their 1971 document, 'Gospel, Politics and Various Types of Socialism', a group of eighty priests (mainly from working-class shantytowns in Santiago) issued a statement praising socialism, backing several of the nationalisation policies of the Popular Unity

TABLE 2

PARTY PREFERENCE AND RELIGIOUS PRACTICE OF CATHOLICS, 1970-1973
(GREATER SANTIAGO, AUGUST 1970, APRIL 1972, FEBRUARY, 1973)

	Regularly Practising			Occasionally Practising			Non-practising		
	1970 %	1972 %	1973 %	1970 %	1972 %	1973 %	1970 %	1972 %	1973 %
UP (Left)	17.0	27.9	34.2	21.1	45.2	35.6	27.7	54.6	43.3
PDC (Center)	29.2	34.1	43.3	22.8	28.7	37.1	27.7	17.5	26.6
PN (Right)	12.9	14.0	10.0	11.4	7.1	11.8	7.6	7.7	7.7
Undecided	40.9	24.0	12.5	44.7	19.0	15.5	37.0	20.2	22.4
Total Sample	N=171	N=129	N=120	N=246	N=394	N=329	N=119	N=194	N=143

Source: Centro de Opinión Pública, Santiago, Chile.

TABLE 3

COMPARATIVE CATHOLIC PARTY PREFERENCE: CHILE (1973), FRANCE (1973), ITALY (1968), and SPAIN (1978)

	Regularly Practising				Occasionally Practising				Non-practising			
	Chile	France	Italy	Spain	Chile	France	Italy	Spain	Chile	France	Italy	Spain
	%	%	%	%	%	%	%	%	%	%	%	%
Left												
Marxist	34.2	13.0	3.5	1.8	35.6	38.0	16.8	6.6	43.3	67.0	46.5	15.5
Non-marxist			12.5	19.0			33.3	34.8			27.8	48.2
Centre												
Christian Democrat	43.3		77.2	41.4	37.1		40.9		26.6		18.1	
Other		16.0	1.2			13.0	1.5	33.8		11.0	2.8	16.9
Right	10.0	70.0	5.6	16.1	11.8	47.0	7.5	4.6	7.7	20.0	4.8	2.4
Undecided	12.5	1.0		21.7	15.5	2.0		20.2	22.4	2.0		17.0
Total Sample	N=120	N=937	N=2,117		N=329	N=667	N=1,251		N=143		N=288	N=1,091

Sources: Data for Chile is from Centro de Opinión Pública in Santiago. Data for France is taken from an IFOP poll of 927 adults conducted in February 1973 and reported in 'Les élections législatives de 4 et 11 Mars 1973', Sondages Vol. 35, (1973), p. 26. The Italian data is a subsample of a poll of 2,500 adults conducted in 1968 by CISER and reported in Samuel H. Barnes, 'Italy: Religion and Class in Electoral Behavior', in Richard Rose (ed)., Electoral Behavior: A Comparative Handbook, New York: The Free Press, 1974, p. 195. Data on Spain is from a subsample of a national survey of 5,898 persons conducted by Juan Linz and associates in September 1978. I am grateful to Professor Linz for showing me his data and giving me permission to cite it.

government, and urging priests to organise in support of them. The bishops warned the priests against resurrecting 'an outdated clericalism' in politics and threatening the 'unity of the Christian people with their pastors'.[24] When the bishops a month later issued their own statement on socialism they explicitly prohibited official church representatives from identifying with any party line.

This did not settle the issue. 'The eighty' published two major critiques of 'Gospel, Politics and Various Types of Socialism', arguing that it was a politically partisan document. They said the bishops were implicitly against socialism since their offer to serve all Chileans actually supported Allende's opposition: 'A church open to all is not really capable of serving the masses: it is intrinsically conservative.'[25] In November 1971 'the eighty' formed the first Christians for Socialism (CpS) movement in Latin America, including clerical, religious, lay, and Protestant members, and announced an international congress to which sympathisers from the rest of the Americas and Western Europe would be invited.

The meeting took place in late April 1972, at the time when opposition to Allende was well under way and just after the Chilean bishops had issued their first public call for moderation and mutual respect between government and opposition. Over 400 people participated, mostly Chileans and the majority priests or nuns. The participants agreed basically with what 'the eighty' had affirmed a year before: official Christian support for socialism; the obligation for Christians to involve themselves in the revolutionary process and identify only with political parties of the working class; the impossibility of achieving unity in the Church without using the methods of class struggle; and the necessity that priests form political movements.[26]

Throughout 1972 the Chilean branch of CpS expanded its mailing list for its monthly bulletin to about 500, and counted 300 active members—most of whom were priests, nuns or ministers (the majority foreigners). CpS also widened its international contacts, acting as a catalyst for the founding of similar groups in Western Europe and North America. Subsequent international meetings were held in Spain and Italy in 1973, and Canada in 1975.

On several occasions in 1972 and 1973, the Chilean CpS publicly contradicted the bishops. During the October 1972 nationwide strike, as the bishops met with Allende to offer mediation, CpS issued a press release praising the efforts of workers and leftist organisations to break the strike and calling upon all Christians to join their side. During the subsequent congressional campaign when the hierarchy called for respect for democratic procedures but remained neutral as to parties, the CpS organisational network actively promoted candidates of the UP. CpS literature indicated that a vote for the opposition was a vote for 'oppressors'. In supporting the 'revolutionary consciousness' of the UP, they said, 'Christ accompanies us and we encounter God'.[27]

In June 1973, after the hierarchy opposed nationalisation of the educational system, Christians for Socialism strongly endorsed ENU as an effective means to liberate society from capitalist ideology. After the nine bishops of the central region the same month criticised government and opposition, warning against statism and economic sabotage, a clerical leader of CpS in *Punto Final*, a journal of the extreme-Left MIR, accused the hierarchy of expressing the 'feelings of the rich' and being 'against revolutionary changes'. The priest demanded that they side with the poor since the 'Chilean process does not admit spectators or arbitrators' or 'ambiguous situations'.[28]

Despite some attempts at dialogue, relations between CpS and the bishops became severely strained, and rumours circulated in early 1973 that the hierarchy was about to condemn the movement. In April they decided to forbid priests and religious from participating further in CpS. They delayed promulgation of the order until a document could be prepared with a complete analysis of the movement.

Allende on several occasions previous to 1973, in conversation with the Cardinal and other bishops, had pointed to CpS as a very positive sign of progressive change in the Church. When he heard in 1973 that the bishops were preparing a public denunciation of the group, however, he urged its leaders to negotiate with their ecclesiastical superiors and to submit eventually to episcopal demands. He could not afford a schism in the Church precipitated by leftist clerics closely identified with his administration. This would leave the UP associated with only a minority of Catholics and would badly hurt its relations with the Cardinal and other bishops, who were far more important politically to Allende than CpS.[29]

There were no further attempts at serious dialogue between the bishops and CpS after April 1973, and the Executive Committee of the Episcopal Conference completed their document of analysis two days after the coup. The Committee decided to table the statement given the drastic changes taking place, but Bishop Carlos Oviedo Cavada, Secretary of the conference, on his own authority released it in mid-October in Chile and sent copies to episcopal conferences throughout Latin America.

In this document, 'Christian Faith and Political Activity' the bishops accused CpS of 'undermining central Christian values of charity, reconciliation and peace'. They flatly rejected the arguments that class conflict could serve to realise these, and that belief in the unity of the Church was 'bourgeois ideology'. They argued that by furthering a unity and charity beyond political and class differences, the Church not only performs its religious mission but also 'makes the moral climate of the country more serene'.[30]

The hierarchy denied that the official position of the Chilean Church was partisan since, they claimed, it offered no political model of its own nor tried to exercise power. Christians for Socialism, argued the bishops, did engage in partisan politics since they used their clerical prestige to mobilise support for the Left. The CpS, said the bishops, was almost 'a Church within a Church' exercising 'a kind of teaching function parallel to that of the bishops'. They concluded with a directive prohibiting 'priest and religious from belonging to that organisation' or from engaging in any 'activity we have denounced in this document'.[31]

The immediate practical effect of this condemnation was minimal since it did not appear until after the coup when all public activities of CpS had ceased and several of its leaders were in hiding or outside the country. The impact of the Christians for Socialism movement and the bishops' reaction to it lies in the boundary lines these imply for future Christian-Marxist synthesis.

During interviews with all thirty active Chilean bishops and a cross-section of seventy-two priests, thirty-three nuns and fifty-one lay leaders throughout Chile in 1975, I discovered that only a minority (twenty-seven of 186, including only two bishops) felt that there was any significant attempt by the UP administration to limit the freedom of church activity. Asked what harm the Church had experienced during the Allende years, only 5.9 per cent (including one bishop) mentioned manipulation of religion or the Church by the government or its followers. But over a quarter considered politicisation of the clergy as the most damaging impact on the Church.[32]

When asked what types of political activities by priests they felt to be most harmful for the Church since 1965, a quarter mentioned political sermons, clerical participation in public demonstrations and the use of religious symbols for political purposes—activities predominantly of clerics with socialist sympathies during the early 1970s. Another fifth specifically mentioned clerical involvement with leftist parties or the actions of Christians for Socialism and 'the eighty'. Only two respondents out of the whole sample singled out public support of priests for the PDC, and only one mentioned clerical involvement with rightist parties as having hurt the Church over the previous decade.[33]

Thus, a cross-section of the clerical, religious and lay leadership of the Chilean Church two years after the Allende experience felt the most serious threat to the Church during his administration had been, not the leftist regime itself, but those within the Church (primarily clerics and religious) who attempted to make a synthesis of Christianity and Marxism and who used their ecclesiastical prestige for partisan political purposes.

LESSONS FOR WESTERN EUROPE

The political, economic and religious context in Western Europe in the early 1980s is different in many respects from Chile ten years ago, but there are suggestive parallels. What lessons might the European Left draw from Chile?

A Left-Christian rapprochement can be more than rhetoric, since there are some common goals that can contribute to peaceful coexistence.

In Chile, the Communists and Socialists who espoused forms of democratic socialism respected civil liberties and democratic processes once in office. The promise to respect freedom of worship was also kept.

Chile also shows that the hierarchy can offer legitimation for both constitutionalism and socialist economic objectives to a leftist government, or one with leftist participation. Such moral support can be important if illegal domestic opposition emerges or if international forces attempt to subvert a government trying to move its country in a socialist direction.

Finally, Chile indicates that the religious cleavage in electoral politics can be reduced if the Left and the official Church adopt conciliatory stances. This lesson perhaps is not as crucial for Communist and Socialist parties in Western Europe whose base of strength is still predominantly among those with little or no contact with the Church. Nevertheless, Chile shows that religion's negative impact on voting for the Left can be reduced where it has long been a significant impediment. In closely contested elections in Western Europe even small changes could be important in the 1980s.

Tensions between the Church and a democratically elected leftist government are almost unavoidable, but need not reach a point of all-out confrontation.

In areas where the Church enjoys special privilege or receives public funds (e.g., in education) there will be tension between it and a leftist government. Disagreement between Mitterrand's government and the Church in France over the school issue appears as inevitable as it was in Allende's Chile.

Moreover, if society polarises over the pace or style of a leftist government's programme, all relations between the administration and those not sharing power will be affected—including those between Church and State. As in Chile, the political opposition is likely to use church structures to further its interests.

If the political pressures which the Allende government experienced are absent from or not as severe on a leftist government in France, Italy, Spain or Portugal, perhaps mutually provocative actions by sectors of the Church and those in the government might be avoided. Even the issue of church privileges might be resolved with less tension than it was in Chile, where the educational question quickly unified all opposition groups in an atmosphere of rapidly escalating polarisation and international pressure.

The fact that the Socialists in France received a strong electoral mandate in 1981 and hold a clear majority in parliament makes the contemporary French situation quite different from that during the Chilean Popular Unity government. Parliamentary support for executive policies, the predominance of one party within the administration, and the ability to rely on a commanding electoral mandate, all give the Mitterrand government assets that Allende's never had. Whatever international pressures develop, domestic political opposition in France may have less leverage than it did in Chile. This may incline the Church to negotiate more readily with the government on the school question since it may not be able to find formidable political allies on this issue.

The most serious leftist challenge to the Church in Chile came from within, not from outside. If this occurs in Western Europe, it is also likely to draw strong condemnation by the hierarchy.

It was not so much the secular Left which caused anxiety to Chilean church leaders, but rather attempts by leftist clerics to identify the authority of the Church with the specific policies of the administration and the UP electoral coalition, and to join Marxism with Christianity. At both the doctrinal and pastoral levels these caused the most serious threats to the Chilean Church during the Allende years.

By challenging church unity, its universal mission, a politically non-partisan position for its official leaders, and its service of reconciliation in society, Christians for Socialism appeared to be attacking elements central to the core symbolic system of Vatican II Catholicism—a threat the Popular Unity administration never raised.

Moreover, the fact that a majority of Chilean CpS were clerics and religious created additional problems since they represented the official Church in a way that lay persons did not. When they repeatedly ignored episcopal orders, they also directly challenged the authority of the bishops.

Should this pattern be repeated by radical clergy in France, Italy and Spain—whether the Left comes to share power or not—the hierarchy will eventually take strong disciplinary action against them as in Chile. It is not so much that Catholic bishops are politically centrist or conservative (most of them are) that explains such condemnations. Rather, the hierarchy resists all efforts to create a radically different Church that is not in continuity with traditional beliefs and subject to their authority. This lesson must be pondered by radical priests and religious in Western Europe and their allies on the political Left. It is perhaps the most crucial of the negative lessons which Chile offers to Europe.

NOTES

Substantial portions of this essay are taken from two chapters of the author's *The Church and Politics in Chile: Challenges to Modern Catholicism* to be published by Princeton University Press, and are copyrighted © 1982 by Princeton University Press.

1. Episcopal Conference of Chile, 'El deber social y político en la hora presente', September 1962, No. 21, *Mensaje* Vol. 11, (November 1962), p. 583.
2. Brian H. Smith, *The Church and Politics in Chile: Challenges to Modern Catholicism*. Princeton: Princeton University Press, 1982, Ch. 5, Table 5.2.
3. On Frei's reforms and various responses to them, see Paul E. Sigmund, *The Overthrow of Allende and the Politics of Chile, 1964-1976*. Pittsburgh: University of Pittsburgh Press, 1977, pp. 50-76.
4. Luis Corvalán, 'Seguir avanzando con las masas', Informe Central al XIII Congreso del PC, 1965, p. 65, mimeo; *Programa del Partido Comunista de Chile*. Santiago: XIV Congreso Nacional del Partido Comunista, November 1969, pp. 57-8.
5. 'UP Program of Government', *New Chile*, New York: North American Congress of Latin America, 1972, pp. 137-8.
6. Ibid., pp. 134-5. Under laws passed in the 1950s when Conservatives and Liberals controlled Congress, the Chilean government has provided subsidies to private primary, secondary and vocational schools—including most of those affiliated with the Church.
7. The surveys of Greater Santiago conducted by the private research firm, Centro de Opinión Pública, were based on door-to-door canvassing of the same random stratified sample used in August 1964, August 1970, April 1972, and February 1973.
8. US Congress, Senate, Select Committee to Study Governmental Operations with Respect to Intelligence Activities, *Alleged Assassination Plots Involving Foreign Leaders*. Report No. 94-465, 94th Congress, 1st Session, 1975, pp. 225-54.
9. Episcopal Conference of Chile, 'Declaración de los obispos sobre la situación actual del país', 24 September 1970, in Bishop Carlos Oviedo Cavada (ed.) *Documentos del Episcopado: Chile 1970-1973*. Santiago: Ediciones Mundo, 1974, pp. 29-30.
10. This Statute of Democratic Guarantees provided for continuation of the multiparty system, for freedom in education, (including continued state subsidies to private schools), trade unions, and the media, and for the independence of the armed forces from political interference. Sigmund, *Overthrow of Allende*, (1977), pp. 112, 119-20.
11. 'El saludo al Presidente Allende', *Iglesia de Santiago*, Vol. 8, (October 1970), p. 11; Cardinal Silva, 'Queremos ser constructores de un mundo más solidario', *Iglesia de Santiago*, Vol. 8, (November 1970), p. 4.
12. Episcopal Conference of Chile, 'Evangelio, política y socialismos', Nos. 25, 54, 64, 67, 88, in Oviedo Cavada (ed.), *Documentos del Episcopado*, pp. 71, 85, 89-91.

13. Ibid., Nos. 35, 44, 48, 53, 69, 70, 88, pp. 76, 79-82, 84, 92, 99. This cautious but generally positive 1971 statement by the Chilean bishops regarding Christian-Marxist cooperation pre-dated by six years comparable positions taken by the French and Spanish hierarchies respectively in 1977. Executive Council of the French Episcopal Conference, 'Le marxisme, l'homme et la foi chrétienne', *La Documentation Catholique*, Vol. 74, 17 (17 July 1977), pp. 684-90; Executive Council of the Spanish Episcopal Conference, 'Les chretiens et la politique', *La Documentation Catholique*, Vol. 74, (6 March 1977), pp. 239-50.

14. Cardinal Silva, 'Estados Unidos debe contribuir a que Chile conquista su desarrollo', *Iglesia de Santiago*, Vol. 9, (November 1971), p. 13; 'Presidente de la Republica se refiere a actitud de la Iglesia', *Iglesia de Santiago*, Vol. 10, (November 1972), pp. 12-13.

15. Episcopal Conference of Chile, 'Por un camino de esperanza y alegria', 11 April 1972, in Oviedo Cavada (ed.), *Documentos del Episcopado*, pp. 133-6.

16. Cardinal Silva, 'Congoja y esperanza', 2 September 1972, *Mensaje* Vol.21, (October 1972), p. 618.

17. Executive Committee of the Episcopal Conference of Chile, 'Pedimos un espíritu constructivo y fraternal', 21 October, 1972, *Mensaje*, Vol.21, (November 1972) p. 682.

18. Ministry of Public Education, 'Informe sobre Escuela Nacional Unificada', *Cuadernos de la Realidad Nacional*, No. 17, (July 1973), pp. 23-46.

19. Executive Committee of the Episcopal Conference of Chile, 'Declaración del Comité Permanente del Episcopado de Chile sobre la Escuela Nacional Unificada', 27 March 1973, in Oviedo Cavada (ed.), *Documentos del Episcopado*, pp. 152-3.

20. *La Tribuna*, 26 March 1973.

21. Jorge Tapia Valdes, Minister of Public Education, 'Carta al Excmo. Señor Cardenal Raúl Silva Henríquez', 12 April 1973, in Oviedo Cavada, (ed.) *Documentos del Episcopado*, pp. 156-8.

22. Episcopal Conference of Chile, 'El momento actual de la educación en Chile: documento de trabajo', June 1973, *Mundo '73*, No. 61, (July 1973), appendix.

23. Cardinal Raúl Silva Henríquez, *et al.*, 'Solo con amor se es capaz de construir un país', 1 June 1973, *Mensaje*, Vol. 22, (July 1973), p. 336.

24. 'Declaration of the Bishops of Chile', 22 April 1971, in John Eagleson (ed.), *Christians and Socialism: Documentation of the Christians for Socialism Movement in Latin America*. Maryknoll: Orbis Books, 1975, pp. 12-15.

25. Secretariat of 'the eighty', *El compromiso político de los cristianos*. Talca: Fundación Obispo Manuel Larraín, July 1971; Juan Luis Segundo, S.J., *La iglesia chilena ante el socialismo*. Talca: Fundación Obispo Manuel Larraín, October 1971, p. 23.

26. Christians for Socialism, 'Final Document of the Convention', 30 April 1972, in Eagleson (ed.), *Christians and Socialism*, pp. 165, 166, 168, 170, 173, 174.

27. National Secretariat of Christians for Socialism, 'Comunicado del Secretariado Nacional "Cristianos por el Socialismo"', 20 October 1972, *Boletín de CpS*, (November 1972); 'Cómo cristianos: ¿ por qué nos importan las elecciones de marzo?', (January 1973), 2 pp. (mimeographed).

28. National Secretariat of Christians for Socialism, *La ENU: ¿ control de las conciencias o educación liberodora?* Talca: Fundación Obispo Manuel Larraín, May-June 1973; Revd J. Pablo Richard G., 'Los obispos y la prédica de la pequeña burguesía', *Punto Final*, No. 188, (1973), pp. 26-7.

29. This information was provided to me by Revd Arturo Gaete, S.J., of the Jesuit monthly magazine, *Mensaje*, who was an advisor to the Cardinal on Christian-Marxist dialogue during the Allende years.

30. Episcopal Conference of Chile, 'Christian Faith and Political Activity', 16 October 1973, in Eagleson (ed.), *Christians and Socialism*, Nos. 14, 19, 23, 58, 68, 79, pp. 187, 190, 192, 207, 211, 216.

31. Ibid., Nos. 35, 36, 37, 40, 47, 74-75, 80, pp. 196, 197, 198, 199, 202, 214, 215, 217.

32. My sample included all thirty active Chilean bishops, seventy-two priests working among different social classes in eighteen of the twenty-three dioceses (including a random stratified sample of thirty-one in Santiago), thirty-three nuns active in direct pastoral work in seven provinces, and fifty-one lay men and women leaders of small base communities (mainly in Santiago). Smith, *The Church and Politics in Chile*, Ch. 7, Table 7.2 and Ch. 8, Table 8.2.

33. Ibid., Ch. 8, Table 8.3.

Dutch Pillarisation on the Move? Political Destabilisation and Religious Change

Mady A. Thung, Gert J. Peelen, Marten C. Kingmans

PILLARISATION: THE DUTCH SCENE

It is hardly possible to study religion and politics in the Netherlands without giving attention to pillarisation, a phenomenon for which Dutch society has provided the 'ideal type'. We will therefore suggest a definition, sketch its history and some views on its consequences for Dutch politics, consider current changes and their relation to other shifts in Dutch politics, and finally attempt in a preliminary way to disentangle 'the religious factor' from this complex picture.

Pillarisation in the Netherlands may be described as the situation in which people's social lives, from childhood to old age, are organised on the basis of religion (particularly Catholicism and Protestantism). This leads to the coexistence of strongly separated social groups, religious as well as non-religious (e.g. socialist). This has also been characterised as 'segmented pluralism' or as 'vertical pluralism' in contrast to horizontal class divisions.[1]

The situation is not peculiar to the Netherlands but has probably been more extreme there than in any other country. Not only were social activities with obvious ideological dimensions organised this way, such as politics, education, broadcasting and the press, but also less obvious ones, like sports clubs, insurance companies and agricultural associations. This often appeared surprising, even ridiculous to outsiders. But—as Billiet recently remarked—any such judgement implies a conviction as to what does and what does not belong to the sphere of religion and embodies its own ideological bias.[2]

Another specificity of the Dutch case is the relatively long period over which this system has lasted: from about 1920 until the 1950s at least, when pillarisation reached a height. But its basis also was disputed and probably increasingly so, here as well as in other pillarised countries.[3] How strongly this has affected the whole system is one of the questions raised here. It appears that in the Netherlands the pillars began to crumble; in Flanders, however, they seem to remain intact, although their internal set-up has changed.[4]

HISTORICAL REVIEW

An important condition for the development of pillarisation is the coexistence of at least two ideologically, culturally or religiously distinct groups, each of considerable size.[5] In the Netherlands there have been at least three such groups since the Reformation: a liberal-humanist, an orthodox-Calvinist and a Catholic group. The last was strong in numbers (never less than one-third of the population) but used to have low status. The rise of socialism added a fourth element from the nineteenth century on. But it was among the orthodox Calvinists that pillarisation started.

Throughout the nineteenth century, orthodox groups criticised the Dutch Reformed Church for modernising and updating the Church and theology. This led to a first schism in 1834. This had few significant social consequences despite the fact that most of the orthodox separatists belonged to the lower social classes. In the second part of the century there was another attempt to return the Reformed Church to the 'eternal and unchangeable' principles of the Reformation. This also failed, and a second schism took place in 1886. This time the social consequences were far reaching. The separated Calvinists founded their own reformed church (referred to as the 'Neo-Calvinist Church' in this paper), a university (primarily for theological education) and a political party called the 'Anti-Revolutionary' party. It particularly fought for schools 'with the Bible' to receive state subsidies.

As in 1834 these Calvinist separatists were mainly lower-class people. But by contrast with 1834, they became fully aware of their low status, not only as a minority within the Church but also as a highly disadvantaged powerless group within society. Thus their struggle became both religious and social. They pursued social emancipation and political power as well. Although separated from the Reformed Church, they still had the ambition of bringing Dutch Protestantism back to the 'ancient truth' and 're-Christianising' the nation. Paradoxically, their strategy was to develop an almost complete social isolation from the 'hostile' outside world. In the words of the Calvinist leader Abraham Kuyper: 'Isolation is our strength', and this unyielding striving for isolation directly produced a great variety of social organisations based on Calvinist principles.

Their struggle for social emancipation appeared to be successful in the first decades of the twentieth century. The struggle for subsidised orthodox Protestant schools was won and the Protestant organisations flourished. The Neo-Calvinists became a minority to be reckoned with. But this also marked the beginning of a certain rigidity. Isolation—initially intended as a means—became the main purpose. The aims of social and religious domination were dropped as unrealistic.[6] This left little to strive for, and may have been an important reason for the pillar's gradual decay.

The rise of a Roman Catholic pillar also dates to the second part of the nineteenth century. But the two religious minorities have even more in common than timing. Even Catholic authors have suggested that in trying to remedy social and economic backwardness, the Catholics applied methods and tactics used by their most fanatic religious opponents. Ever since the Reformation, the Dutch Catholics had been discriminated against more or less openly, even after freedom of religion was officially decreed in 1796. But now they began to resist oppression with social action. Resistance served a two-fold purpose: a show of power to the outside world; and a growing self-respect within the group itself. In their case, too, the struggle for emancipation led to isolation in pillar organisations. The main difference between the Neo-Calvinists and the Catholics was that the latter did not aim at religious domination in the beginning. The purpose, rather, was social emancipation and maintenance of the Catholic identity within a pluralistic society. They were to achieve this in the middle of the twentieth century.

Together these pillars embraced about half the population at that time. The numbers involved in confessional organisations varied across different sectors of society: confessionally-based education attracted nearly all Neo-Calvinist and Catholic, and about half of the Dutch Reformed youth. Confessional schools outnumbered 'neutral' ones. In the press the proportions were quite different: there were more subscribers to 'neutral' than to Catholic and Protestant newspapers combined.[7] The pillars thus were complicated networks of organisations with only partly overlapping clienteles or memberships. In the orthodox Protestant pillar, the denominational backgrounds of members or clients also varied across sectors.

The 'neutral' pillar (i.e., the non-religious or secular) can hardly be considered one at all, since it comprised non-ideological private organisations in, for example, the recreational sector, and governmental agencies in, for example, health care (such as municipal or academic hospitals), as well as a range of socialist organisations paralleled by a competing set connected with the Conservative party.

The terms 'pillarisation' or 'vertical pluralism' therefore suggest a neater division of the population into three equally organised groups than has actually been the case. This also becomes clear if one examines some of the indicators that are often used to measure pillarisation.

Indicators

Three factors are most frequently considered:
(1) 'Degree of pillarisation' is an indication of the extent to which social tasks are fulfilled by competitive pillar organisations, for example, the ratio of confessional schools to the total number of schools.
(2) 'Pillar commitment' is an indication of preferences for social organisations of one's own religion. It has been measured by a scale of intensity of commitment[8] and also by the number of people expressing sympathy with confessional organisations.
(3) 'Degree of saturation' is an indication of the extent to which confessional organisations attract their potential membership.

As will be seen below, these indicators do not always coincide. Parents who express 'pillar commitment' to Christian schools may well send their children to a 'neutral' municipal school which happens to be nearer.

Another complication is the great variety in the confessional or ideological bases of pillar organisations. In some of the literature, socialist organisations are categorised as pillarised, and rightly so. In this paper we will confine ourselves to confessionally based organisations and will use this term in a general sense, i.e., for all organisations that claim to have a Protestant, Catholic, or Christian background. We will use the terms 'Christian' for organisations that no longer distinguish among the denominational backgrounds of their membership (this is increasingly frequent); 'Protestant' for organisations confined to a non-Catholic membership; and 'denominational' for organisations related to the membership of one specific Church only, such as a Lutheran hospital or a Dutch Reformed Church school.

PILLARISATION AND POLITICS

The best known theory about the effect of pillarisation on Dutch politics is that given by Arend Lijphart. This author argues that both class and religious differences have caused deep cleavages in Dutch society, stronger and of longer standing than in many other Western democracies.[9] Nevertheless, the political system has been remarkably stable.[10] He tries to explain this by a theory of the 'politics of accommodation'.[11] Pillarisation produced a situation in which disputes which in principle were irreconcilable from a religious point of view, had to be settled. This was achieved by rigidly isolating one group from another and by coupling political passivity of rank-and-file members with close cooperation at the level of the elites. Thus the powerful, practically autonomous elites of the various pillars ruled the country together, while keeping their followings strictly apart.

This political situation has also been characterised as 'pacification'. Hans Daalder, too, has indicated a number of reasons why it lasted so long.[11] Very relevant was the political passivity among the people in combination with a long-standing 'regent mentality' among the rulers, who tended to settle problems among themselves in secrecy, with arrogant imperviousness to criticism. Both passivity and 'regent mentality' were nourished by the huge gap between the pillars, by a diffusion of political responsibilities, by treating essentially political matters as non-political, and by the paradox of colourless group compromises coupled with the great individual influence of the political leaders. The 'politics of accommodation' and the political passivity of the people were mutually reinforcing over a long period.

If this policy succeeded, it was due, among other factors, to the fact that religious and class differences were not overlapping.[12] Among sociologists of religion, Yinger is one of the few who has pointed to the importance of this phenomenon.[13] He contrasts the Dutch 'model' with a horizontally divided society in which socio-economic cleavages are reinforced by others such as religion, language, ethnicity. These types of societies may be very explosive, although Yinger raises other possibilities as well. He discusses a third type of society, in which all possible social cleavages cross-cut each other. Religion tends to play a marginal role in these cases; what the effects on political stability or instability might be, he carefully avoids discussing (see Figure I).

DESTABILISATION OF DUTCH POLITICS

Daalder, in 1964, accused the Dutch of a lack of interest in politics and their leaders of a misplaced 'regent mentality'. Ten years later he stated that the tides had turned.[14] Lijphart in 1968 also observed that the political climate was changing.[15] Demonstrations against the monarchy, riots and unauthorised strikes, student rebellions and grim sit-ins at the universities—these were the more visible signs. Beneath the surface, various other shifts were noticeable. The political scientists J. Th. J. Van den Berg and H.A.A. Molleman tried to analyse them systematically and characterised the situation as nothing less than a 'crisis' in Dutch politics.

This analysis pointed to nine aspects which the authors—somewhat artificially—allocated to either the cultural or the social structural sphere.

FIGURE I

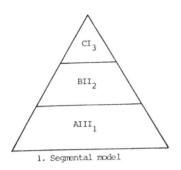

1. Segmental model

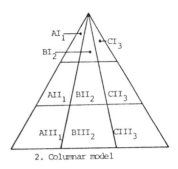

2. Columnar model

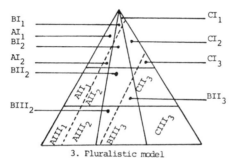

3. Pluralistic model

Source: Yinger (1970): Models of social structures using three religions (A, B, C), three classes (I, II, III), and three ethnic-linguistic groups (1, 2, 3) as differentiating characteristics (p. 426).

They suggested that the cultural crisis had become a structural one and that both were rooted in the remarkable societal changes of the 1960s, of which one was the shift of religious orientations.[16] For that reason their theory is briefly reported here.

The cultural crisis

According to these authors, two sets of factors initiated a process of cultural change and brought pressure to bear upon the political system. First, the demand for a new ideology and the desire for new styles of democracy—this international phenomenon in the Netherlands led to the formation of new parties and a variety of pressure groups. More specific to the Dutch case, however, was the process of deconfessionalisation in political life. It can be measured, among other ways, by the so-called p.o. (political orthodoxy) index, roughly equivalent to what was called 'degree of saturation' above.

The figures presented by Van den Berg and Molleman show a remarkable drop in the p.o. index among Catholics—from 90.5 per cent as voters for a Catholic party in 1948 to 38 per cent in 1972, with the strongest shift occurring between 1963 and 1967. An important drop also occurred among Neo-Calvinists which, however, started later (from 82 per cent in 1967 to 56 per cent in 1972), and a slight drop among the Dutch Reformed who had always been 'politically orthodox' only in their Right wing (from 24 per cent in 1967 to 18 per cent in 1972).[17]

Although there is some relationship here with the decrease in the rate of church-going, it is not possible to explain the declining p.o. index only by this fact. Rather, as research has shown, the motivations for party choice were changing. It is no longer self-evident, the authors state, for a member of one denomination to vote for the party traditionally associated with that denomination. In their words: the 'pillar motive' decreased.[18]

Parallel with this process were two other changes in the confessional pillars: first, a decreasing loyalty between organisations of the same confession. A politician of the Catholic party, for instance, could not in all matters count upon loyal support from the Catholic trade union, as he could have in the past. The confessional pillars had lost cohesion while the ideological basis of the constituent organisations was gradually changing or even disappearing. Second, there was a decreasing loyalty within the confessional parties themselves. Fundamental discussions about the meaning and content of their creed had already more than once led to divisions.

The structural crisis

At the time of 'pacification', political decisions were made by coalitions of the five main political parties: three confessional ones, a Conservative and a Labour party. From shortly after World War II until the 1950s, these coalitions won the support of 86-92 per cent of the electorate. After 1959 this support began to wane and was reduced to 73 per cent by 1972.[19] The drop can be almost wholly explained by deconfessionalisation: votes for the confessional parties decreased from 55 per cent in 1948 to 31 per cent in 1972, and there was a sudden rise of new parties.

Another symptom of instability was the enormous increase in the floating vote. In 1970 moreover, the obligation to vote was abolished. At the next elections one-third of the electorate failed to show up. Together all these phenomena constituted a crisis at the level of political parties. The people made it clear that they distrusted the political style, its lack of transparency and its rather authoritarian character. Thus there was also a legitimacy crisis, and it had important consequences for the effectiveness of the political system.

The great parties grew further apart and this especially affected relations between the Labour party and the other four. Cabinet formation, already a lengthy process in the Netherlands, became more problematic, as did the task of maintaining power. The widespread desire for greater democratisation and a gradual disappearance of the passivity which had characterised the politics of accommodation, led to rapid change in the political climate; indeed, within ten years, two generations of politicians had retired from the scene.

Another indication of the crisis was the above-mentioned proliferation of pressure-groups, a form of extra-parliamentary opposition which now cannot be overlooked in Dutch society. It suggests a great dissatisfaction with the functioning of the political system.

The 'politics of accommodation' had operated according to certain rules, as described by Lijphart. Tolerance was one; allocation of state subsidies according to the proportion of members in the pillar organisations was another. Secrecy and depoliticisation of emotional issues were also important. The crumbling of the pillars, the demand for democracy, and the growing distrust of political leaders undermined this system. The principles of tolerance and proportionality made way for polarisation. The parties no longer resigned themselves to a minority status, thus reducing the former readiness to compromise; efforts were made to form cabinets based on narrow majorities with the exclusion of political opponents. The stability and durability of the cabinets did not increase.

Another complicating factor in the 1970s was the so-called social crisis. Negotiations among government, unions, and management over major socio-economic issues changed completely in style and in content. Trade unions made political demands, old loyalties lapsed, and it became fashionable to disclaim peaceful settlement and to bargain according to the 'conflict model'. These and other factors combined to produce permanent pressure on the government to increase its expenditure. Since 1971 the Minister of Finance's budget was in deficit, while old mechanisms to limit it no longer functioned. Because of all these symptoms of crisis, Van den Berg and Molleman suggested that the Dutch political system of pacification was already in the 'tomb'.

THE RELIGIOUS FACTOR

The authors discussed above assigned an important role to religious changes in the destabilisation of Dutch politics. This contrasts with the more recent analysis of L.E. Dutter. He suggests that the Dutch situation can be explained by the theories of plural societies, as developed for the politics of pre- and post-colonial countries—countries divided by strong cleavages between ethnic groups. Among these 'pluralist' hypotheses, the one developed by A. Rabushka and K.A. Shepsle is especially interesting, Dutter argues. These authors suggest that political stability in a plural society results when the so-called 'multi-ethnic' leaders try to win votes from more than one ethnic, linguistic, or religious subgroup and therefore put forward ambiguous programmes. Next, they claim that instability results when so-called 'political entrepreneurs' try to gain votes from their own subgroup by stressing the favourite issues of only one subcommunity.[20] The theory is particularly designed to explain political violence: if none of these leaders has his way, resort to extra-legal methods will be likely. It assumes internal homogeneity within the subcommunities and conflicting political preferences between them.

In Dutter's view these assumptions are valid in the Netherlands, although the subcommunities here are not ethnic or linguistic but religiously distinctive blocs. According to the theory of Rabushka and Shepsle, political entrepreneurs could well succeed in winning support by exploiting the political preferences of their blocs.[21] They therefore challenged the secrecy of the former accommodating elites (who were behaving like the ambiguous leaders of the Rabushka and Shepsle theory) and the tendency to depoliticise hot issues. In this way at least one party—the Labour party—was won for non-accommodation politics and 'polarisation of Dutch voters and elites on ethnically related issues began'.[22]

In this view, the decline of the pillars has played a minor role. Indeed it is argued that the religious subcommunities have remained homogeneous, thus sensitive to 'ethnically related issues'. Applied to the Dutch case this, of course, would have to be 'religiously related issues'. But—as Dutter states—the 'political entrepreneurs' were drawn from the secular bloc and it was the non-confessional Labour party that was the one most critical of accommodation politics. Is it plausible that these actors would advance religious issues in order to gain votes in their own (secular) bloc? Although an inventory of the most debated issues would be necessary, it is our impression that, on the contrary, socio-economic problems and the demands for radical democratisation have predominated in the recent polarisation of Dutch politics.

Crucial in Dutter's argument is his view of the composition of the pillars. He suggests that the confessional pillars were indeed shrinking, but maintained their former cohesiveness. He sees the 'secular bloc' as another pillar, comparable to an 'ethnic', 'linguistic' or 'religious' bloc. Misled perhaps by Lijphart ('Deep religious and class divisions separate distinct isolated and self-contained religious groups in the Netherlands. Social communication across class and religious boundary lines is minimal.'[23]), he may have overlooked the columnar character of the Dutch system, as depicted by Yinger. It implied that class-cleavages were to a great extent bridged within the confessional pillars, although there were class differences, e.g., between one Protestant party associated with the Dutch Reformed Church and another one associated with the Neo-Calvinists. It was only within the secular bloc that social communication across class boundaries was minimal: here a socialist and a conservative 'pillar' could be discerned, as suggested above. Adapting Yinger's figure to the Dutch situation, one might chart it in a simplified fashion for the period of pacification (see Figure II). One should add that the so-called 'secular bloc' included about half of the population, whereas the percentage of non-church-affiliated was only about 20 per cent since 1948. Thus, more than half of those voting conservative or socialist were members of a church.

All this makes it unlikely that the recent polarisation in Dutch politics is due to a revivification of cleavages between the pillars and that religiously related issues served as the catalysts. It does not, however, preclude the relevance of 'political entrepreneurs' in destabilising politics, but rather suggests the familiar questions about charismatic leadership as an element in social change.[24] The social scientist must still analyse the social conditions that enable an 'entrepreneur' to win followers. So far, the social conditions mentioned by Van den Berg and Molleman seem more salient for the Dutch case than the entrepreneur theory. Among these conditions, depillarisation stood out as an important one. What its exact role was, is difficult to decide, however.

FIGURE II

Adaptation of Yinger's model II for the Netherlands, showing class divisions, four 'pillars' and Church affiliation. 'Pillars' indicated: Cath(olic), P(rotestant), Conserv(ative) (in political sector), Social(ist) (ibid.). Church affiliations: Cath(olic), Prot(estant), N(eo)-C(alvinist), D(echurched) + O(thers).

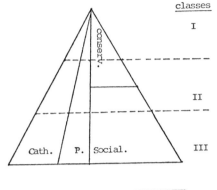

Distribution of Church affiliation in total population.

DEPILLARISATION

Thus far we have assumed that the Dutch 'pillars' have started to crumble. But what does this mean, if, as argued above, Dutch society was not divided as neatly as the terms 'segmented pluralism', 'pillarisation', 'division into three blocks' suggest? Indeed, 'depillarisation' is not so simple a process. The three indicators mentioned above illustrate this and suggest that at least three processes are involved, and that they need not always coincide.

First, a decreasing *degree of pillarisation* may occur in various sectors of society. It may mean a substitution of 'neutral' for confessionally-based social organisations or it may mean that organisations from different denominational backgrounds (Protestant and Catholic for instance, or Lutheran and Reformed) merge to form an organisation designated as 'Christian'. Thus the former Catholic party has recently federated with the two main Protestant parties to form a 'Christian Democratic Appeal'. This federation participated as such in national elections in 1977 for the first time. It then formed a coalition cabinet with the Conservative party, while the Labour party went into opposition.

Noteworthy as an illustration of how complicated developments are, is the fact that the Catholic trade union federation followed another pattern. It merged with the Labour-related federation, the biggest in the country. Thus, class divisions started to become manifest in the 'Catholic bloc'. They remained less so in the Protestant world. There was one Protestant federation; it participated in the negotiations for merger but in the end it remained independent.

There were realignments among individual unions too, but with a great variety of pattern. In general, Catholic middle-class unions (of higher employees, civil servants, military officers) preferred other partners than Labour-related trade unions. Thus, the decrease of the 'degree of pillarisation' is in itself a complicated process: it seemed to be accompanied by growing tensions between social groups with opposing interests.[25]

Another indicator was *pillar commitment*: what people think or say about confessionally-based organisations. Decline of pillar commitment may be measured in several ways, and many individual organisations have measured their own sector of society, but the results have apparently not yet been systematically collected. J.M.G. Thurlings mentioned, for example, a 1967 public opinion survey on the extent to which religiously-based organisations were considered desirable in various sectors of society. As expected, church-affiliated respondents were most affirmative but there were great differences between denominations as well as in opinions about different sectors of society, as Table 1 shows.

TABLE I

PERCENTAGES AFFIRMING THE DESIRABILITY OF CONFESSIONAL ORGANISATION AMONG CATHOLIC, REFORMED, NEO-CALVINIST WOMEN AND MEN

	Catholic		Reformed		Neo-Calvinist	
	F	M	F	M	F	M
	%	%	%	%	%	%
Broadcasting companies	46	53	49	47	92	82
Sports associations	29	26	21	21	69	53
Trade unions	40	41	30	36	83	75
Youth clubs	62	71	65	69	95	90

Source: Thurlings (1978), p.144.

Pillar commitment thus varies considerably for different sectors of society, and it would be premature to pronounce an overall decrease. For instance, Thurlings mentioned the results of a 1969 survey in which 47.3 per cent of the total sample (including non-church-affiliated) expressed a preference for the confessional broadcasting companies.[26] This was a small decrease from the figures reported earlier by J.P. Kruyt and W. Goddijn. A government report, compiling data from various surveys, suggests that pillar commitment remains very strong in the sector of primary education (see Table 2).

Finally, *degree of saturation* is an indicator of pillarisation. It should be examined separately because the number of people expressing agreement with or preference for the existence of confessional organisations does not always parallel the number of those actually involved. For example, Van Kemenade observed in 1966 that among parents who sent their children to Catholic schools, some 26 per cent did not mind very much about how Catholic their education was.[27] The tables presented in this article show the same discrepancy between confessional party choice and verbally articulated preferences for confessional parties.[28]

Thurlings, studying the Catholic pillar especially, reports that with respect to the press, the degree of saturation changed very little in the turbulent period between 1955 and 1968: in Catholic households subscriptions to national newspapers fell by only 1 per cent, from 76 per cent to 75 per cent.[29] For other sectors he only reported growth or decrease, not the relationship to potential

TABLE 2

OPINIONS ABOUT THE RELATIONSHIP BETWEEN RELIGION AND SOCIAL ORGANISATIONS AMONG RESPONDENTS
WHO CLAIM TO BE CHURCH AFFILIATED, PERCENTAGE OF THOSE WHO AFFIRMED THE DESIRABILITY OF
CONFESSIONAL ORGANISATIONS

		1966 %	1970 %	1971 %	1972 %	1975 %	1977 %
a)	Should send a child to a confessional school	76	60			61	
b)	Religion and politics should not be separated	41	32			28	
c)	Broadcasting should be based on religion	52	34			40	
d)	Trade unions should be based on religion	41	27			31	
e)	A political party should be based on religion	45	38			35	
f)	Confessional parties should exist, among others			66	63		59

Source: Sociaal en Cultureel Rapport 1978, Sociaal en Cultureel Planbureau Rijswijk, Den Haag, 1978.

members (i.e., not exactly the same measure as 'degree of saturation'). The figures, however, suggest, first, that confessionally-based organisations remained strong in the sector of medical help in the home, since Catholic and Protestant organisations increased even more than the 'neutral' ones (30 per cent, 30 per cent and 25 per cent respectively). Secondly, the data show that Catholic organisations lost much support in the youth sector. This sector showed an overall decrease, but Protestant and 'neutral' organisations did not shrink as much. Between 1950-63 the decreases amounted to 33 per cent for Catholics, 19 per cent for Protestants, and 17 per cent for 'others'.[30] Finally, both Catholic and Protestant trade unions lagged behind the growth of Labour-related unions, the groups expanding between 1961-68 by 4 per cent (Catholics), 8 per cent (Protestants), and 10 per cent (the Labour-related federation).

On the whole, therefore, the variations between denominations and between various sectors of society were considerable. This poses a problem for sociologists of how to account for the differences. One explanation, by Thurlings, especially refers to 'the religious factor' and is therefore related here.

THE 'CRISIS HYPOTHESIS'

Thurlings claims that two hypotheses account for the differences in depillarisation between various sectors of society. The first starts from the fact that pillarisation in the nineteenth century began in sectors most obviously related to religion, such as education and the press. Only later did confessional organisations proliferate in all kinds of other activities. It would, therefore, be logical if depillarisation started in organisations hardly related to religion itself (such as sports clubs) while pillar organisations with a specific task in maintaining religious values would survive longer. This would correspond to the preferences reported in Table 1: most groups described there were in favour of a confessional basis for youth clubs first, mentioned broadcasting companies secondly, which were then followed by trade unions and sports clubs. Depillarisation would consequently affect the corresponding sectors of society in a reverse order.[31] Thurlings calls this the 'hypothesis of differential affinity'; it lies at the basis of many studies on the depillarisation process. But this hypothesis fails to account for the figures on youth organisations: deconfessionalisation seemed stronger here than elsewhere, though this is a sector very close to religious concerns. The 'differential affinity thesis' apparently does not explain enough.[32] The author notes the same problem with respect to the Catholic press, which had declined strongly, while the Protestant and Catholic broadcasting corporations were also threatened by a loss of support.

This phenomenon seems less surprising if one takes into account changes in Catholic theology and Church life since Vatican II. These refer to the second explanation: the 'crisis hypothesis.' It suggests that conflicts and divisions within the Church between protagonists of renewal and conservatives have caused a crisis in the very heart of the Catholic pillar. This has confused the ordinary church member. What it means to be a Catholic is no longer certain. For this reason the pillar organisations related to religion would be the first to decline. Figures reporting the drop in church-going, baptisms, entries into the priesthood, etc., support this thesis.[33]

However, one may question what this means for politics. Is this a sector closely related to religious values or not? Or does it occupy an intermediate position in this respect? Curiously enough, it is in this sector that (Catholic) depillarisation began.[34] Neither of the two hypotheses seems able to explain this. Thurlings then raises a third hypothesis: the so-called 'defence hypothesis.' It suggests that Catholic pillarisation had primarily served the purpose of maintaining Catholic group life and that the Catholic political party stood in the front line of the fight.[35] Once the threat had disappeared and Catholicism had gained respectability, the necessity to close the ranks inevitably waned.

Is this an adequate explanation of the early depillarisation in the political sphere? If, indeed, the political party was the main instrument for this defensive policy, would it be one of the first pillar organisations to lose its *raison d'être* once the battle was won? Lorwin, discussing depillarisation in politics, also looks in this direction for an explanation.[36] He mentions other reasons as well. Increased communication among members of the various blocs, rising costs in sectors such as the press, professionalisation of welfare services, intensified contacts between the elites as government intervention in economic and social life furthered collective bargaining, and so forth. He also notes growing disaffection among the youth about the ideological blocs.[37] But these apply to depillarisation in general; whereas the 'defence hypothesis' was to account especially for depillarisation in politics. What does this mean with respect to our quest for the role of 'the religious factor'?

PROBLEMS FOR DISCUSSION

We are thus left with two theories explaining the recent destabilisation of

Dutch politics. One points to polarisation processes that are generally occurring in plural societies and disregards religious change (Dutter). The other points to depillarisation as one important factor at least (Van den Berg and Molleman). In the latter theory 'the religious factor' enters the picture in a very explicit manner. But with respect to politics it may work two ways:

(1) According to the 'defence hypothesis' present-day religious changes are not of primary importance. The fact that the rationale of the pillars' existence has evaporated is decisive. The war has been won; the army can be sent home. If religious change is occurring as well, it may be just an epiphenomenon, a coincidence.
(2) According to the 'crisis hypothesis', however, the recent changes in religion are decisive. Depillarisation and the destabilisation of politics would not have taken so rapid a course, had not these changes occurred.

To the sociologist of religion the 'crisis hypothesis' seems very plausible. The religious scene indeed has changed dramatically in the Netherlands. The country was exceptional for its high and early rate of decline in religious affiliation as can be seen from census data (see Figure III). Recently the Catholic Church, exceptional again until about the 1950s for its loyalty to Rome, for a high rate of practice and for a strict observance of Catholic morality, underwent dramatic changes. The new religions found an easy foothold in this country, too. But how, exactly, do these religious changes relate to politics?

Is there any way, then, to examine the relative importance of religious change? Thus far, we have only attempted to disentangle 'the religious factor' from three other variables in the data of two comparable investigations. These data were obtained from Dutch election studies: large-scale surveys, carried out since 1967 by political scientists on the occasion of national elections.[38] They allow for a longitudinal analysis of changes in political attitudes and behaviour.

The variables selected were sex, class, and age. *Class* was considered important because it seemed that with declining pillarisation, class cleavages would more and more displace religious ones (cf. quotations above from Thurlings). Yinger's three types of society would then have to be supplemented by a fourth: one divided by differences in social class and (more or less parallel?) differences in political ideology.[39] Dutch society might then be evolving to this fourth type.

Age was considered important because religious changes as well as depillarisation seem to develop fastest among the young. *Sex* was included on the chance that the feminist movement might have led to noticeable differences in survey responses by men and women.

The investigations compared were from the years 1972/3 and 1977. Earlier material is available and may well be more interesting; perhaps the present data reflect the so-called reaction to the turbulent 1960s, the 'apathy' of the 1970s. Nevertheless Tables 3, 4, and 5 suggest some interesting changes. In these tables the religious factor appears in the form of answers to the question of whether respondents regarded themselves as church-affiliated. Religious convictions, devotional practices, religious attitudes—all these aspects are

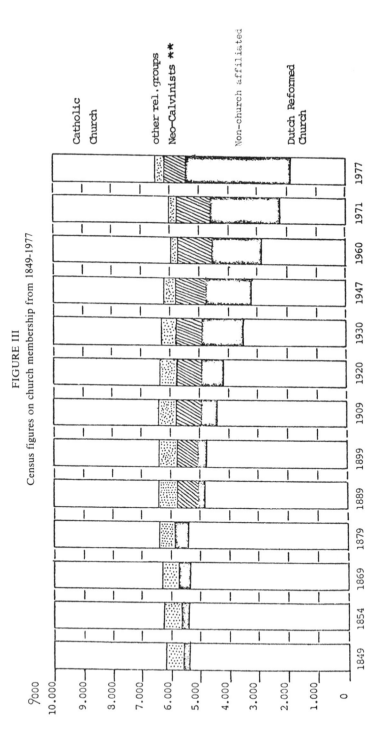

FIGURE III

Census figures on church membership from 1849-1977

Source: 13e Algemene Volkstelling deel 7, p. 21

* Data from Dutch election studies (sample: N = 1,856)

** Criteria fluctuate since there are various small Neo-Calvinist Churches.

absent, as are macro-sociological factors (negotiations between churches and the State, church stances on political issues, and so forth) which should also be taken into account in relation to politics. Despite these limitations, the data raise interesting suggestions about political interest, pillar commitment, and degree of saturation.

Political interest (Table 3)

Of the questions on political participation in the Dutch election studies, four were selected which approached the problem of political interest (so crucial in Lijphart's and Daalder's theories) from different angles:
'Are you interested in political subjects?' (very much, rather, no; recode: yes, no)
'How often do you read about national problems?' (almost always, often, sometimes, seldom or never; recode: much, little)
'People like me have no influence on governmental politics.' (true, not true)
'Do you feel affiliated with a certain political party?' (yes, no)
First, the overall answers for 1972/3 and 1977 from the different denominational groups were inspected. Second, the degree to which these may be imputed to sex, class or age differences, was examined. The more remarkable results are noted in the table. They suggest the following observations:

(1) Calvinists (and non-church-affiliated to a certain extent) showed considerable political interest in 1972/3. This raises a question about the Lijphart and Daalder theses on the lack of political interest among the Dutch and its possible relationship with pillarisation. At least one strongly pillarised group (the Neo-Calvinists) cannot be seen as politically passive, according to these figures.
(2) For both years, the rank order of interest was: Neo-Calvinists, followed by non-church-affiliated, and Dutch Reformed, while Catholics ranked low in 1972/3 and lowest in 1977. On the whole, differences among denominations decreased. The Lijphart and Daalder theses may apply best to the latter group.
(3) Strong Neo-Calvinist political interest even seems to override differences between men and women.
(4) Class differences had effects on both the Catholics and the non-church-affiliated. Among the former, however, these differences increased.
(5) Age differences did not matter very much in 1972/3 but became significant for Catholics and non-church-affiliated in 1977. It was again among the Catholics that the differences were strongest. Although the Dutch Reformed Church is very heterogeneous, the greatest increases in heterogeneity with respect to the issue at stake took place among Catholics.
(6) The significantly low party identification of the young seems to support the suggestion by Van den Berg and Molleman of a crisis on the level of the political parties. But their sense of personal political influence increased. This crisis therefore need not reflect a decline in political participation. Lijphart's suggestion may thus be reversed: depillarisation and decreasing

TABLE 3
POLITICAL INTERESTS, 1972/3 COMPARED WITH 1977

	Indicators used	Percentage interested		Possible intervening variables						Observations on denominational groups
				Sex %		Social class %		age %		
		1972/3	1977	1972/3	1977	1972/3	1977	1972/3	1977	
CATHOLICS	Interest expressed	52	57	14 M>F	17 M>F	26 H>L	28 H>L	n.s.	n.s.	Lowest percentage on all indices in both years (except reading in '72/73).
	Reads about politics	49	40	28 M>F	28 M>F	15 H>L	21 H>L	n.s.	14 E>M>Y	Differences between classes increased.
	Perceived influence	30	46	n.s.	13 M>F	15 H>L	25 H>L	n.s.	16 E>M	Age differences became significant in 1977.
	Expresses party affinity	31	31	n.s.	n.s.	n.s.	n.s.	n.s.	25 E>M>Y	
DUTCH REFORMED	Interest expressed	54	63	21 M>F	18 M>F	n.s.	18 H>L	n.s.	n.s.	Increase in interest on three indices; interpretation is difficult.
	Reads about politics	46	48	30 M>F	24 M>F	16 H>L	n.s.	n.s.	n.s.	
	Perceived influence	35	53	n.s.	n.s.	n.s	n.s	n.s.	n.s.	
	Expresses party affinity	43	41	n.s.	n.s.	n.s.	n.s.	n.s.	18 E>M>Y	
NEO-CALVINISTS	Interest expressed	77	74	n.s.	n.s.	n.s.	23 H>L	n.s.	n.s.	Highest percentage on all indices in both years (except reading in '77). Women are about as interested in politics as men.
	Reads about politics	66	40	n.s.	n.s.	n.s.	n.s.	n.s.	n.s.	
	Perceived influence	51	51	25 M>F	n.s.	n.s.	n.s.	n.s.	n.s.	
	Expresses party affinity	66	52	n.s.	n.s.	n.s.	n.s.	50 E>M>Y	n.s.	
NON-CHURCH AFFILIATED	Interest expressed	64	66	14 M>F	15 M>F	19 H>L	20 H>L	n.s.	n.s.	Level of interest remained more or less constant; class differences already present in 1972/3 (diminishing a little by '77).
	Reads about politics	56	48	22 M>F	23 M>F	28 H>L	19 H>L	n.s.	12 M>Y	
	Perceived influence	41	47	n.s.	n.s.	19 H>L	11 H>L	n.s.	n.s.	
	Expresses party affinity	38	37	n.s.	10 M>F	n.s.	n.s.	n.s.	5 E>M	

General observations: —Percentage differences between confessional groups decreased on all indices.
—Men more interested politically than women except among Neo-Calvinists; High class more interested than lower class; wherever age differences exist, interest is lower the younger the group.
—Age differences are especially important with respect to 'affinity to a political party'.
—'Reading' decreased in most groups.
—'Perceived influence' increased in three groups (steady among Neo-Calvinists whose rate was high already.)

Operationalisations Denomination: 'Do you feel affiliated with a certain religion or denomination? To which one?' *Soc. class* (self-rating): 'Could you indicate to what social class you think you belong?' (Categories: higher-middle; middle; lower-middle; lower. (Recode H;L). *Age:* 1972/3 sample: Elderly – born before 1916; middle-aged – born between 1916-1935; young – born 1936 and after; 1977 sample: Elderly – born before 1920; middle-aged born between 1920-38; young – born 1939 and after.
Legend: >: percentage of affirmations higher; if three groups are mentioned, percentage differences between extreme groups indicated n.s.

TABLE 4

INDICATORS OF (DE-)PILLARISATION, 1972/73 COMPARED WITH 1977

Pillar commitment: A. Political sector (approval for the existence of Christian trade unions and parties)

		Support for Christian organisations %		Possible intervening variables						Particulars of the three denominational groups	Overall observations
				sex %		social class %		age %			
		1972/3	1977	1972/3	1977	1972/3	1977	1972/3	1977		
CATH.	Tr. Un.	46	38	n.s.	n.s.	n.s.	n.s.	n.s.	23 E>M>Y	Only group to decrease in commitment to confessional trade union and party. Only denomination to show increasing age differences.	Percentage differences between denominations increased (because of declining pillar commitment among Catholics). Rank order in pillar commitment: Neo-Calvanist; Dutch Reformed; Catholics (in both years).
	Pol. p.	53	47	n.s.	n.s.	n.s.	n.s.	n.s.	n.s.		
DUTCH REF.	Tr. Un.	57	54	n.s.	n.s.	n.s.	n.s.	n.s.	n.s.	Steady in pillar commitment	
	Pol. p.	64	63	n.s.	n.s.	n.s.	n.s.	n.s.	n.s.		
NEO-CALV.	Tr. Un.	82	83	n.s.	n.s.	n.s.	n.s.	n.s.	n.s.	Steady in pillar commitment. Only group to be nearly as interested in Christian Trade unions as in Christian party	
	Pol. p.	89	87	n.s.	n.s.	n.s.	n.s.	n.s.	n.s.		

Pillar commitment: B. Education (percentage support for the existence of Christian schools)

	1972/3	1977	sex % 1972/3	sex % 1977	social class % 1972/3	social class % 1977	age % 1972/3	age % 1977	Particulars of the three denominational groups	Overall observations
Catholics	60	63	n.s.	n.s.	n.s.	11 H>L	19 M>Y	16 E>M>Y	Only denomination to show class and age differences. Slight increase in pillar commitment.	Percentage differences between denominations did not change. Rank order in pillar commitment as in political sector.
Dutch Ref.	67	72	n.s.	n.s.	n.s.	n.s.	n.s.	n.s.	Increase in pillar commitment.	
Neo-Calv.	93	95	n.s.	n.s.	n.s.	n.s.	n.s.	n.s.	Steady/slight increase in pillar commitment.	

Legend: (see also Table 3)
Tr. Un.: Trade union—percentage respondents expressing preference for Christian trade unions
Pol. p.: Political party—percentage respondents expressing preference for Christian political parties

differences between denominations might well be accompanied by increasing political interest.

Pillar commitment (Table 4)

The questions in the Dutch election studies were:
'Should Christian parties be separate, merge, or should there be no religious ties at all?' (recode: religious ties or none).
'Should Christian trade unions be separate, merge or should there be no Christian unions?' (recode: Christian unions or none).
'Should Christian schools be separate, merge or should there be no Christian schools?' (recode: Christian schools or none).

The answers are illuminating with respect to the differences in (de-)pillarisation of different sectors:

(1) The rank order in pillar commitment was: education, political party, trade union—in all three groups, for both periods surveyed.
(2) Interest in confessional parties and trade unions decreased, but the contrary was true for Christian schools.
(3) Class differences did not replace denominational differences. Again, the Catholics provided an exception, surprisingly not with respect to the political sector, but with respect to the educational one. Here class turned up as a significant intervening variable.
(4) Contrary to the findings about political interest, the data on pillar commitment suggest consistent and continuing differences among the three denominational groups.

Degree of saturation (Table 5)

Finally, we considered answers to the question: 'For which party did you vote at the last election?' (All three Christian parties were coded together.) The answers confirmed Thurlings' observation: involvement in confessional organisations need not correspond with a verbally expressed preference for such organisations. Interestingly, among Catholics the differences between 'pillarised' voting and verbally expressed pillar commitment were opposite to those among Protestants. Did old habits outlive changed opinions?

Other implications are:

(1) 'Degree of saturation' as measured by this variable increased. This does not mean that the total rate of votes for Christian parties also increased. Figure III shows considerable shrinking of the denominational groups, and the election figures show a decline of Christian Democratic votes (see Table 7).
(2) There were more votes from all three denominations for Labour and the Conservatives in 1977 than in 1972/3 (see Tables 6 and 7). The elections in 1977 were exceptional in that they—for once—halted the fragmentation of the electorate into many new parties.
(3) The rank order of pillarised behaviour by groups has changed, although Neo-Calvinists were first again (see Table 4).
(4) Differences did not decrease between denominations.

TABLE 5

INDICATIONS OF (DE-) PILLARISATION, 1972/3 COMPARED WITH 1977

Figures on 'degree of saturation'	Percentage voting for Christian Democrats		Possible intervening variables						Observations on the three denominations
			sex %		social class %		age %		
	1972/3	**1977	1972/3	1977	1972/3	1977	1972/3	1977	
Catholics	48*	54**	n.s.	n.s.	n.s.	n.s.	n.s.	36 E>M>Y	More voters than respondents choose Christian parties. Age differences increased.
Dutch Reformed	30*	31*	n.s.	n.s.	n.s.	n.s.	20 E>M>Y	n.s.	Fewer voters than respondents favour Christian parties. Age differences decreased.
Neo-Calvinists	76*	78*	n.s.	n.s.	n.s.	n.s.	32 M>Y	n.s.	Same pattern as Dutch Reformed but on higher level of pillarisation.

* 100 per cent: non-voters excluded, hence the differences with Table 6.
** Combined percentages for three Christian parties.

TABLE 6

VOTING BEHAVIOUR IN FOUR DENOMINATIONAL GROUPS, 1972/3 and 1977

	Labour %		Christian Democrat %		Conservative %		Non-voters and other parties %		Total electorate %	
	1972/3	1977	1972/3*	1977	1972/3	1977	1972/3	1977	1972/3	1977
Catholics	13	22	43	49	8	11	36	18	100	100
Dutch Reformed	25	34	28	30	19	19	28	17	100	100
Neo-Calvinist	—	7	76	76	3	8	21	9	100	100
Non-church-affiliated	45	51	4	7	16	14	35	28	100	100

* Combined percentages for three Christian parties

TABLE 7

VOTES FOR THE THREE MAIN CHRISTIAN PARTIES
(CHRISTIAN DEMOCRATIC APPEAL IN 1977) IN PARLIAMENTARY ELECTIONS
PERCENTAGE OF ALL VALID VOTES

Parties	1946-1959*	1963	1967	1971	1972	1977
Catholic	30.8	31.9	26.5	21.9	17.7	Christian Democratic Appeal
'Anti-Revolutionary' (= Neo-Calv.)	11.3	8.7	9.9	8.6	8.8	
Reformed	8.5	8.6	8.1	6.3	4.8	
Three combined	50.6	49.2	44.5	36.8	31.3	31.9

* Averages of five elections
Source: Figures compiled by Dutter: p. 569.

(5) Class differences did not increase, except for the votes that went to Labour and the Conservatives (Table 6). Among Catholics, age differences changed again, and in a direction opposite to that of Protestants.

FINAL CONSIDERATIONS

The data from the two election studies do not unequivocally show continuing depillarisation, substitution of class for denominational differences, nor confirm the theories on lack of political interest. These data, however, pertain to years later than those in which the theorists of depillarisation wrote. Moreover, the time-span analysed here is quite short. Figures from earlier (and later) years would be necessary to confirm our conclusions.

What stands out, in spite of these somewhat puzzling outcomes, is that the denominations still behave quite differently in politics. Furthermore, sex, class and age differences intervened only in a few cases in explaining the data for the denominational groups. Finally, the Catholics showed the greatest increase in heterogeneity. It was in this group that class and age differences most frequently appeared to matter. Age was more influential than class here. For all these reasons, we suggest that religious change does play a significant role in present-day Dutch politics, in so far as the variables we have analysed are the appropriate ones. We also suggest that of these transformations, the dramatic ones in the Catholic world may well be the most important. Thus far, little attention has been focused on what may well be the equally important sequels of the turbulent transformations at work in the Neo-Calvinist world. The effects of these shifts, however, have yet to show up in the data.

NOTES

This paper was presented at the fifteenth Meeting of the CISR (Conférence Internationale de Sociologie de Religion) in Venice, 1979. We owe many thanks to Dr Peter McCaffery from Aberdeen University and Professor Suzanne Berger from MIT, for careful screening of our English grammar and idiom.

1. V.R. Lorwin, 'Segmented Pluralism, Ideological Cleavages and Political Cohesion in the Smaller European Democracies', *Comparative Politics*, Vol. 1, (1970), pp. 141-75.

2. J. Billiet, 'Beschouwingen over het samengaan van secularisatie en verzuiling', *De Nieuwe Maand*, (1976), p. 245.

3. Lorwin, op. cit., p. 163.

4. J. Billiet and K. Dobbelaere, *Godsdienst in Vlaanderen: van kerks Katolicisme naar sociaal-kulturele Kristenheid*. Leuven: Davidsfonds, 1976.

5. Lorwin, op. cit., p. 148; L.E. Dutter, 'The Netherlands as a Plural Society', *Comparative Political Studies*, (1978), p. 557.

6. Cf., e.g., J. Hendriks, *De emancipatie van de Gereformeerden, sociologische bijdrage tot de verklaring van enige kenmerken van het huidige Gereformeerde volksdeel*. Alphen aan de Rijn: Samson Uitgeverij, 1971.

7. J.P. Kruyt and W. Goddijn, 'Verzuiling en ontzuiling als sociologisch proces', in A.N.J. de Hollander *et al.*, (eds.), *Drift en Koers, een halve eeuw sociale verandering in Nederland*. Assen: Van Gorcum & Co. N.V., 1968, pp. 227-63.

8. J.A. van Kemenade, *De Katholieken en hun onderwijs, een sociologisch onderzoek naar de betekenis van Katholiek onderwijs onder ouders en docenten*. Meppel: J.A. Boom & Zn, 1968, p. 117ff.

9. A. Lijphart, *Verzuiling, pacificatie en kentering in de Nederlandse politiek*. Amsterdam: J.H. de Bussy, 1968, p. 19ff.

10. Ibid., p. 76.

11. H. Daalder, *Politisering en lijdelijkheid in de Nederlandse politiek*. Assen: Van Gorcum & Co. N.V., 1974.

12. Lijphart, op. cit., p. 95.

13. J.M. Yinger, *The Scientific Study of Religion*. London: Macmillan, 1970, p. 426.

14. J. Th. J. Van den Berg, 'Tien jaar later: anti-Daalder', *NRC/Handelsblad*, 9 February 1974. 1974).

15. Lijphart, op. cit., p. 9.

16. J. Th. J. Van den Berg and H.A.A. Molleman, *Crisis in de Nederlandse politiek*. Alphen aan de Rijn: Samson Uitgeverij, 1974.

17. Ibid., p. 65.

18. Ibid., p. 67; the concept is comparable to the concept of pillar commitment above.

19. Ibid., p. 134.

20. Dutter, op. cit., p. 556-61.

21. Ibid., p. 582.

22. Ibid., p. 582.

23. Ibid., p. 563.

24. A body of theory which Rabushka and Shepleseem to pass over, while admitting that they do not know how to account for the emergence of the 'political entrepreneur'. Ibid., p. 560.

25. J.M.G. Thurlings, *De wankele zuil, Nederlandse Katholieken tussen assimilatie en pluralisme*. 1st ed., Nijmegen: Dekker & v.d. Vegt and Amersfoort: de Horstink, 1971, and 2nd ed. Deventer: Van Loghem-Slaterus, 1978.

26. Ibid., p. 140.

27. Van Kemenade, op. cit., p. 225.

28. Cf. also Thurlings, op. cit., p. 143.

29. Ibid., p. 142.

30. Thurlings mentions a total number of 885,754 members of youth clubs which must probably be 855,754 (ibid., p. 141).

31. Ibid., p. 145.

32. Ibid., p. 147.

33. Ibid., p. 170ff.

34. Ibid., p. 210.

35. Ibid., p. 148.

36. Lorwin, op. cit., p. 164.
37. Ibid., p. 167.
38. *De Nederlandse kiezer '72*. Alphen aan de Rijn: Samson Uitgeverij, 1973 (Dutch election study 1972/73); compilation of first results by L.P.J. de Bruyn, J.W. Foppen, (eds.), Instituut voor Politicologie, Nijmegen; *De Nederlandse kiezer '73*. ibid.; *De Nederlandse kiezer '77*. Voorschoten: VAM, 1977, (Dutch election study 1977); compilation of first results by G.A. Irwin, J. Verhoef, C.J. Wiebrens, (eds.), Vakgroep Politieke Wetenschappen Juridische Faculteit, Leiden.
39. Of course, the problem of what types of differences this involves, how the concept of 'class' should be interpreted and what the relationship with different political ideologies is, should be taken into account. Furthermore, the growing number of migrant labourers from Mediterranean countries and immigrants from the former Dutch West Indies will in the future constitute important minorities with whom we could not deal here.

Politics and the Pulpit: The Case of Protestant Europe

John Madeley

Confounding the assumptions and doctrines of Enlightenment secularism (in both its original liberal-bourgeois and later Marxist guises), religion has continued to play an important role in the politics of the 'Old World'. Both Northern Ireland and Poland stand as contemporary reminders that, despite rumours to the contrary, God is not dead so far as European politics is concerned. The partial retardation of secularising processes by revivals of different kinds in Catholicism and Protestantism in the nineteenth century, not only confounded the expectations of secularist thinkers, it also had significant political effects in the formative years of the European party systems, which reflected the continuing importance of religious cleavages and the contemporary salience of religious issues in politics. These religious elements in partisan politics have shown a remarkable ability to survive, despite general trends toward secularisation; and even where they have declined or disappeared, the religious factor in a number of significant cases continues to operate as a sort of 'hidden agenda' in the pattern of voting behaviour.[1]

In an important 1969 article on social cohesion, political parties and strains in regimes, Rose and Urwin attempted to assess the relative impact of religion on politics with the aid of quantitative data. They developed a measure for the social cohesiveness of political parties and applied it to the secondary analysis of broadly comparable survey data from seventeen different Western countries.[2] This analysis showed that religion—measured variously in terms of confessional affiliation, church attendance and pro/anti-clerical opinion— provided a positive basis for cohesiveness in a greater number of parties than any other variable, including class. They were thus able to conclude that, contrary to Lipset's well-known claim for the primacy of the class factor in democratic politics, 'religious divisions, not class, are the main social basis of parties in the Western world today'.[3] Two years later a complementary study by Lijphart of the political cohesion of social groups (i.e., the reverse relationship), which was based on a secondary analysis of data from ten European countries, confirmed the contemporary political importance of the religious factor.[4] He concluded that by contrast with divisions based on age, sex and urban/rural residence 'class and religion are clearly the most significant variables'.[5]

In addition to demonstrating the overall importance of the religious factor in post-war European politics, the Rose-Urwin and Lijphart studies also provided a basis for measuring its incidence as between the different regions of Europe. In terms of the broad confessional categories of Catholic and Protestant, Western Europe has, as Rokkan pointed out, been divided into three major areas since the Reformation and the Thirty Years War: 'a Protestant north (Denmark-Norway, Sweden-Finland, Prussia); a religiously mixed zone from Ireland to the Alps (Britain-Ireland, the Low Countries, the Rhineland, large sections of France until 1685, the Swiss cantons); and the counter-Reformation countries in the east and south (the Hapsburg territories, Spain and the Italian territories, France after 1685).'[6] This subdivision has remained remarkably stable, at least in so far as the various populations are concerned, even though the state boundaries have shifted as recently as 1945 in such a way as to affect the confessional balance in individual states. Despite the changes entailed in the unification and division of Germany, and the secession from the United Kingdom of the Republic of Ireland, the basic lines of subdivision are still such as to provide the most natural breakdown of Europe into confessional culture areas.

The Rose-Urwin European data (augmented from other sources) are aggregated in Table 1 in terms of these areas. There is clearly a wide variation between the three areas in the distribution of parties cohesive by religion and class. In the Catholic and mixed-confession groups of countries an equal proportion of all parties (72 per cent) are cohesive by religion, while in the Protestant group an almost identical proportion (71 per cent) are not. Cohesiveness by class shows the reverse pattern though not quite as strongly: in the Protestant group, 64 per cent of parties are cohesive by class, as against less than half that proportion (28 per cent) in the other two areas. Lijphart's data, augmented from other sources (see Table 2), reflect a similar pattern: 'Class voting and religious voting are negatively correlated with each other. In general, the higher the index of class voting the lower the indices of religious voting, although this relationship is by no means perfect.'[7] In all cases, class voting is markedly higher than religious voting in Protestant countries, while in the mixed-confession and Catholic countries the reverse is the case.

This contrast in the overall weight of the religious factor between the largely mono-religious Protestant countries and those countries with at least a significant minority of Catholic citizens, is well known and is reflected in the fact that most of the work on the religious factor in European politics has focused on Catholic populations and the largely Catholic post-war phenomenon of Christian Democratic parties.[8] Any attempt to provide a general explanation for the varying incidence of the religious factor must, however, account for its relative weakness in the north of Europe, as well as its relative strength in the middle and south. It must take account of the exceptional, but nonetheless significant, cases where religion has provided the base for Protestant confessional parties in the north. Such an undertaking is made difficult by the fact that what will here be called 'Protestant Europe' has historically contained a much greater variety of confessional types, patterns of Church-State relations, degrees of religious pluralism and levels of religious observance, than has been the case in Catholic or counter-Reformation Europe. This article is a first attempt to redress the balance in studies of the religious factor by: (a) providing a summary overview of the most salient features of the religious structures and cultures of Protestant Europe; and (b) relating these constellations to the emergence or non-emergence of the religious factor in politics.

The term Protestant Europe is used here to identify collectively both the mono-religious Protestant countries of the north and the mixed-confession

TABLE 1

COHESIVENESS OF PARTIES IN FOURTEEN

WEST EUROPEAN COUNTRIES BY RELIGION AND CLASS

	Cohesive by religion only	Cohesive by both religion and class	Cohesive by class only	Other	Total
Protestant countries					
Britain 1966			Lab	Con,Lib	3
Denmark 1956/70	Christians*	Left Socs[+]	Soc,Con,Lib	Rad	6
Finland 1966	Christians*	SKDL +	Soc,Agn,Lib,Con	SPP	7
Norway 1965	Christians	CP	Lab,Agn,Con	Lib	6
Sweden 1964	Christians	CP	Soc,Con,Lib	Agn	6
Total and percentage	4=14%	4=14%	14=50%	6=21%	28=99%
Mixed-confession countries					
Germany 1965	FDP	SDP		CDU	3
Netherlands 1964	KVP,ARP,CHU	PVDA,VVD		Farmers	6
Switzerland 1972**	EVP,Cath,Rad	Soc		Indep, Nat Actn	6
N.Ireland 1968	Unionist, Nationalist		NLIP		3
Total and percentage	9=50%	4=22%	1=6%	4=22%	18=100%
Catholic countries					
Austria 1968	OVP	SPO		FPO	3
Belgium 1965	PSC,Volks-U, Lib	Soc,CP			5
France 1956	SFIO,Rad, MRP,RPF,Ind	PCF			6
Ireland 1965				FG,FF,Lab	3
Italy 1963/67	DCI,PRI,MSI	PCI,PSI	PLI	PSDI,Mon	8
Total and percentage	12=48%	6=24%	1=4%	6=24%	25=100%
All country total	25=35%	14=20%	16=23%	16=23%	71=101%

* These parties did not compete in national elections until the early 1970s

+ These attributions are made on the basis of Rose and Urwin (1969),p.45, Note 1.

**Data for Switzerland are reported in H.Kerr, <u>Switzerland: Social Cleavages and Partisan Conflict,</u> Sage Professional Paper in Comparative Political Sociology, Vol.1, No.06,002.

TABLE 2

INDICES OF PARTISAN CHOICE IN ELEVEN COUNTRIES OF WESTERN EUROPE

	Class	Church affiliation (Cath/Prot)	Church attendance
Mono-religious, Protestant			
Gt. Britain 1959	+ 37	+ 7	− 1
Sweden 1955	+ 53	—	+ 16
Norway 1957	+ 46	—*	+ 21
Mean scores	+ 34	+ 2	+ 12
Mixed Protestant and Catholic			
W. Germany 1959	+ 27	+ 29	+ 40
Netherlands 1956	+ 26	+ 50	+ 73
Switzerland 1963, 1972[x]	+ 26	+ 15	+ 59
N.Ireland 1968**	+ 14	+ 82	n.d.
Mean scores	+ 23	+ 44	+ 57
Mono-religious, Catholic			
Italy 1959	+ 19	—	+ 51
France 1956	+ 15	—	+ 59
Belgium 1956	+ 25	—	+ 72
Austria 1967	+ 31	—	+ 54
Mean scores	+ 22	—	+ 59

* Lijphart gives a score of + 26 here but it is based on an expected correlation between membership in fundamentalist and dissenters' associations and conservative voting in Norway and does not refer to Catholic-Protestant divisions; Lijphart (1971) pp.7-8.

[x] The figures for class and church attendance voting are from Lijphart, based on a 1963 survey: Lijphart (1971), p.8. The figure for church affiliation voting comes from Kerr (1974) and is based on a 1972 survey.

** The Northern Ireland figures are calculated from the table in Rose and Urwin (1969), p.64.

countries of the middle belt. The Westphalian settlement of 1648 finally established the *cuius regio eius religio* rule recognising the right of state authorities to establish as the religion of each state the particular confessional form to which the State's ruler(s) adhered. The application of this rule meant that in the mixed-confession territories of Europe, one or other Protestant church was established as the institutional expression of the official religion. Thus in the Netherlands and Switzerland large regionally-based Catholic minorities were constrained by the existence of a Protestant official religion and Protestant central elites deriving from Protestant majorities. Ireland with its largely Catholic native population also suffered (until 1869) from the imposition of a Protestant state church. Only after 1921 did it take its place among the Catholic countries, while the north of the country remained part of the United Kingdom, dominated by a self-consciously Protestant local elite. In Germany the intricate patchwork of states, principalities and free cities, each with their own established religion, was simplified only in 1870 by the German Reich under the leadership of Protestant Prussia.

THE RELIGIOUS STRUCTURES AND CULTURES OF PROTESTANT EUROPE

The religious settlements of the mid-seventeenth century not only marked the broad spatial subdivision of Europe between Catholic and Protestant populations, they also cemented the divisions within Protestant Europe between different types of confession and different patterns of Church-State relationship. While Lutheran state churches were maintained in Scandinavia and northern Germany, Anglican state churches were re-established in England, Wales and Ireland, and Calvinist church establishments were confirmed in Scotland (1690), the Netherlands and Switzerland. These differences in confessional culture and ecclesiastical structure provided the context for the emergence of quite distinct patterns of religious cleavage among the several Protestant populations in more recent times.

Each of the major types of Protestant confession possessed certain distinct features which *a priori* might be expected to have affected the impact of religion on modern electoral politics.[9] Among the characteristic features of Calvinism are its activist ethos and its insistence on the will of God as expressed in the Bible as the absolute guide for all human conduct. The combination of these two features has been a particularly powerful historical force. Mainstream Lutheranism, by contrast, has tended to be marked by a quietist ethos, an emphasis on personal piety and, through the doctrine of the calling, the belief that the Christian can best serve God by obediently and conscientiously performing the duties attaching to his or her social position which God himself has determined. Anglicanism is distinguished from the other two confessional types by its claim to represent a *via media* between all extremes, including those of activism and quietism. Its historic ability to embrace diverse elements within a single pattern of liturgical order is associated with its origin as the national Church of a single country (England) which, in the century after the Reformation, attempted to achieve comprehensive membership among a religiously diverse population.

Lipset has implied that confessional type does indeed provide part of the explanation for the differential propensity of particular populations to generate religious parties. He focuses, however, less on ethos than on the different confessions' doctrines and their implications for Church-State relations:

> The more a church conceives of itself as God-ordained and has an ecclesiastical constitution that is completely separated from state power, the more likely is it to be interested in government action. In the West, the Catholic Church best fits these conditions. As a church in the sociological sense, it assumes that it is God-ordained, and it claims authority over all persons born within it, rather than (as with Protestant denominations, which have sectarian origins) over those who voluntarily give it allegiance. Unlike other Christian *churches* (the Lutheran, the Anglican and the Greek Orthodox), it is genuinely supranational, accepting an authority outside the nation: the Pope. The other state-supported churches have been closely linked to those who hold power in the state and their tie to state power prevents them from playing an independent political role.[10]

Among non-Catholic churches, however, 'seemingly Calvinism where it retains its ancient strong faith, retains more of the attributes of the God-ordained universalistic Church than any other Protestant group', and in the Netherlands it provides the basis for two independent confessional parties.[11] Lutheran churches, on the other hand, seem to diverge most from this pattern and demonstrate a very low potential for generating political involvement in the form of support for explicitly religious parties.

This hypothesis is problematic, particularly if the range of variations found in Protestant Europe is considered. First, almost all churches, or for that matter sects, denominations or cults, regard themselves to be in some sense 'God-ordained', and there are difficulties in judging to what *degree* a religious body conceives of itself in this way. Second, with regard to the 'structural' element of the hypothesis, it is by no means clear that churches with a 'constitution that is completely separated from state power' have tended to be more 'interested in government action' than, for example, state churches which depend for their support on government action. Other things being equal, church independence from state power is likely to be significant in so far as it affects: (a) the ability of religious communities to act independently; and (b) the probability that a religious community will see its own interests as being distinct from those of the State. Third, Lipset's claim that Calvinists have more consistently provided support for religious parties, raises the question of the contrast between the relative weakness of the Evangelical People's Party in Calvinist Switzerland and the relative strength of the Christian People's Party in Lutheran Norway. This comparison suggests that variations are perhaps to be accounted for, less by the confessional character of the dominant churches, than by other factors which only partially, if at all, coincide with confessional type. Lastly, and most importantly, by restricting the scope of his hypothesis to churches, Lipset fails to take account of non-church religious groups such as independent denominations or groups within churches which have been a feature of Protestant countries and have occasionally, as will be seen, provided the inspiration and support for religious parties.[12] Despite these problems, the hypothesis does raise interesting questions about the influence of narrowly religious and ecclesiastical factors on the development of patterns of political opposition.

Lipset also proposes a supplementary hypothesis to help explain the likelihood that religious parties will arise within any given population: 'Where a cultural community is threatened by outside values, and there is a close identity between the community and a given religion, religious parties are more likely to emerge.'[13] He adds that this generalisation applies particularly to the situation of various colonial peoples in the Third World, but it would seem to apply equally well to the situation of certain religious communities in Western Europe at junctures which have been crucial for the development of religious parties, for example, the Catholics in the German Reich during the *Kulturkampf*, and both Catholic and Protestant communities in the various parts of Ireland at different times. This point does not only apply to situations where Catholic and Protestant communities coexist, however. As will be seen, the religious cultures of Protestant Europe have generated a wide range of separate religious traditions and communities within certain Protestant populations which were once largely uniform in matters of religion. It will consequently be interesting to examine the degree to which the pluralisation of religious forms is associated with the development of competing communal identities.

Taken together, Lipset's two hypotheses provide a useful starting point for the examination of the preconditions for the emergence (and non-emergence) of the religious factor in the politics of Protestant Europe. The first suggests the importance of the varying confessional and ecclesiastical heritages of the different countries, while the second directs attention to the linkages between the national and other forms of religion and developing elements of cultural and subcultural identity. The rest of this section considers these features. Since the territory of Protestant Europe as defined above contains eleven modern nations, this can of course be undertaken only in the most summary way. The analysis is, however, facilitated if these countries are grouped according to confessional and ecclesiastical type.

Despite the differences of confession (Anglican, Lutheran and Calvinist) and the traditional association of each with contrasting theories or doctrines regarding the proper relations between the Church and the State, these relationships were, in Europe of the late eighteenth century, remarkably uniform. If 1770 is taken as a first datum point for comparing these patterns, the similarities among all confessional areas, including the Catholic, are striking. There was a near-universal tendency for church and state establishments to be closely interlocked even where, as in Calvinist Holland or Catholic France, the dominant confession encapsulated claims for church independence.[14] If the triangular relationship between Church, State and Nation is examined, on the other hand, broad contrasts between Catholic and Protestant Europe begin to emerge. Despite the attempts of eighteenth-century Catholic monarchs to claim power over the Catholic Church within their own countries, they never succeeded in binding the myths of Church and

Nation together in the Protestant manner. The Reformation had brought the use of vernacular languages into the churches of Protestant Europe at a time when the spread of printing facilitated the development of national literatures and cultures. In the cases of the Calvinist Netherlands and Scotland, Anglican England and Lutheran Sweden, the myths of Nation and Church had been further bonded by struggles for national autonomy and power during the wars of religion. In Protestant as opposed to Catholic Europe, therefore, the established churches tended to be strongly national as well as state dominated.

In the following century (1770 to 1870), a range of patterns of religious and social cleavage developed under the impact of the forces unleashed by the French and Industrial Revolutions (in particular secularist radicalism, nationalism and various strains of religious revivalism). The variations in these patterns in large part account for the uneven incidence of the religious factor in the era of mass politics (beginning roughly in 1870). In all parts of Europe liberalising reforms were introduced but their manner and timing had important and varying consequences for the resultant cleavage structures.[15] In line with the broad implications of Lipset's first hypothesis, a factor of particular importance in accounting for the contrasting patterns appears to be the degree of independence from the State which different types of church establishment enjoyed. There were two polar types: countries (usually Protestant) which inherited Erastian church regimes, where the Church was directly subject to the authority of the State; and independent church regimes (Catholic and Protestant), where the established Churches retained a significant degree of autonomy. In Catholic Europe where, during the nineteenth century, the Church managed to regain much of the independence it had tended to lose in the eighteenth, the patterns have been much studied. The central tendency there was toward what Martin describes as 'spirals of antagonism' resulting in situations of conflict where 'coherent and massive secularism confronts coherent and massive religiosity'.[16] The case of Protestant Europe has received less attention, at least in comparative terms, and we now turn to examine the more varied contexts to be found there. First the broad patterns of Church-State relations are described, then the characteristic types of religious cleavage system which developed within the frameworks set by the constitutional patterns.

In the Lutheran states of Scandinavia and northern Germany, the classic pattern of Church-State relations dates back to the Reformation when the reduction of the Catholic Church had been carried through particularly thoroughly. Not only were church properties sequestered, religious orders suppressed, and the authority of the Pope rejected, but the succession churches were laid completely under the crown, even the vestigial rights of local parish autonomy in appointments soon disappearing. The classic Lutheran doctrine of the institutional Church which legitimated this subjection, stated that the Church constituted only the human framework for the working of God's free grace; it possessed as an institution no inherent or derived authority to dispense miraculous benefits or to interpret the will of God, such as was claimed by the Catholic Church. The prince, as father of his people in spiritual as in secular matters, was responsible to God alone for his stewardship as *summus episcopus* of the Church. No longer a state within a state, the Church ceased to exist as an independent legal corporation and became instead a branch of the royal bureaucracy, charged with the proper administration of the sacraments, the preaching of the word and the general oversight of the moral welfare of the population. Until the late eighteenth century this arrangement provided for almost complete uniformity and a relatively high degree of conformity in religious matters. The church officials' trade-off of church independence for a complete monopoly of religious functions, guaranteed and upheld by the civil power, ensured them a central role in their localities, while their responsibility for the administration of numerous state functions further reinforced a secure and exalted position in the framework of traditional society.[17]

The Anglican succession churches of England, Wales and Ireland were also stripped of any effective independence from the State, although the clergy there did not take on the same character of an ecclesiastical state bureaucracy. While bishops were appointed by the Crown, and the Church lost all influence in the process of their election before appointment, the episcopal office retained a greater degree of dignity and larger independent means. The existence of a wide range of patronage rights vested in the bishops, landowners, colleges and corporations (as well as the Crown) also made for a less rigid subservience to the State, while the development of parliamentary government with jurisdiction over the Church made for a much less uniform style of religious establishment than was the case in the absolutist states of Lutheran Europe. The early development of religious toleration, although it did not dislocate the relationship between the establishments in Church and State, did ensure the freedom of most dissenting Protestant minorities to enjoy their own forms of worship.

The Calvinist countries of Europe—Scotland, the Netherlands and Switzerland—exhibited a wide range of church regimes. Although the theory of Presbyterian church government through a hierarchy of independent synods was anchored in the creed of the Calvinist churches, only in Scotland in the eighteenth century was the theory approximated in practice. There, after the struggles of the previous two centuries against episcopalianism, a structure of local consistories, regional synods and national ecclesiastical courts, headed by the General Assembly in Edinburgh, maintained a degree of independence from the State unknown elsewhere in Protestant Europe. An established Church, supported with a wide range of guarantees by the civil power, it refused to accept the authority of the Crown in its internal affairs, although in the eighteenth century the Crown-in-Parliament did encroach in the matter of church appointments. In the Netherlands, by contrast, the national church synod was not convened for almost 200 years after 1619, and the government of the Church at local and regional level was inextricably intertwined with the civil administration. The denial to religious minorities—including the large Catholic minority in the south—of the rights of citizenship ensured that only members of the Dutch Reformed Church were involved in the management of civil and ecclesiastical functions, but this scarcely compensated the Church for the truncation of its synod structure.

In Switzerland the creeds of the Protestant cantonal churches were Calvinist, but the church constitutions generally took the form of the other,

Zwinglian branch of the Swiss Reformation. The thirty-sixth of Zwingli's sixty-seven theses ran: 'the jurisdiction which churchmen have unduly claimed belongs entirely to the secular authority, provided it is Christian', and it was a Zwinglian theorist of Church-State relations, Erastus, whose name has conventionally been given to the most thorough-going state control over churches. In the Catholic cantons, however, the Church retained more of its wonted independence, protected by the territorial segmentation of political authority from the attentions of the Protestant national majority.[18]

Around 1800 several contrasting changes occurred in the patterns of Church-State relations in the Continental part of Protestant Europe where the impact of the French Revolution was most directly experienced. In northern Germany, for example, the Hohenzollern monarchy imposed throughout its expanded territories a unification of Lutheran and Calvinist churches in a demonstration of pure Erastian statecraft. The effect of this policy was to re-establish a uniform, albeit hybrid, identity of Church and State after the territorial gains had led to the presence in the Hohenzollern territories of a degree of ecclesiastical pluralism. In the Netherlands, on the other hand, after a period of Church-State separation during the French occupation, the national synod of the Dutch Reformed Church was finally reconvened in 1816 and, although its jurisdiction was initially closely circumscribed, in 1852 many, and in 1876 most, of the restrictions were removed. It thus eventually became an independent established church on the pattern of its sister Calvinist church in Scotland.

The significance of the contrasting patterns of Church-State relations for modern politics appears most clearly when the church authorities' responses to the challenges of religious revivalism on the one hand, and secular indifference or hostility on the other, are examined. The introduction of religious toleration at various times was part cause, part consequence of very diverse patterns of religious cleavage. Toleration in all cases entailed a renunciation on the part of state authorities of the effort to maintain conformity and orthodoxy. It was generally conceded or promoted by political elites whose own attachment to confessional orthodoxy was suspect, and many of the groups which took advantage of the new toleration did so in order to revive or re-establish the orthodoxy which latitudinarian church leaderships had ceased to guard. Orthodox Protestant dissent was generally born in opposition to the laxity of the official church authorities and, from the late eighteenth century on, this conflict was fairly common in large areas of Protestant Europe. Its form and its consequences varied widely, however, as between Erastian and independent Protestant churches.

The classic Erastian response is best seen in Scandinavia, northern Germany and Protestant Switzerland.[19] In these countries religious revivalism in various guises had generally already appeared before religious toleration; indeed toleration itself was often the product of wearying experience on the part of the authorities with the difficulties of imposing conformity against the resistance of revivalist groups. One consequence of the relatively late timing of toleration in these countries was that the growth of non-conformity, and the pluralisation of the religious cultures which attended it, occurred largely within the ambit of the state churches and in this way the ideal of comprehensiveness, according to which all members of a society were to be accommodated within a single Church, was maintained. Thus while many small sectarian groups took advantage of eventual toleration to establish their own identity outside the official churches, the groups who were mobilised by the revivalist movements tended to remain within. State church authorities were generally willing to accommodate them, owing to a greater concern for comprehensiveness than for the maintenance of orthodoxy.

In the independent Protestant national churches of the Netherlands and Scotland on the other hand, a different pattern emerged. With their independent Presbyterian modes of self-government, the conflict between revivalist elements and latitudinarian church leadership led initially to bitter struggles within the ecclesiastical governing bodies, constituted as they were to allow representation of varying church views. The schisms which resulted led to the establishment by uncompromising revivalists of a remarkable number of rival churches, each claiming to embody the true national church and maintain traditional orthodoxy. Thus by contrast with the intra-ecclesiastical pluralism of the Erastian churches, there developed a competitive, institutional pluralism. Paradoxically this institutional pluralism did not lead to the proliferation of confessions, except at the margin; in both countries the religious culture remained overwhelmingly Calvinist.

Developments in the United Kingdom, taken as a whole, followed neither of these patterns exclusively. There, religious toleration had been introduced as early as the late seventeenth century after a period of indecisive struggle between national church authorities and dissenting bodies. In Scotland the independent Presbyterian Church was established, while elsewhere the Erastian Anglican Church retained its established status. The early abandonment of the effort to impose religious uniformity meant that when evangelical revivalism appeared with Methodism in the mid-eighteenth century, it was able to develop outside the state Church alongside the old dissenting sects. Unlike the situation in the Netherlands and Scotland, the competitive pluralism generated by a series of important religious revivals did lead to increasing confessional diversity. Furthermore revivalism had an impact within the state Church, and this was accommodated in the same way as in the other Erastian churches. Thus within a single political community one had intra-ecclesiastical pluralism as in the other Erastian churches *and* competitive pluralism as in countries with independent Protestant church regimes. As will be seen, this degree of religious fragmentation was to have important political consequences, in part, because of the association of some alternative traditions with the cultural identity of subgroups, defined variously by class, region, and nationality.

By 1870, therefore, the religious structures and cultures of Protestant Europe showed a much greater degree of variation both within and between different countries than a century before. In the mixed-confession countries, Catholic minorities which had benefited from measures of religious toleration continued to represent distinct religious (and regional) subcultures, made all the more assertive by the revival of ultramontanism and papalism from around mid-century. In the Protestant populations of Switzerland, northern Germany and Scandinavia, both religious revivalism and secularism had developed (albeit at different rates and to different degrees) in the space allowed by the relaxation of the old religious laws, although most of the religious revivalist groups had remained within the ambit of the relatively tolerant Erastian churches. In the Netherlands and Scotland, on the other hand, the challenges of revivalism had led to the emergence of a number of schismatic counter-churches in direct competition with the independent established churches. As in the case of the Erastian countries just mentioned, though not quite to the same extent, religious division had meanwhile failed to generate a wide range of confessional contrasts, Calvinism retaining its historic dominance as the embodiment of the national religious tradition. Finally, in England, Wales and Ireland, while the Anglican Church retained its established status (in the case of Ireland only up to 1869), a greater variety of religious contrasts had emerged by 1870. In addition to the traditions of Irish Catholicism and of Old Dissent which had already been present a century before, a large number of distinct alternative religious traditions developed, spanning a far greater range and embracing a far higher proportion of the population than in any other part of Protestant Europe.

What was the significance of these different patterns for the development of political parties and voting behaviour in the new era of mass politics which was emerging around 1870?

THE TRANSLATION OF RELIGIOUS INTEREST AND VALUE CLEAVAGES INTO POLITICS

Religious groups, like groups identified by ethnicity, class, spatial location and so forth, have certain interests, which are usually legitimised by an explicit doctrine or implicit theory about the world and the group's place within it. In the view of the theory or doctrine, these interests appear not simply as claims but as rights. Where different religious groups develop in situations of religious inequality, such as still existed in Protestant Europe around 1870, the rights of one group often conflict with the pretended rights of another. Most centrally, for example, the rights of established churches as 'the conscience of the state' (as in Anglican and Lutheran countries) or as the guardian of a national covenant with God (as in Calvinist countries), will conflict with the rights claimed by dissident groups, whether within or outside the confessional tradition of the dominant church. The rights of dissident groups within the same confessional tradition will generally be based on claims to represent the *true* conscience of the state or to be the *proper* guardians of a national covenant with God. The rights of dissident groups of a different confessional colour, on the other hand, will generally be argued on the grounds of natural law or other theories of human rights.

Religious groups or institutions differ from other types of collectivity in that they are classic value-generating bodies.[20] The theories or doctrines embodied in their belief systems are of interest not only because they have generally been used to justify individual group or church claims to particular rights, but also because they typically provide the basis for what are claimed to be universal values. In the case of Roman Catholicism these universal values derive from an ancient tradition of social teaching which spans most aspects of human life but which also emphasises the universal status of the Catholic Church as the vehicle of divine grace. In divided Protestantism these universal values have been refracted through the particular ethos of the different confessions: in Calvinism, obedience to the commands of God as revealed in the Bible; in Lutheranism, the patient dependence on divine grace unrelated to works; and in Anglicanism, the cultivation of spiritual life in connection with the ministrations of the Church. By virtue of common ancestry, however, all these Christian traditions also hold a large number of universal values in common—most notably, in recent times at least, values related to what one might broadly call family morality.[21] The development of alternative non-religious value and belief systems, particularly since the French Revolution, has challenged these common claims to represent values of universal application and relevance; and these contests have become a source of ideological political conflict.

In examining the impact of the religious factor on the politics of Protestant Europe, there have been two modes or phases in the 'translation' of religious cleavages which are associated with the dual nature of religious groups as the proponents of interest and value claims; historically, interest claims have always tended to be pressed first.

By 1870 the enforced religious uniformity which had once characterised the Protestant population of northern Europe had largely disappeared, but the privileges and penalties which had once underpinned it had nowhere been completely removed. The religious monopoly provisions of the established churches had been virtually dismantled, more or less gradually in various countries. In the mixed confession countries, large Catholic populations had managed throughout to maintain, and then more and more to assert, their separate religious identity, despite a range of disabilities and disadvantages. Among the Protestant populations the elementary right of religious toleration—to leave the established church and join some other religious body or none—was conceded as early as 1689 in the United Kingdom, and as recently as 1923 in overwhelmingly Lutheran Finland.[22] In most countries this dates to the middle or late eighteenth century. However, the concession of this elementary right hardly touched the main body of laws and provisions which supported the special status of the established churches and their members. The juxtaposition of an emergent religious pluralism with the remaining legal, financial, and other advantages of the dominant churches (and the corresponding disabilities and disadvantages of non-established groups) was in the nineteenth century to prove a most fertile source of contentious religious-political issues. The broadening of the franchise and the opening of access to parliamentary representation for members of disadvantaged groups facilitated the translation of these interest issues into political cleavages. The emergence of a secularist opinion opposed to any connection between the state and religious bodies, reinforced the tendency for these contentions over interest to become political questions.

Three broad types of issue associated with the interests or rights of religious bodies encouraged the oppositional alignment of church establishments, disadvantaged religious groups, and secularists. First, there was the basic issue of the elementary right of religious toleration. Second, there was the removal of the many legal and other disabilities attaching to religious non-conformity and dissent, such as the denial of the right to perform wedding or burial services or the obligation of all to contribute to the upkeep of the established churches through tithes, dues, and taxes. Third, there was the demand for positive equality of treatment for the members of all religious groups, and none. This third type of issue became a particularly potent source of political conflict with the development, in the late nineteenth century, of public education.

The value claims of churches and other religious groups tend to be distinct from their interest or right claims, in so far as they are taken to be of universal rather than particular or sectional scope. Struggles to promote or defend the right of religious communities to follow their own forms of religious service or to influence the religious education of their children, are essentially self-regarding, whatever the tendency to identify the interests of whole societies with the interest of particular groups. Struggles to promote or defend such values as human dignity or social welfare which different religious groups have converted into campaigns against alcohol or pornography or for the defence of the Christian religion generally, are, by contrast, typically oriented to altering arrangements affecting whole societies. While groups or parties organised initially to pursue religious interest claims will usually also make value claims and vice versa, the earlier appearance of interest claim groups and their closer association with particular religious constituencies provide them with a stronger and more stable hold on their electorates.

The structures of religious cleavage reviewed above, define the number, strength, and type of religious groups which by their very existence could be the source of interest claims, the pursuit of which might affect the patterns of political opposition. On a priori grounds one would expect religious interest claims to have a political impact proportional to: (a) the numerical and organisational strength of the religious group concerned; (b) the degree of difference in confessional type which distinguishes it, if at all, from that of the established church; and (c) the extent of the disadvantages and disabilities suffered. The impact of religious value claims, on the other hand, should be related to more general factors, such as the overall level of secularisation within a society and the countervailing strength of mainstream religious opinion. Because of their more general character, religious value movements often differ according to whether religious groups, previously divided by competing interest claims, have been able to combine and pool their strengths. Value movements are often characterised by cross-group cooperation among the different religious groups of a particular society; where this cooperation is not achieved for whatever reason, such movements will be correspondingly weak or non-existent.

The emergence of the Catholic parties of Protestant Europe was directly related to the emergence of religious interest issues on the political agenda. The Catholic populations of Ireland, the Netherlands, Germany and Switzerland were characterised by a numerical and organisational strength which was associated with their relative geographic concentration, by the fact that they were confessionally quite distinct from the Protestant established churches, and by the significant extent of the disabilities from which they suffered. In predominantly Protestant Germany, Bismarck's attempt to

[1]TABLE 3: SUMMARY, BACKGROUND CONDITIONS, RELIGIOUS PARTIES, RELIGIOUS VOTING AND ISSUE TYPES

	Background conditions (ca. 1870)			Interests of Religious Groups	Values of the Religious community	Parties
	Dominant confession	Church regime	Religious Pluralism			
England	Anglican	Erastian	High; internal and external	XO		
Wales	Anglican	Erastian	High; external	X		
Scotland	Calvinist	Independent	High; external	XO		
Ireland (after 1921 N. Ireland)	Anglican	Erastian	High; external (+Catholics)	000 (Nationalists, SDLP) XXX (Unionists, DUP)		Social Democratic Labour Party Democratic Unionist Party
Denmark	Lutheran	Erastian	Low	X	XX (CCP)	Christian People's Party
Finland	Lutheran	Erastian	Low	X	XX (FCL)	Finland's Christian League
Norway	Lutheran	Erastian	Moderate; internal	XX (Mod. Left P.)	XXX (CPP)	Christian People's Party
Sweden	Lutheran	Erastian	Low	X	XX (CDL)	Christian Democratic League
Germany	predominantly Lutheran	Erastian	Low; (+ Catholics)	XX (SCWP) 000 (Zentrum)	CDU	Social Christian Workers' Party Christian Democratic Union
Netherlands	Calvinist	Independent	High; external (+ Catholics)	000 (KVP) XXX (ARP)	XXX (CHU) XX (SGP) XX (GPV) CDA	Catholic People's Party(KVP) Anti-Revolutionary Party Christian Historical Union Christian Democratic Appeal Political Reformed Party(SGP) Reformed Political League (GPV)
Switzerland	Calvinist	Erastian	Low; (+ Catholics)	000 (SCPP)	(CDPP) XX (EVP)	Swiss Conservative People's Party Christian Democratic People's Party Evangelical People's Party (EVP)

Legend: X indicates Protestant; O indicates Catholic
X or O: impact on voting
XX or OO: minor religious party
XXX or OOO: major religious party

subject the Catholic Church to the new State raised all three types of interest issue simultaneously. Although he did not attempt to suppress the mass as such, he did expel the Jesuits, tried to control the church's organisation and forbade churchmen to speak from the pulpit on matters of State. On those who resisted these and other attacks on the autonomy of the Catholic Church, which included several bishops and hundreds of priests, the civil courts imposed severe penalties. An important element in the campaign was the attempt to deprive the Church of its former control over primary education. These assaults led directly to the founding and explosive growth of the Catholics' own party of religious defence, the Zentrum, which was to last until the end of the Weimar Republic.[23]

In Switzerland also the Catholic Church came under attack from a liberal Protestant elite. After the Catholic secession war of the 1840s, the Jesuit Order was expelled (1848) and in 1874, in imitation of Bismarck's campaign, restrictions were placed on the freedom of monastic orders. The result was the same as in Germany: a Catholic party was set up which rapidly became the second largest party in the country. Despite its electoral success, the Swiss Conservative People's Party (since 1971 known as the Christian Democratic People's Party) failed to achieve the removal of the anti-Catholic clauses of the constitution. Today it remains a Catholic interest party, though it has also engaged itself in more general religious value issues.

In the Netherlands where in 1815 formal religious toleration had been granted and in 1848 full freedom of religious organisation conceded, the Catholic Church was not subjected to the same sort of attack from the Protestant liberal elite, although the re-establishment of the hierarchy in the 1850s led to a storm of protest. It was, instead, the third type of interest issue, education, that led to the organisation of the Catholic party alongside the orthodox Calvinists of the ARP (see below). Since 1945 this party has been called the Catholic People's Party (KVP).[24]

In Ireland the three types of interest issue arose separately. The first Catholic political organisations were concerned initially with the struggle which led to the Catholic Emancipation Act (1829), and then with the fight to remove the remaining disabilities. This fight focused on relief from the obligation to pay tithes for the upkeep of the established (Anglican) church and culminated in disestablishment in 1869. The education issue, remarkably, was less contentious. The government established a system of state schools, managed by a national board representative of both Catholic and Protestant communities, and clergymen of the different confessions participated in this system for the purposes of religious instruction. Because of the relatively early settlement of the religious group interest issues, the nationalist movement and party did not develop as an explicitly Catholic organisation. But the nationalist movement did derive much of its strength from the historic association of foreign domination and discrimination against Irish Catholics *qua* Catholics, and the resulting identity between Catholicism and Irish Nationalism has ever since reinforced the religio-political polarisation which has dominated the affairs of Northern Ireland since its creation in 1921. Although religious group interest issues continue to feature in the rhetoric of conflict among the militant Protestants there, the bitterness of the protracted conflict between Catholics and Protestants apparently owes more to the dynamics of competing nationalisms, to which religion is essentially incidental, than to the dynamics of religious group interest conflicts.

Among the Protestant populations of Protestant Europe there was by 1870, as has been seen, a wide variation in the number, strength and type of religious groups. Few non-conformist groups, either singly or collectively, approached the numerical or organisational strength of the Catholic minorities, however, and even in the exceptional cases, such as late nineteenth-century Wales where they did, the degree of difference in confessional type between the established church and non-conformity was less than that obtaining between Catholic and Protestant in the mixed-confession territories. Finally, the extent of the disabilities suffered by Protestant non-conformity was rarely as great as that experienced by Catholics. It is therefore not surprising that the translation of religious into political cleavages was much less common among Protestants than among Catholics. Certain translations did nevertheless occur.

In Switzerland and Germany, where the degree of religious pluralism, both internal and external to the established Erastian churches, was relatively low, the comparative absence of important cleavages between religious groups accounts for the weakness of Protestant religious parties. Tension between Church and State was also low because the interests of the established churches were generally well served by precisely those privileges and penalties which elsewhere were a cause of resentment to significant religious minorities (including of course Swiss and German Catholics).[25] Although the usual intra-ecclesiastical differences subsisted between liberals, latitudinarians, high churchmen and more or less orthodox revivalists, these had generally been accommodated in the classic Erastian manner. Religious revivalism furthermore tended to take the form either of world-renouncing pietism or of humanitarian inner-mission movements. Certain religious group interest issues, nevertheless, did emerge to affect patterns of political alignment. Thus Stoecker, despite his Lutheran background and his position (until 1890) as court preacher in Berlin, voiced demands for giving the established church a measure of autonomy, albeit under the authority of the Kaiser as *summus episcopus*.[26] Stoecker's Christian Social Workers' Party, which received its greatest support among the old Reformed (i.e. Calvinist) groups within the Church in Siegerland, was thus, in part at least, a religious interest party. It was also, however, like the short-lived Christian People's Service Party of the Weimar period, as much or more concerned to promote universal religious-social values, particularly social welfare. Like the Swiss Evangelical People's Party (EVP) (which still exists), these parties remained extremely small.[27] In West Germany the religious-political tradition of these parties was taken up in 1945 by the Protestant groups which combined with Catholic Christian Democrats to form the modern CDU. This inter-confessional party has been a classic religious value party, principally committed so far as religion is concerned to promote non-sectarian Christian values, although its development into a catch-all conservative party tends to overshadow its specifically religious character.

The weakness and strength of the religious factor among the Protestant populations of Switzerland and the Netherlands—both overwhelmingly

Calvinist in confession—is instructive. The orthodox Protestants of the Netherlands with a history of independent church government and schism have, throughout the modern period, provided the basis for strikingly successful religious parties.[29] As for the Dutch Catholics, the issue of education provided the initial stimulus when, in 1878, a Liberal government attempted to bar denominational religious education from the school system. A massive petition campaign on this one issue led to the foundation of the country's first mass party, the Anti-Revolutionary Party (ARP). Its founder, Kuyper, was an orthodox clergyman who was as opposed to the lukewarm leadership of the established church as to the programmatic liberalism of the government. Within a decade of founding the party, he had also led the latest in a series of fundamentalist secessions from the Church. The fissiparousness of Dutch Calvinism was also reflected in politics. In 1894 the ARP split when the Christian Historical Union was founded by the politically more conservative, but religiously less fundamentalist, Calvinists who continued to identify with the Dutch Reformed Church. Other smaller parties were formed in 1918 (SGP, the Political Reformed Party) and 1948 (GPV, the Reformed Political League). Their base has been among the smaller Calvinist sects, which have been able to secure separate representation only because of the extremely low-threshold electoral system.[30] Among Protestants as among the more cohesive Catholics, therefore, the Netherlands has seen the direct transposition of religious into political cleavages.[31]

For most of the twentieth century the main confessional parties (ARP, CHU and KVP) have cooperated in government and jointly entrenched the interests of their respective religious constituencies. In 1976, they allied to form the interconfessional Christian Democratic Appeal (CDA). The steady loss of support, which they had suffered collectively, precipitated the foundation of the CDA, but it also reflects the contemporary irrelevance of religious group interest conflicts as traditional Christian values come under attack by movements, for example, to liberalise, the abortion laws.[32] Here, as in Germany, one sees a shift from political patterns set in the period of interest conflicts to patterns more suited to the defence of values which are held in common by all the mainstream denominations.

In the other predominantly Calvinist country, Scotland, a pattern of religious cleavages similar to the Dutch produced quite different consequences. The pattern of a Calvinist church establishment faced by a number of rival secessionist bodies, each claiming to be the true representatives of the national religious tradition, failed to produce a religious political party partly, at least, because religious group interest issues were handled so differently. The 1872 Education Act, which entailed state control of the schools provided by the different Presbyterian churches, safeguarded confessional education on the basis of the 'shorter catechism' which was common to all of the principal groups. The issue of disestablishment, on the other hand, proved more divisive and led for a time to the alignment of free and established church opinion behind the Liberal and Conservative parties respectively. The failure of the disestablishment campaign and the re-unification of the several leading Calvinist bodies with the established church, has since removed this issue from politics, however.

In the rest of the United Kingdom where the Anglican Church had long enjoyed the privileges of established status, religious interest issues were rather more contentious. The survival of Catholicism in Ireland and the early granting of toleration to Protestant dissenters had produced a pattern of dissent external to the Church which was matched in the nineteenth century by the growth of religious divisions within it. The first religious political campaigns, which aligned dissenters with the Whigs and Liberals, and the supporters of Anglican privileges with the Conservatives, concerned the removal of civil disabilities, finally achieved between 1828 and 1871.[33] Thereafter education and disestablishment were the issues which affected the differential support of the various religious groups for the major parties. In Wales, where non-conformity, boosted by religious revivals such as those of 1859 and 1904-5, became a vehicle for the resurgence of a sense of distinctive national identity, both issues became major determinants of party alignment.[34] The 1870 and 1902 Education Acts, the second of which occasioned a 'Welsh revolt', led to major political campaigns by dissenting groups opposed to the public subvention of denominational religious education in areas with no state schools. The issue of disestablishment further reinforced the alignment of massive non-conformity with the Liberal party between 1868 and 1914 when the act disestablishing the Anglican Church in Wales was finally passed.

In England the alignment of non-conformity with the Liberal party before 1914 was also largely related to the emergence of religious group interest issues.[35] Disestablishment was a less central issue in England than in Wales because non-conformity and Anglicanism were closer in strength and there was no complicating nationalist factor. The education issue, however, became almost equally disruptive. Non-conformist reactions to the 1902 Education Act led, as in Wales, to a massive campaign which played a great part in the Liberal landslide of 1906. By the time of the 1944 Education Act, the various religious groups were concerned less with denominational differences than with the maintenance of religious education, as such, within state schools.[36]

In terms of religious value issues, temperance played a large part in reinforcing the association of Welsh and English non-conformity with the Liberal and, later, Labour parties in the period before World War I when it was a political issue of some importance.[37] More recently, however, the emergence of such moral issues as pornography and abortion has only led to the foundation of small campaigning organisations like the Festival of Light and the Society for the Protection of the Unborn Child. Because the interest issues were settled early, these organisations have been unable to capitalise on pre-existing religious-political cleavages. Both of the current major parties have treated the value issues as matters for the conscience of individual MPs and have thereby been able to remove them from party-political debate. The failure of any major party to adopt strong positions on them, not least because of strong intra-party differences of opinion, has meant that the religious factor in modern British politics is a mere vestige of old patterns of alignment, surviving principally among the oldest cohorts of voters.[38]

In Northern Ireland, as has already been noted, the impact of interest issues was, from early on, complicated by the national question. Thus, for example, certain non-conformist leaders opposed disestablishment on the grounds that it would undermine the role of Protestantism in Ireland.[39] The education issue, which ceased to be divisive in the rest of the United Kingdom after World War I, was also treated as merely one aspect of continuing conflict between Catholic nationalism and Protestant loyalism. Owing to pressure from Protestant leaders in the 1920s the state schools effectively became denominational, but this subvention of Protestant religious education did not prevent Unionist politicians attacking subsidies for Catholic schools. Thus Ian Paisley's Democratic Unionist Party (DUP) founded in 1970, continues to oppose these subsidies. Over the last decade statements from both sides condemning the use of violence would seem to reflect an emergent interdenominational consensus on common moral and religious values, but the survival of religious interest conflicts within a context of intense community conflict undermines the prospects for a realignment on this new axis.

In Scandinavia as in the other countries with Erastian church systems, conservative politicians and officials in the late nineteenth century regarded support for the established Lutheran churches as a natural corollary of their defence of the status quo.[40] In this they found themselves ranged against not only secular liberals and social democrats but also lay revivalists within the churches and the small groups of dissenters without. Settlement of the issues of toleration and the removal of non-conformist disabilities was achieved relatively late (earliest in Norway in the 1840s, latest in Finland in the 1920s). Only in Norway, however, was a group of fundamentalist revivalists sufficiently large to provide an independent basis for a religious party. In 1888 they broke from the Left (Liberal) party to form the Moderate Left party when it became clear that their interest in church reform and the maintenance of religious orthodoxy was not shared by their more secular former allies. Led initially by vigorous religious entrepreneurs—like Kuyper in the Netherlands, they were revivalist clergymen—the party soon faded and moved to the Right as the national question came to dominate the political agenda. Throughout Scandinavia conflicts between clerical conservatives, 'churchly' revivalists, radical revivalists and dissenters among the religious activists, each with their own particular interests, undermined any attempt to set up a successful religious party. The maintenance of the privileges of the established churches, including the use of state schools for confessional religious instruction, also meant that in the absence of a large body of dissenters outside the state churches there was no basis in a fundamental grievance. The value issue of temperance which, as in Britain, was adopted by Liberal and Social Democratic parties in the early part of this century, did lead orthodox revivalists and dissenters to give a disproportionate support to these parties, although the parties' support for other more traditional religious values was occasionally suspect.

The recent emergence of a range of moral-religious value issues has been reflected in the rise of expressly Christian parties. In Norway as early as the 1930s a Christian People's Party was founded to combat the secularism of the Left, the latitudinarian policies of the church authorities, and the evils of drink. Originating in Norway's Bible belt in the south and west of the country which had earlier been the base area of the Moderate Left party, it became a national organisation in 1945. Its overriding emphasis on religious and moral questions in which religious activists of most backgrounds have a common interest has made it the representative of interdenominational religious opinion on such matters as temperance, abortion and pornography. Furthermore, its success as the leading centrist party has encouraged groups with similar views and concerns in the three other Scandinavian countries to form Christian parties on the basis of common religious values.

This overview has necessarily been brief despite its relatively narrow focus. Taking Lipset's cue we have concentrated on the religious and ecclesiastical preconditions for the impact of religion upon the politics of Protestant Europe. Table 3 attempts a schematic representation of the major patterns. Clearly a full analysis would also have to include many other aspects of the social and political systems within which the religious factor has operated. But this approach has helped to clarify certain centrally important elements which political analysts might otherwise leave for consideration only by ecclesiastical and social historians. The relative strength and weakness of religion in the modern politics of Catholic and Protestant Europe suggested, on first view, the importance of confessional differences but these cannot alone account for a number of significant variations across time and space. It has been argued that the nature of historically entrenched patterns of Church-State relationships and their associated religious cleavage systems, which are only incidentally related to confessional type, must also be brought into any analysis of the preconditions for the translation of religious into political effects. Such translations vary considerably in form, depending on whether religious interests or values are judged to be at stake. While interest conflicts account for the earliest cases, value conflicts have become most common in recent politics.

Perhaps, as Burke declared, 'politics and the pulpit are terms that have little agreement', but in certain times and certain places it is clearly difficult to understand the operation of one without the other.

NOTES

1. This term is used by Converse to describe the operation of 'religious animosities' on the main trends in American party alignments. P. Converse, 'Some Priority Variables in Comparative Research', in R.Rose (ed.), *Electoral Behaviour: A Comparative Handbook*. London: Macmillan, 1974, p. 733.
2. R. Rose and D. Urwin, 'Social Cohesion, Political Parties and Strains in Regimes', *Comparative Political Studies*, Vol. 2, No. 1, (April, 1969).
3. Ibid., p. 12.
4. A. Lijphart, 'Class Voting and Religious Voting in European Democracies', University of Strathclyde, Glasgow, 1971.
5. Ibid., p. 7.
6. S. Rokkan, 'The Structuring of Mass Politics in the Smaller European Democracies. A Developmental Typology', in O. Stammer (ed.), *Party Systems, Party Organisations and the Politics of the New Masses*. Berlin: Institute of Political Science of the Free University, 1968, p. 52. Much of what follows owes a great deal to insights developed in this and other

seminal articles by Rokkan. Most of these articles are listed in the bibliography appended to S. Rokkan, *Citizens, Elections and Parties*. Oslo: Universitetsforl., 1970.

7.   Lijphart, op.cit., p. 9.
8.   See, for example, M.P. Fogarty, *Christian Democracy in Western Europe, 1820-1953*. London: RKP, 1957; R.E.M. Irving, *The Christian Democratic Parties of Western Europe*. London: Allen and Unwin, 1979; and J.H. Whyte, 'The Catholic Factor in the Politics of Democratic States', *American Behavioral Scientist*, Vol.17, No. 6, (1974). See also the review article by G. Pridham, 'Christian Democracy in Western Europe: a Bibliographical Survey', *West European Politics*, (October 1980).
9.   The classic work on this subject is E. Troetsch, *The Social Teachings of the Christian Churches*. (trans. by O. Wyon), London: Allen and Unwin, 1931. A shorter presentation of the same subject can be found in E. Molland, *Christendom*. London: Mowbray, 1959.
10. S.M. Lipset, *Revolution and Counter-Revolution*. New York: Basic Books, 1968, p. 219.
11. Ibid., p. 220.
12. I have argued elsewhere that Lipset's hypothesis should be reformulated in terms of the differential nature and location of authority in or over religious communities. Martin summarises my argument in D. Martin, *A General Theory of Secularization*. Oxford: Blackwell, 1980, p. 97.
13. Lipset, op.cit., p. 220.
14. 'While the churches continued to exercise their traditional functions, it was increasingly as an arm of the secular state. Everywhere, whether in Catholic, Protestant or Greek Orthodox lands, kings and rulers were asserting their authority over their churches and prelates.' G. Rudé, *Europe in the Eighteenth Century*. London: Cardinal, 1974, pp. 159-60.
15. As will be seen liberalisation was not in all cases a unilinear development without reversals. In the three Continental mixed-confession countries, significant deviations occurred.
16. D. Martin, op.cit., p. 6.
17. A useful review of Church-State relations in Scandinavia can be found in A. Aarflot (ed.), *Kirke og Stat i de Nordiske Land*. Oslo: Univ. forl., 1971.
18. Until the nineteenth century Switzerland maintained at the cantonal level the *cuius regio* rule, which had obtained in the rest of Europe as between states.
19. For the history of revivalism and the Protestant churches throughout Europe, see K.S. Latourette, *Christianity in a Revolutionary Age, Vol. II*. London: Eyre and Spottiswoode, 1960.
20. Lipset, op.cit., p. 215. This idea is a commonplace of religious sociology.
21. It is in this field that the mainstream Christian denominations have been most able to make common cause. Secularists have been concerned to remove the traditional bias of legal systems towards the support of religion-based morality and it is in conflict with these that the different religious groups have tended to define their most distinctive value claims.
22. The 1689 Toleration Act only applied to Protestant dissenting groups which accepted the doctrine of the Trinity. In Finland a degree of religious toleration had been introduced in 1869, but only in 1923 was the right to belong to no religious body formally conceded.
23. The Zentrum in fact included a small number of prominent Protestants such as Ludwig von Gerlach in its early period. For most of its history it was unable to avoid the image of being a Catholic ghetto party. See K. Buchheim, *Geschichte der Christlichen Parteien in Deutschland*. Munich: Kösel, 1953.
24. Daalder indicates the development of the KVP from a mere Catholic interest party: 'It started out with a single aim "religious freedom for the children", and developed into a compendious party with a full set of doctrines.' H. Daalder, 'Parties and Politics in the Netherlands', *Political Studies*, (1955), p. 2.
25. The entrenchment of established church interests made for the identification of privileged church groups with conservative political elites but provided no basis for specifically religious parties—only for the association of religious, economic, and social elements within the dominant blocs.
26. See Buchheim, op.cit., pp. 266-7.
27. Gruber identifies the EVP's principal dilemma thus: 'What political options will a party have that has inscribed on its banner not the interests of the farmers, the workers or industry [or even the interests of a strong religious group—J.M.] but pre-eminently, always and everywhere the interests of God?' C. Gruber, *Die Politischen Parteien der Schweiz im Zweiten Weltkrieg*. Vienna: Europa, 1966, p. 166.

28. Heidenheimer argues that the 'relationship between an underlying set of moral values and an elastic fund of working doctrines' has contributed to the adaptability of German Christian Democracy. A.J. Heidenheimer, *Adenauer and the CDU*. The Hague: Nijhoff, 1960, p. 17.

29. See J.P. Kruijt, 'The Influence of Denominationalism on Social and Organisational Patterns', *Archives de Sociologie des Religions*, Vol. 4, No.8, (1959). Like more recent work, he stresses the penetration of confession-based organisations into a wide range of sectors of Dutch society.

30. A. Lijphart, 'The Netherlands: Continuity and Change in Voting Behaviour', p. 235 in R. Rose (ed.), op.cit. Due to lack of information it is difficult to know whether SGP and GPV should be seen as initially interest or value parties.

31. Lorwin uses the term 'segmented pluralism' to describe the organisation of societies along lines of religious and ideological cleavages and points out that the Dutch first developed a vocabulary for describing it. He also implies that it was the churches' interest in 'preserving the faith' that encouraged its development. V.R. Lorwin, 'Segmented Pluralism: Ideological Cleavages and Political Cohesion in Smaller European Democracies', reprinted in K. McRae, *Consociational Democracy*. Ottawa: Carleton Library, 1974.

32. Irving, op.cit., pp. 207-12 emphasises the pragmatic aspects, while mentioning problems associated with contrasting ethos.

33. In 1871 the Universities Tests Act removed 'one of [the Church of England's] last obviously anachronistic privileges' according to one historian. As in the case of Irish disestablishment it was passed by a Liberal government led by Gladstone—himself not merely a staunch Anglican but a High-Church one to boot. His great popularity among non-conformists derived from his image as a Christian statesman. See D.W. Bebbington, 'Gladstone and the Nonconformists', in D. Baker (ed.), *Church, Society and Politics*. Oxford: Blackwell, 1975.

34. See K.O. Morgan, *Wales in British Politics, 1868-1922*. Cardiff: University of Wales Press, 1963.

35. See S. Koss, *Nonconformity in Modern British Politics*. London: Batsford, 1975.

36. Non-conformist dissatisfaction with the 1944 Act was met with the argument: 'The question is not whether people will be Anglicans or Nonconformists, but whether they will be Christians at all'. Quoted in Koss, op.cit., p. 222.

37. In certain peripheral parts of the country temperance retains a degree of importance. See for example P.J. Madgwick with others, *The Politics of Rural Wales*. London: Hutchinson, 1973.

38. D. Butler and D. Stokes, *Political Change in Britain*. London: Penguin, 1971, p. 170.

39. K.S. Latourette, op.cit., p. 399.

40. For a comparative study of the origins and nature of the religious factor in Scandinavian politics, see J. Madeley 'Scandinavian Christian Democracy: Throwback or Portent?' *European Journal of Political Research* (1977). A recent study of the Finnish case is reported in D. Arter, 'The Finnish Christian League: Party or Anti-Party?', *Scandinavian Political Studies*, No. 2, (1980).

From Princes to Pastors: The Changing Position of the Anglican Episcopate in English Society and Politics

Kenneth Medhurst and George Moyser

INTRODUCTION

The political science literature on England generally assumes that religious activities and values do not fall within the discipline's bailiwick.[1] Widely-held assumptions about secularising tendencies within English society and the general absence of overt religious cleavages within the political domain, have combined to produce a situation in which religion tends to be regarded as a matter of marginal significance for practitioners of the discipline.[2] Mass surveys do include some questions about religious practice, and they seem to reveal correlations between particular forms of religious allegiance and particular partisan loyalties. Thus, ordinarily Anglicans are regarded as likely to be disproportionately identified with the Conservative party and Roman Catholics and non-conformists as likely to align with the Labour or Liberal parties.[3] Even here, however, in recent times such correlations may be of diminishing significance.

These responses may need to be questioned in the light of two factors. Firstly, even today churches command larger regular audiences and can count on a greater degree of popular support than almost any other voluntary association.[4] Secondly, relevant mass survey data tend to lose sight of potentially important distinctions between the values and activities of nominal church members, church activists and national ecclesiastical elites.[5] Indeed, a major purpose of this study is to indicate the existence of an emergent consensus within the upper reaches of the established Church of England, a consensus tending to point the Church in politically new directions with limited yet potentially significant consequences for English elite political culture. Differences of perception between the elites in question and their rank-and-file followers may create difficulties for the former, and, to some extent, limit the impact of historically novel initiatives. On the other hand, our evidence indicates that, at certain levels, Anglican activists are quite disproportionately involved in the political process thus opening up the possibility of a considerable ecclesiastical impact, direct or indirect, upon the polity. In certain areas of public debate, at least, it is not fanciful to see church leaders, including Anglican leaders who are the subject of this article, as contributing fairly significantly towards some redefinition of—and thus towards some potential changes in—the content of public policy.

The bulk of the evidence here is drawn from the authors' long-term study of the Anglican Church's internal politics and of its more general political role. This project has involved an extensive survey of members of the Church of England's legislative body, the General Synod, and a detailed investigation of the Church's episcopal leaders. The authors have been interviewing all forty-three English diocesan bishops, a process which is likely to produce a unique body of evidence concerning the current thinking of bishops.[6] Equally, this research should shed light upon the influences which have moulded episcopal attitudes and upon the nature of recruitment into this ecclesiastical elite.

This elite displays characteristics that in substantial measure mark it off from its predecessors.[7] Historically, of course, the Anglican Church, not entirely without justification, was popularly regarded as the 'Conservative Party at prayer'. Even when its leaders have not been formally identified with a particular party, they have tended to be generally very supportive of the status quo and of prevailing political assumptions. The Anglican bishops in the House of Lords voted by a large majority against the Reform Bill of 1832, and even in the early twentieth century, English bishops were not as a rule identified with political protest or with serious challenges to conventional political wisdom. Socially or politically critical prelates can be identified as in the cases of Bishops Wescott and Gore, but such figures were exceptional. The Church of England has also nurtured currents of radicalism, notably in the shape of the Christian Socialist tradition associated with such figures as Charles Kingsley and F.D. Maurice. Moreover, during the inter-war period, prelates like Bishop Percival of Hereford and Bishop Barnes of Birmingham testified to certain radical currents within the episcopate. But it is only with Archbishop William Temple that the Christian Socialist tradition can claim to have made a truly significant impact at the very highest levels of the English ecclesiastical establishment.

Only in the years since Temple's reign at Canterbury (1942-44) have one or more generations of bishops emerged with genuinely radical views. This study seeks to identify the factors making for this change and the stages by which the change has come about. Equally, it is concerned to evaluate possible future implications of such shifts as well as their likely limitations.

THE EMERGENCE OF THE 'NEW RADICALS'

The emergence of a perhaps more politically questioning episcopate appears to coincide with some change in prevailing conceptions of the episcopal function and in the expectations surrounding the episcopal office. This transition in shorthand, and probably over-simplified terms, is the shift from the 'Prince-bishop' to the 'pastoral bishop'.[8] By 'Prince-bishop' we mean a traditional conception of the episcopal function manifested in a distinctive cluster of attitudes to internal church affairs and a more or less parallel set of attitudes towards Church-Polity relationships.

Under the first heading can be identified a strictly hierarchical, even quasi-monarchical view of the bishop's part in the governing of the Church. This view assumes great deference towards the bishop as the traditional hierarchical source of virtually all ecclesiastical authority within a given diocese and denies any widely-shared clerical, still less lay, responsibility for the Church's government. In so far as clerical or lay participation might be involved, it would be largely a matter of private or sometimes informal interaction with limited ecclesiastical or socio-political elites involved, for example, in the traditional patronage system, and appointments to clerical livings. Such a traditional hierarchical conception has been symbolised and expressed by the custom of referring to bishops as 'My Lord' and by the great social distance interposed between the episcopate and church members. Such conventions point secondly toward traditional definitions of the bishops' more public functions. These definitions are clearly of medieval origin and stem initially from the 'Christendom situation' in which Church and State cooperate to sustain one relatively well-integrated religio-political system. In this system political authority receives some measure of religious legitimation, and church leaders also operate as temporal authorities. In England, of course, strong residues of this persist in the Anglican Church's established position and its association with the monarchy and the House of Lords.[9] We see 'the Prince-bishop' as one who would tend to conceive of the Church's public or political role in such traditional terms. The stress would be laid on bishops as peers of the realm operating largely within the context and confines of established elite relationships—relationships likely to provide informal private access to national political leaders, legislators, civil servants, and other opinion-formers, as well as to local perhaps land-owning or commercial elites. Within such a network of relationships, the bishop would be as, or more, likely to reflect prevailing currents of opinion than to challenge such orthodoxies by reference to a mass audience. The bishop, in other words, would be coopted as a relatively well-integrated member of a traditional elite and one whose ecclesiastical authority would be more likely to legitimise than to question national policy-makers or governmental actions. Moreover, the characteristic 'Prince-bishop' might, in practice, be recruited from a relatively limited upper-middle or even aristocratic social stratum and might well come from established 'ecclesiastical dynasties'. This social base would, in its turn, be associated with links with a limited number of well-known public schools as well as with the Universities of Oxford and Cambridge.[10]

In speaking of 'pastoral bishops' we imply a relatively substantial redefinition of the traditional episcopal function, first tending to affect internal church relationships and, secondly, tending to entail some fresh understanding of the linkages between the Church and society, or the Church and polity. Established hierarchical models of church government and authority give way to, or, at the least, coexist with, more participatory, collegiate or quasi-democratic arrangements. Traditional conceptions may persist, but are likely to be confined to relatively restricted, if important, areas of ecclesiastical activity and decision-making. The stress here comes to be much more on minimising the social distance between the bishops and the rest of the Church, and upon sharing responsibility with representatives of both clergy and laity. Likewise, as our terminology implies, there tends to be an emphasis on the bishop as a coordinator, animator and facilitator of corporate activity rather than a simple equation of the Church with the activities or pronouncements of its hierarchy. Equally, there may be some stress on the task of helping church members to identify and tackle problems in their own situations rather than seeing episcopal initiatives or administrative action as the prime mode of decision-making.[11]

Such conceptions of ecclesiastical authority may embrace potentially new modes of social or political involvement. An emphasis on participation and shared problem-solving may lead to the identification of problems in the political environment which could not readily be tackled through traditional uses of episcopal authority. Shared responsibility for the Church's life may point towards the identification of the church community with the perceived needs of those for whom it claims some responsibility. The Church's ministry, in other words, may be conceived less in terms of a hierarchical transmission of authority through such traditional activities as confirming new members and more in terms of concern for the general welfare of the community.[12] In contrast with the triumphalist posture of the 'Prince-bishop', his 'pastoral' counterpart is more accepting of ideological and religious pluralism. This general conception of ecclesiastical leadership represents an attempt to deal with the general collapse of the traditional Christendom synthesis and to engage with society on new terms. Such efforts may compel ecclesiastical leaders to de-emphasise traditional legitimating functions and to assume fresh, more socially or politically critical, roles. If episcopal leaders are less well integrated into established elites, they may be more likely to join in new coalitions and perhaps more likely to seek to mould and mobilise opinion in opposition to conventional wisdom or current public policy. All this may also be accompanied by some change in the social bases of recruitment and the creation of a relatively more open elite.

We are here talking essentially in terms of ideal types and broad generalisations. Thus, 'Prince-bishops' may cover those closely tied to the State and those sometimes prepared to challenge secular authorities while retaining authoritarian postures within the Church itself. Also, one can find early examples of 'pastoral bishops'. Finally, the contemporary episcopal elite in general, and particular individuals within it, may represent an uneasy combination of traditional and non-traditional traits. Such combinations clearly point to, as yet unresolved and perhaps ultimately unresolvable, tensions within the existing ecclesiastical structures and within individuals manning those structures. Likewise, the transition from one model to the other may be a protracted multi-stage and complex process leaving different individuals located at different points along the trajectory. We intend to discuss and illustrate such patterns of change and the dilemmas they pose, and to show how in any situation there are elements of differing approaches or models and symptoms of uncertainty in the face of transition. For example, it might be logically assumed that disengagement from traditional modes and networks, and the process of re-engagement along fresh lines, would be separated by a period of reflection during which a distinctive and more autonomous role would be defined *vis-à-vis* traditional allies. In fact, however, the large residue of inherited traditions and practices means that change does not proceed along such apparently logical lines and that the episcopate as a group, and as individuals, are left to varying degrees in ambivalent situations, embracing a range of perhaps inconsistent functions or postures.

First, it is necessary to try to identify the factors giving rise to the processes of change. Such factors form a complex pattern within which it is difficult to disentangle cause from effect or to allocate priorities. For purposes of analysis, however, a distinction may be drawn between factors in the Church's general environment and internal factors. Under the former heading, reference should be made to long-term 'secularising' tendencies at work within English society which have combined to erode the traditional prestige and authority of religious bodies including the established Church. This is part and parcel of a situation characterised by religious and ideological pluralism, with which the Church and its leaders have been forced, albeit hesitantly, to come to terms. Such conventional indices of commitment as church attendance have shown a general long-term decline.[13] Electoral demands for extended state intervention have involved a progressive loss of functions in such traditional areas of ecclesiastical responsibility as education and welfare. The net result seems to have been the erosion of institutional certainties and self-confidence, and a marked diminution of the institution's general social salience.

This may be linked to, and at least partially account for, some accompanying long-term shifts in the basis of clerical recruitment. Here there is an interplay of factors so that changes in the Church's environment are reflected in its own institutional life. The clerical profession has apparently become much less closely linked to traditional aristocratic, land-owning or upper-middle-class elements, for whom a career in the Church no longer confers a sufficient degree of prestige.[14] Conversely, the Church has recruited relatively high percentages of clergy from lower-middle and even working-class origins, for whom an ideological motivation rather than considerations of social prestige may be more pronounced. It is very significant, for example, that, in recent years, a majority of the Anglican Church's newly-ordained clergy has been composed of non-graduates.[15] Particularly within the past decade, such changes have been reflected in the pattern of recruitment to the episcopate. That body remains, of course, largely composed of university-trained men and, indeed, is still largely of Oxford or Cambridge origin. But there is now a larger sprinkling of bishops from other backgrounds. Thus, in our work, we have identified two bishops with working-class origins and two without university education. However small a component of the total, this nevertheless testifies to developments that would have been almost unthinkable only one generation ago. Moreover, there are more substantial numbers of their colleagues who, though conventionally educated, come from more modest middle-class backgrounds than most of their predecessors. Finally, the attitudes of even those bishops of relatively privileged origins have probably been affected by the general economic crisis through which the Church has been passing. The long-term decline in prestige has been accompanied by great difficulties in keeping pace with inflationary pressures, so that even the Church's most highly remunerated servants are subject to financial constraints not generally shared by counterparts in other professions or those with similar educational achievements. A recurrent theme in talking with bishops has been the extent to which relative financial hardship has led them to more sympathy with their own clergy. Equally, they have admitted that they now identify more closely, in historically novel ways, with the difficulties of less well paid groups in society at large. It may well be that in so far as the Church's leaders have in recent times espoused socio-economic and political values of a relatively radical or even egalitarian character, this has been quite substantially due to changes in their own material rewards and expectations.

Though economic factors, or constraints, seem to have been significant in catalysing changes in attitudes among Anglican leaders, our evidence suggests that such changes cannot be wholly accounted for in material terms. Economic changes have been accompanied by, and have probably interacted with, changes in perceptions and ideological shifts. In this connection, it seems interesting to note some of the influences which the bishops themselves regard as formative, as well as some of the experiences they report as important. Firstly, there is the possible impact of Archbishop William Temple, who has already been mentioned.[16] A number of bishops alluded to his influence upon their general approach to social, economic and political questions as well as to his more general impact on ecclesiastical colleagues. This may in part be a generational matter, for those episcopal leaders who matured during Temple's most active years most often acknowledged his influence. Possibly general changes in the intellectual and political climate of post-war Britain combined with this particular and powerful ecclesiastical force to shape attitudes of a somewhat more Left-leaning variety than had previously been common in the upper reaches of the Anglican Church.

The impact of such Christian thinkers as William Temple seems to have been particularly felt by recruits to organisations lying outside of the Church's conventional territorial structures. One particularly significant example is the Student Christian Movement which, in the immediate post-war world, enjoyed considerable influence in university circles and attracted a number of able clerics who were subsequently to move on to influential academic or administrative posts and who included some future bishops. The theologically liberal, and politically somewhat radical, ethos of an organisation of this type seems to have played a significant part in crystallising the thinking of a number of the Church's subsequent leaders.

An important element in the general ethos of such bodies was identification with the burgeoning ecumenical movement which, in the immediate post-war period, found expression in the World Council of Churches. That body, though initially dominated by European and North American churches, came increasingly to be a forum for Third World Christians with distinctive interests and perceptions that have taken a politically radical form. Certainly a number of future church leaders were profoundly affected by earlier ecumenical strivings and some have been influenced by relatively extensive first-hand experience in Third World countries. Sensitivity to Third World issues may also, in its turn, help to explain the small, but unprecedentedly significant, number of English bishops with extended experience of other parts of the Anglican Communion, and the apparently increased willingness of their colleagues to draw on such experience. The net effect of all this seems to have been to produce a historically unusual degree of sensitivity toward other Christian churches, as well as toward other non-Christian faiths. Likewise, in some important cases, it seems to have facilitated the espousal of relatively radical political views.

One other discernible group of bishops, which in some cases overlaps with the groups mentioned above, shares a common experience of wartime service in the Armed Forces. Several bishops were in the Royal Naval Volunteer Reserve, and the present Archbishop of Canterbury received the Military Cross as an army officer. A number of his colleagues, underlined the importance of such episodes in shaping their general outlook and expectations. On one hand, military service involved life with men from a wide variety of socio-economic backgrounds, some at least of whom would have remained largely outside the acquaintanceship of conventionally-recruited clerics. On the other hand, these men, as de-mobilised officers, were affected to a greater or lesser degree by events of the immediate post-war world which included the acceptance of the achievements of the 1945-50 Labour government. While there is no generalised support for the Labour party, there is an acceptance of social change generally uncharacteristic of predecessors. Thus the war and its aftermath helped to remould the world-view of future church leaders, including some whose backgrounds might, at an earlier stage, have disposed them to adhere to more traditional postures.

Finally, in seeking to explain changing episcopal values, attention needs to be drawn to several interrelated developments in the Church's institutional life which relate to long-term shifts in the Church's position within English society and the redefinition of its responsibilities. Firstly, note must be taken of changes in the traditional Church-State nexus which have put greater distance between these two historic partners, and which have recognised the appropriateness of greater ecclesiastical autonomy. This independence has been expressed in the recent creation of a synodical system of church government, and, in particular, in the establishment of the General Synod of the Anglican Church as the only authoritative national legislative body in England outside of Parliament itself. Parliamentary sanction is still finally required for ecclesiastical legislation but, de facto, a great majority of this is enacted on the initiative of the Synod. Within this Synod, the bishops sit as one 'house' alongside the other two houses representative of the clergy and the laity.[17] These two latter houses are largely elected bodies, with a mandate from a grass-roots church electorate, so they reflect a more participatory and even quasi-democratic element in the Church's government.

An unresolved tension created by this situation arises from the need to reconcile traditional hierarchical (episcopal) conceptions of authority with the new quasi-democratic models. Certainly, most earlier bishops would have found it extremely difficult to come to terms with this new situation. Though it is not by any means an entirely generational matter, we do have some reason to suppose that the oldest generation of existing bishops, who were appointed to the episcopate prior to the establishment of synodical government in 1970, are on balance the most likely to have difficulty in working within the new framework. Rather different attitudes and skills are required for the relatively successful functioning of the now more widely shared collegial form of church government; and a new set of expectations is held by those responsible for episcopal appointments as a result of these major institutional innovations. This may be particularly important since the recent change in the appointment system, which still leaves the final and formal word in the traditional hands (the monarch on the advice of the Prime Minister), but provides for consultation with church representatives including clerical and lay spokesmen of the relevant diocese.[18]

The second factor in this general context is the changing career patterns of those within the Church who finally emerge as bishops. Historically, large proportions of the episcopate were drawn from ordained men who, except for very brief periods, did not share in the Church's conventional pastoral or parochial work but who pursued alternative pathways as academics or possibly as public school teachers and headmasters. Two rather distinct career patterns existed which meant that clergy with extensive grass-roots experience of parish life rarely reached the positions of greatest influence within the Church. Since World War II, however, and particularly in the last one or two decades, there has been a significant change on this front. Thus, ex-headmasters are an extinct category and even ex-university professors account for a much diminished and now extremely small proportion. Bishops have suggested that this, too, may reflect economic considerations, for today a considerable financial sacrifice is involved in any move from academic to ecclesiastical life. In so far as appointments of an academic kind are concerned they now, on an extended scale, involve the promotion of theological college principals as opposed to university chair holders. This testifies to increasing professionalisation of the clergy, but also, to some extent, to the emergence of some bishops for whom the pastoral oversight of their diocesan clergy is likely to receive a higher priority.

Such shifts are partly due to the perceived need to recruit from a different and wider base. Thus, it is increasingly common to appoint bishops whose previous experience has almost exclusively been in conventional pastoral activity. Our evidence suggests that this experience may sometimes be a better training for the new forms of episcopal responsibility than the training of their predecessors. Equally, the evidence makes it safe to infer that exposure to such pastoral experiences helps to explain, at least in part, the shift in values previously noted. Earlier generations of bishops, for example, generally had relatively little first-hand experience of less privileged elements in English society and tended to move in relatively restricted upper-strata circles. Clearly this has had a bearing on the shift in episcopal commitments and values. Also, it mirrors the general tendency on the Church's part to acquire enhanced degrees of autonomy, for it both reflects and possibly accelerates a process whereby the clergy tends to perceive itself more as a discrete professional entity and less as an integral part of wider and diffused elite groupings.

Finally, brief mention should be made of some theological influences which have probably been both cause and effect of these changes. For the Catholic wing of the Anglican Church, the Second Vatican Council was very important. In these quarters, debates within the Roman Communion have probably contributed to changing perceptions of the episcopal office as well as to changing social and political values. In the longer run, the Church of England at large has, perhaps, been affected by theological currents pointing in the direction of a redefined pastoral role. This may in part reflect limited but significant experiences of ministering to less-privileged sections of English society. Both the Catholic and Evangelical wings of the Church have precedents to draw on in this sphere.

THE NEW RADICALISM?

Having acknowledged a shift in the general attitudes of Anglican leaders, and having investigated possible explanations of this development, we now examine the nature of the new values, attitudes or commitments. Equally, it is necessary to examine the limitations to this radicalisation as well as the factors impeding or facilitating the wider dissemination of such outlooks. It is from the start important to note that not all the English episcopate has been uniformly, or extensively, affected by the process. A significant proportion of bishops are essentially 'apolitical' in the sense that they principally define their role in relatively conventional terms of internal ecclesiastical responsibilities and pastoral tasks. Such bishops may intermittently interact in a relatively informal fashion with local, and on rare occasions, national business, trade union, political or opinion-forming elites, but they would not as a rule expect to use such contacts for the purposes of propagating overtly political values or for pursuing avowedly political causes. Their political intervention would be at most very spasmodic and more likely take the form of pronouncements in local diocesan publications or occasional efforts to influence such locally significant figures as the Member of Parliament.

In such cases, efforts to exert influence would be largely ad hoc responses to very specific or isolated problems, and would not entail an effort to implement a coherent ideology or strategy. In so far as political initiatives did occur, they were most likely to involve the use of informal private contacts of the sort we associate with traditional modes of episcopal activity in this realm. Today it is likely that such traditional activities would be brought to play in the pursuit of values of a less traditional variety. An example might be lobbying local authorities on behalf of groups of homeless people. In the odd limiting case radicalisation in the ecclesiastical, theological or political senses has scarcely occurred. It is possible to identify the occasional bishop whose attitudes towards the episcopal function, church government, ecumenism, social or economic matters, and political involvement, very largely fit the model of the traditional 'Prince-bishop' sketched above.

Likewise, even those who cannot be adequately comprehended in terms of the traditional model approximate to the alternative model to quite varying degrees. At this stage, perhaps only a minority of bishops, though a seemingly growing one, see their task as having a truly substantial political, or socially critical, component. Moreover, it cannot be assumed that there is a uniformity of view on all, or even some, of the salient political or social issues in terms of which one might expect to discern or define radical postures. Some bishops give special priority to matters in which they have particular interest or expertise, at the expense of other issues which some other bishops might regard as of greater importance. Episcopal priorities and enthusiasms differ. By the same token, the current approach of the Anglican hierarchy must generally be regarded as largely issue-oriented. Attitudes to a specific issue, or range of issues, may sometimes reveal a stance that can be characterised as critical or radical but they need not, in most instances, be seen as directly or intimately linked to a single global or more or less coherent political ideology. Such positions may be linked to a relatively coherent theological stance, but this need not be mediated through a highly developed political belief-system when it comes to intervention in the public domain.

Radicalisation or a degree of politicisation should not be confused with strong or openly avowed partisan affiliations. The recently retired Bishop of Southwark was on public record as being a member of the Labour party but he was exceptional in this respect. In the House of Lords, for example, the bishops occupy the cross-benches and they usually operate in a non-partisan fashion. This does not preclude commitments to, or against, governmental initiatives but it does preclude sustained association with any one partisan cause.

The majority of current bishops see themselves as occupying positions ranging from the Centre to the moderate Left. Some believe that most of their colleagues, in so far as they would claim any partisan allegiance, are in general sympathy with the Liberal party, or perhaps (this is our conjecture) the Social Democratic party. Some may object that this does not signify a markedly radical episcopate. Certainly there is virtually no sign of active sympathy with more left-wing Labour party tendencies. Even relatively left-wing prelates may espouse some positions that would be conventionally regarded as conservative. (As will be seen below, this is particularly true of attitudes to such questions as abortion.) Likewise, all the bishops that we interviewed adhere to a consensual model of politics which stresses the continuity and preservation of most traditional British political institutions and emphasises the accommodation of competing sectional and class interests. This model rejects an exclusively class-based analysis of political realities or objectives and draws substantially on established liberal traditions asserting the primacy of individuals and the defence of freedoms against impersonal entities. Nevertheless, these political values do represent a quite substantial shift when measured against the values of their predecessors. Also, recent pronouncements have shown some active concern for underprivileged groups at home and in underdeveloped societies abroad which point away from classic liberalism and sometimes toward a general, if ill-defined, ideology of a socialist variety. This leads us to surmise about potential Social Democratic leanings and suggests the plausibility of our earlier assertions about the formative experiences of contemporary bishops.[19]

On the other hand, the individualism associated with classic liberalism is compatible with the marked degree of individuality which some bishops still embrace as an almost positive virtue. The traditional 'Prince-bishop' was regarded as virtually sovereign within his own diocese and there was relatively little sense of coordinated episcopal activity or an orchestrated episcopal presence in national affairs. Bishops were primarily active in national affairs, and in particular in the House of Lords, as individual peers of the realm rather than corporate spokesmen. To some, if to a diminishing extent, such attitudes still characterise episcopal involvement at that level. Certainly one cannot speak in terms of an episcopal bloc vote in the House of Lords. Until the present at least, efforts to marshall episcopal forces on a planned or coordinated footing have been limited. Our interviews suggest the possibility of a more collective or collegiated approach to decision-making, not least as it affects political engagement within the House of Lords, but this is, at most, a matter for the future.

Although the mode of political involvement bears traces of traditional approaches, most of the contemporary episcopate has moved away in part from the preoccupations of the traditional 'Prince-bishop'. The latter frequently gave considerably higher priority to Parliamentary affairs than is currently the case. A newly-appointed nineteenth century bishop might delay his first visit to his diocese by as long as six months because of involvement at the centre in national public life. With few exceptions, contemporary bishops give a much lower priority to this dimension of their task and a higher priority to local ecclesiastical and pastoral responsibilities. Our interviews suggest that as few as five bishops bear the main brunt of work in the House of Lords and that others attend spasmodically, and then because of matters of particular personal interest or national importance.[20] This stems partly from increasing administrative responsibilities but also from the increasing professionalisation which tends to stress pastoral concern for the Church's own at the expense of a wider political vision. The promotion of theological college principals may have had some bearing on this conception of pastoral responsibilities. Contemporary bishops also differ from their predecessors in that their interest in matters of a social, economic or political nature may frequently manifest itself through the appointment of specialised clerical staff-officers or chaplains with particular expertise in the relevant area. Industrial chaplains fall into this category. This clearly represents a growing professionalism and differentiation of functions and a quest for greater efficiency and more informed judgements. In the case of a few bishops with special responsibilities for the management of church affairs, such practices include consultation with specialists from outside the Church's formal advisory arrangements.

With all these qualifications, we can now briefly identify recent examples of the Church's political engagement which testify to an embryonic new consensus of its leaders. Firstly, there is a range of issues involving the Church's traditional institutional interests and often relating to its established position. A recent example of this was the attempt of some backbench, and mainly Conservative, MPs to ensure the continued use of the old 1662 Prayer Book services in the face of opposition from the General Synod of the Church of England, including its episcopal members. Senior cabinet members took the lead in successfully resisting the initiative, which was perceived by most official spokesmen for Church and State as a contravention, at least in spirit, of the agreement between the two parties on the locus of authority in most ecclesiastical matters.[21] In this instance, leaders in Church and State combined to defend established institutional arrangements. In another relatively recent case, by contrast, church leaders in the House of Lords successfully defended church interests in the face of a perceived threat emanating from the government itself. This was the case in which the government's attempt to interfere with established busing arrangements for schoolchildren in rural areas was viewed as a breach of the spirit of a 'concordat' between the Church and the State enshrined in the Butler Education Act of 1944.[22] This was undoubtedly a defensive institutional response of a rather traditional variety. But what was at least equally interesting was the willingness of Anglican Bishops to take part in mobilising and leading a coalition of forces which not only embraced affiliates of other religious traditions but also extended to secular opponents of government policy. This suggests the contemporary Anglican Church's willingness to accept the religious and ideological pluralism of modern English society. Not least it shows a willingness to meet head on with a Conservative government.

A propensity to criticise some aspects of Conservative policy is also evident in ecclesiastical responses to issues that go beyond institutional matters of immediate concern to the Church. There is a willingness to be socially critical in public debate on issues with a clearly political character. A prime example of this is the Church's official response to the government's (at the time of writing) pending Nationality Bill. There appears to be a fairly solid consensus of episcopal leaders on the potentially discriminatory nature of the Bill.[23] Indeed, in immigration and race relations, Anglican Church leaders, including the normally 'apolitical', manifest a particular unity of view and purpose. This derives in part from the liberal ethos but also is grounded in particular theological reformulations which are obviously at odds with some traditional Christian responses to colour. This issue indicates a rather new willingness to mobilise in alliance with other Christian leaders and with secular political leaders, principally of the Liberal and Labour parties. Indeed, a quite common view of bishops is that on such matters the Anglican Church need not define a distinctive Anglican position but should articulate a generally shared Christian viewpoint, if not the viewpoint of a broadly-based coalition of all liberal-minded elements in English society.[24] Thus, the case is another example of a willingness to adjust to a pluralistic society, though the modes of political involvement are more diverse and sometimes less traditional than those evident in the case of education cited earlier. Episcopal engagement in this area includes conventional legislative activities and recourse to the perhaps diminished, but still present, opportunities for gaining informal private access to national political leaders. In addition, the bishops have moved to less traditional modes of participation, characteristic of an age of open, secularised, and mass politics. Thus, some episcopal leaders have made use of the mass media and some of them have engaged in peaceful demonstrations or marches.

Two other areas of domestic social or economic policy will further illustrate our point. Firstly, a number of church leaders, including the Archbishop of Canterbury have, through the media and public manifestations, opposed official housing policy as inadequate for the homeless and for lower socio-economic groups.[25] They have resisted selective aspects of current efforts to decrease public expenditure and the government's general priorities in this area. Similarly, some Anglican leaders, perhaps with encouragement at the highest level, have publicly identified themselves with protests against the consequences of government policy for unemployment and for particular communities.[26] Such interventions in public economic debate would certainly be regarded by some as going beyond the Church's conventional spheres of activity and of legitimate concern. Probably such criticism is substantially motivated by the identification of certain Anglican dignitaries with organised political movements of the Left (and even of the extreme Left) as well as with the trade union movement and specialised pressure groups.

Similar criticisms are sometimes expressed concerning recent ecclesiastical interventions in the debate about the British government's overseas aid contributions to developing countries. The Anglican Synod, in general, and the Archbishop of Canterbury in particular, have voiced strenuous opposition to what they see as the government's unduly modest efforts.[27] At the very top levels of the Church, at least, there also seems to be something of a consensus on this issue. Here, too, the Church's contribution to debate has expressed itself through alliances with other religious and secular agencies. Together they have constituted a relatively formidable lobby which, both in private and in public, has subjected the government to serious criticism and pressure.[28] Indeed, in this area, there are grounds for thinking that the Church has played a significant role in crystallising a general climate of opinion which has been at least a short-run problem for the government.

Another area of policy-making in which prevailing orthodoxies are visibly subject to some questioning is defence, and, in particular, unilateral nuclear disarmament. Here Anglican leaders have recently made quite significant contributions.[29] But they have spoken with a less unified voice. There is a general reluctance to assume the unilateralist position and support exists for different approaches. The Church has contributed to creating in this area a climate of opinion in which questioning established orthodoxies, is legitimate.

The Church's critics may question the appropriateness or legitimacy of ecclesiastical intervention in the public debate of economic, international or defence matters, but the legitimacy of such interventions in the discussion of sexual morality is readily conceded as a traditional sphere of proper theological concern. In this domain, more traditional postures are often struck. The responses of Anglican leaders have not, however, been wholly unambiguous opposition to liberalising trends. Church leaders were involved in discussions that led to liberalising the divorce laws while they still favoured less flexible provisions for the Church's own members. In this sense, the Church acknowledged secularising trends in the wider society and its inability to enforce its own moral standards in the community at large. At the same time, a substantial proportion of the bishops we have interviewed have indicated at least a limited willingness to liberalise the Church's own internal regulations. This may suggest an accommodation to prevailing secular trends but some church leaders maintain that the proposed changes represent a legitimate reinterpretation of traditions which are not the less legitimate for being arrived at from secular directions. Such claims to have reformulated a fresh, yet still distinctively Christian position may gain credibility in view of the fact that even the more liberal of ecclesiastical spokesmen do not envisage surrendering to secularism. Our conclusions thus differ from those of, for example, Dr E.R. Norman who regards most recent innovations in church political and social thinking as no more than a response to, or a reflection of, current fashions of the secularised intelligentsia.[30]

Such an interpretation is perhaps better justified in the matter of abortion. Ecclesiastical spokesmen did play some part in preparing opinion for the legitimising of the 1967 liberalisation of the laws.[31] It is also true, however, that the Church's part in this process was as much a tribute to the naïvety of some of its leaders as a measure of radicalism. Cautious commitment to a liberalisation of the law, as the lesser of evils, was not intended, or expected, to give rise to the degree of change that in fact occurred. Our own interviews with bishops make it plain that they agree on the need to tighten up post-1967 provisions. Even those subscribing to relatively radical political views tend to be somewhat conservative and cautious on this matter. Here, apparently, theological understandings collide with the views of secularised radicals.

THE LIMITS OF RADICALISM

Anglican leaders, as we have seen, employ a range of methods for participation. Traditional forms of activity, such as interventions in the House of Lords, or lobbying other national elites, coexist with a new consciousness of the importance of the mass media or of public demonstrations. Likewise, attitudes and responses vary from the continuing espousal of very traditional values to identification with processes of change. Such mixtures point to possible ambivalences or potential contradictions in the episcopate's overall position, and inevitably raise questions about both the extent of change and the Church's capacity to mobilise its own followers as well as wider sections of society.

Clearly one significant set of constraints stems from the Church's still established position. Though prominent Church leaders have recently openly criticised state leaders, the scope of such criticisms is likely to be limited by the ties still binding Church and State. In part, some bishops see themselves as having important functions as unifying symbols within the national community. They still attach importance to the concept of a 'national Church' which articulates values of an integrating character within the national polity. The Church now recognises the legitimacy of alternative religious or secular systems of belief but it still retains the idea of a community bound together by shared values of Christian origin which the established Church has a special responsibility to defend and express. To stray too far beyond conventionally accepted political or social norms would, from this perspective, be at odds with this essentially consensual vision.

The importance which church leaders attach to such notions is underlined by the fact that, on the basis of our evidence, only two, or at most three, bishops would not mourn the complete passing of the traditional Church-State partnership. On the contrary, most of them see the link as a guarantee of some continuing church influence in national affairs and as an expression of the continuing significance of Christian values in England's cultural heritage. Thus, for example, the bishops agree about a continuing Anglican presence in the House of Lords, even though some bishops wish that representatives of other religious groups sat alongside them. Likewise, they see value in the limited access to national political leaders which still sometimes flows from the existing Church-State nexus. The perpetuation of such links would clearly seem to limit the critical public role of the Church in national politics even if, as our evidence suggests, there are occasions where criticisms are privately pressed at the highest levels. The possibility of a break between Church and State is considered very remote, and an event which church leaders see as coming about only if the State were to take such an initiative. Certainly, recent frictions do not amount to a major disruption in the relationship, though such cannot ultimately be precluded. One possible source of crisis might be what would be considered as undue state interference in such internal church matters as senior appointments or liturgical practices. Controversy surrounding the recent appointment of a new Bishop of London suggests that the idea of such interference cannot be ruled out as entirely fanciful. Nevertheless, restraint on both sides would seem sufficient to perpetuate the relationship, and the episcopate's conception of the Church's place in English society suggests that they have strong incentives to display such restraint.[32] Church leaders, in accordance with some of their reformulated theological positions, do talk of a 'prophetic' role for the Church as a guardian of public morality or as the potential denouncer of injustice or infringed human rights. But the same leaders acknowledge a latent tension between this role and the Church's residual, yet still significant, functions as a partner and legitimator of state authority.

Another set of constraints arises from the nature of the Church's membership, and difficulties in mobilising it. Thus our investigations indicate a considerable gap between values held by the bishops and those of the faithful, who in principle accept the former's authority. On a whole range of issues the relative 'radicalism' of much of the episcopate is at odds with the values of 'rank-and-file' church members. Mass survey data suggest that most of the Church's constituents, both in a partisan and a general attitudinal sense, are more consistently conservative than the Church's official spokesmen. One should distinguish here nominal from active members and active local members from those clergy and laity who are elected to the Church's 'Parliament' (the General Synod). The latter are somewhat closer to the position of the episcopate than the former. But these elites are themselves divided and by no means unified in support of episcopal positions. Thus our evidence indicates that most bishops subscribe to theological positions correlated with political positions that can be generally defined as liberal/radical. Indeed over half the episcopate is at least informally associated with that group within the General Synod that is heir to the Anglican Church's liberal theological tradition.[33] That group, however, accounts for only a minority of General Synod members, especially among the clergy, and, particularly since the 1980 elections, it has been somewhat overshadowed by spokesmen for the Church's Evangelical and Catholic wings. On social and political matters, as opposed to doctrinal or theological questions, the latter groups contain elements broadly sympathetic to episcopal thinking. To that extent, the political initiatives of bishops might expect more broadly based support. But divisions remain, the effect of which is to inhibit the episcopate's capacity to mobilise even elite Anglican opinion.

This difficulty principally arises from the nature of recruitment to the episcopate. Thus, in a Church with a diversity of theological or partisan traditions, and with a continuing tendency towards some partisan polarisation, leaders capable of promoting consensus and compromise are highly valued. Leaders are appointed who are not completely committed to one or other of the more polarised tendencies. The episcopate does contain powerful spokesmen for both the Catholic and Evangelical wings. If the episcopate is to be at all representative, such appointments will continue. Indeed there is a concern to preserve an ideological balance at this level. But the pressures and experience of episcopal office tend to push even those trained in a particular tradition toward a more 'centrist' position which, in terms of traditional Anglican allegiances, means some move toward the more liberal camp. This does not mean open identification with the formally organised Liberal group, for that too would be regarded as an act of unacceptable partisanship, but rather support for 'centrist' groupings who see it as their responsibility to promote dialogue between competing traditions as well as to respond to changes in the Church's environment. An open election of bishops might perhaps throw up leaders of a different type, but, in the present state of the Anglican Church, there is a relatively strong tendency to promote figures who, because of 'centrist' leanings, are likely to be at odds with others in the rather well-organised and vocal partisan Evangelical and Catholic groupings. Maintaining unity in diversity has long been presented as one of the Anglican Church's most characteristic achievements. But such 'coalition politics' inhibits very radical initiatives from the top and at worst perpetuates immobility.

The specialised demands of the episcopal office within the Anglican framework, then, throw up leaders who, despite markedly different personal traits and individualistic styles, are ideologically quite homogeneous. Their path to the top involves common experiences and the fostering of similar perceptions. Thus they come to share in a common elite culture close to the educated opinion of secular intellectuals (though, as has already been stated, not necessarily sharing wholeheartedly or indiscriminately all the latter's assumptions, as Edward Norman sometimes appears to suggest). It is not surprising that these men find themselves out of step with second-order ecclesiastical elite groups in the General Synod, and perhaps still more out of step with rank-and-file worshippers. However substantial the community of outlook of the episcopate and the General Synod on political or social matters, there is a much smaller set of assumptions shared by Anglican bishops and grass-roots Anglican opinion. This limits the possibilities of mobilising Anglicans in support of the episcopate's relatively radical postures and even more, raises doubts about reaching mass opinion beyond the confines of the Church. It is possible to exaggerate the extent of secularising trends in English society and to underestimate the residual respect still accorded to Church pronouncements. Nevertheless, massive problems of communication remain which are not rendered less intractable by the fact that church leaders are not necessarily expert in public relations or in the use of the media.[34]

All this suggests that, in so far as the Anglican Church may have some limited national political role, its impact is most likely to be felt within relatively limited elite circles. In part, this is simply a question of the Church's leaders operating through traditional institutions and alliances in defence of relatively circumscribed ecclesiastical interests. In part it is also a matter of applying private or public pressure in alliance with the leaders of other interested groups of a religious or secular variety in order to affect public policy. The Church also brings a distinctive perspective to public debate and so contributes to the formation of elite opinion.[35] What the impact of elite views are on the general climate of opinion may be difficult to specify, but a situation may be created within which certain new initiatives become possible. The way in which this happens is, perhaps, too little investigated by social scientists, as are the ways in which relatively sudden shifts in public perceptions of policy sometimes occur. This is true of the relatively massive shift in opinion which made it possible to discuss, and then enact, that body of liberalising legislation popularly associated with 'the permissive society'.[36] Similarly, on such issues as aid to the Third World, a certain momentum seems to be gathering force that may oblige policymakers to adopt a more liberal stance. Here church leaders, along with others, have done their bit in changing the climate of opinion.

The importance of ecclesiastical contributions to the crystallising of relatively new currents of opinion can be underestimated. This is particularly so as our research suggests that those non-episcopal ecclesiastical elites, represented most notably in the General Synod, and relatively close in outlook to the episcopate, do tend to participate in political life to disproportionate degrees.[37] The relatively very high propensity of such people to participate, at various levels, in public debate (a considerably higher propensity than the educated middle classes as a whole), does suggest that attitudes and values, at least partially engendered within an ecclesiastical milieu, may subsequently permeate national political processes and help to determine the terms of public debate. Such matters require much more thorough investigation, but it seems that, however indirectly, the Church may play a role in shaping the nation's political agenda. It may be that ecclesiastical leaders respond to cues emanating from the Church's general environment, but to some extent the Church may also help identify issues for serious public discussion or, at least, contribute a distinctive voice and direction to that debate.

The Anglican Church's small but not insignificant role in conditioning the terms of national political debate, and in marginally affecting priorities on the national political agenda, is not the outcome of a carefully orchestrated and coherently implemented ecclesiastical political strategy. Until recently, ecclesiastical public interventions were ad hoc responses to specific pressures, incidents, or crises. But there is now more serious and even relatively systematic thinking about public issues.[38]

The General Synod and its advisory boards, committees or agencies not infrequently debate issues of a political kind. Such thinking and debate, however, has not been readily translatable into coordinated strategies for mobilising church opinion or influencing the wider public. Indeed, some bishops have acknowledged that, though considerable relevant expertise is available to the Church, a higher priority might be given to using such expertise. Similarly, they admit that church leaders have some propensity for random pronouncements on public issues without consultation with experts. Not least, there are hints of inadequate consultation amongst the bishops themselves, with the result that the Church ends up appearing committed to positions which some of its leaders do not support. Some may object that the Church largely exists for other purposes and that political involvement is secondary, hence that no such strategy is required. But the Archbishop of Canterbury has implicitly acknowledged the need for some more effective machinery to equip the Church for a role in the public arena. The expert advisory staff he has assembled for this, as for other matters, points in that direction. The question is whether such a staff, and other parallel church bureaucracies, have the resources needed to raise the Church's corporate self-consciousness to a point where its potentialities as a source of creative political activity can be realised. For most of the new 'pastoral bishops' the demands of their jobs may result in a low priority for participating in wider public debates. Vastly changed conditions outside and inside the Church make largely impossible and inappropriate the type of public presence once associated with some of the 'Prince-bishops'. Even so, the Church of England still remains important in politics, within the limits we have discussed. If the Church wished, it could play a modestly enhanced role as the source of possibly innovative or critical political thinking. The Church's general historical circumstances, and the general state of British politics today, clearly preclude a radical option approximating to the radicalism of some Latin American hierarchies. It might not be wholly unrealistic, however, to expect the Church to contribute in a small but positive way to redefining a new consensus within British society.

NOTES

We wish gratefully to acknowledge the financial assistance of the British Social Science Research Council in undertaking the research on which this article is based. We would also like to thank all those bishops of the Church of England who have given so generously of their time and have shown to us such courtesy, kindness and friendly cooperation.

1. Our remarks refer to England not the rest of the United Kingdom, even though our observations may sometimes have implications for other areas. The Anglican Church, unless otherwise stated, refers to the Church of England and not to other parts of the worldwide Anglican Communion.

2. For some questioning of the secularisation thesis, see David Martin, *A Sociology of English Religion*. London: Heinemann, 1967. On the same general subject, see also David Martin, *A General Theory of Secularization*. Oxford: Blackwell, 1978; and Alan D. Gilbert, *The Making of Post-Christian Britain*. London: Longman, 1980.

3. For a detailed survey of such relationships see W.L. Miller and G. Raab, 'The Religious Alignment at English Elections between 1918 and 1970', *Political Studies*, Vol. XXV, No. 2, (June 1977), pp. 227-51.

4. For an elaboration of this point, see our own article, 'Political Participation and Attitudes in the Church of England', *Government and Opposition*, Vol. 13, No. 1, (Winter 1978), esp. pp. 81-2. For a more up-to-date comment and survey, see *Prospects for the Eighties*. London: Bible Society, 1980, esp. pp. 28-9; and Peter Brierley, *UK Protestant Missions Handbook*. London: Bible Society, 1978, esp. Vol. 2.

5. See Moyser and Medhurst, op. cit.

6. Interviews were held on condition that confidentiality was consistently observed and that no statements which might be quoted would be attributed to named individuals. The interviews, however, have been recorded and transcripts have been made that provide our evidence. The discussion here represents our first findings. They will be elaborated and given statistical content, in a forthcoming book.

7. For changing social characteristics of the Anglican episcopate, see D. Morgan, 'The Social and Educational Background of Anglican Bishops—Continuities and Changes', *British Journal of Sociology*, Vol. XX, No.3, (1969), pp. 295-310. For just one reference to a

background historical study, see G. Kitson Clark, *Churchmen and the Condition of England, 1832-85*. London: Methuen, 1973.

8.   The richness of our material suggests the need for a more complex typology which will appear in our projected book.

9.   For a modern discussion of the question of establishment, and its implications, see Owen Chadwick *et al.*, *Church and State*. (Report of the Archbishop's Commission), London: Church Information Office, 1970.

10. See D. Morgan, op. cit.

11. Our categories are close to a typology used by Ivan Vallier when discussing the Roman Catholic Church of Latin America in his article, 'Religious Elites', in Seymour M. Lipset and A. Solari (eds.), *Elites in Latin America*. 1967. Our development of the categories arose out of the logic of our own investigation, rather than from a conscious use of the Vallier typology.

12. Bishops do, of course, continue to give high priority to such traditional sacramental tasks which some regard as their principal function. Others, however, consciously extend their concept of pastoral care beyond the conventional tasks and institutional frontiers of the Church to include some forms of wider social and political engagement.

13. On the subject of changing church attendance, see Robert Currie, A.D. Gilbert and L. Horsley, *Churches and Churchgoers: Patterns of Church Growth in the British Isles since 1700*. Oxford: Clarendon, 1977. See also A.D. Gilbert, op. cit.

14. On the general subject of changes in the clerical profession, and accompanying dilemmas, see Robert Towler and Anthony P.M. Coxon, *The Fate of the Anglican Clergy*. London: Macmillan, 1979.

15. On this subject, see the 'Statistical Supplements' to the *Church of England Yearbook*. London: Church Information Office, annually.

16. For an example of William Temple's thinking, see his *Christianity and the Social Order*. London: SCM Press, 1976, with an introduction by Ronald H. Preston. For more general references to Temple in the context of the politics of his own era, see Paul Addison, *The Road to 1945*. London: Quartet, 1977.

17. More precisely, the House of Bishops not only contains the forty-three diocesan bishops, but also nine representative suffragan bishops. For the details, see *The Church of England Handbook*, op. cit.

18. The controversy surrounding a recent appointment to the very senior Bishopric of London indicates the possibility of friction arising in this new situation should state and church leaders find themselves out of step, or should the Prime Minister take some personal initiative or interest in the matter in ways opposed by important churchmen. Perhaps if such an instance were to be frequently repeated, or the State seek insistently and clumsily to override ecclesiastical advice, one could imagine a major crisis in Church-State relations. So far, however, the new system has generally worked without such major frictions and, it is worth noting, sometimes thrown up bishops of radical views. For the case of the London appointment, see *Church Times*, 3 April, 1981.

19. Certainly on such issues as decentralisation, participation and the perceived need to resist some centralising or bureaucratising tendencies within modern society, the expressed views of a number of bishops converge with the thinking of Social Democrats like David Owen and Shirley Williams as respectively formulated in *Face the Future*. London: Jonathan Cape, 1980, and *Politics is for People*. London: Penguin, 1981.

20. For published evidence supporting our view, see G. Drewry and J. Brock, 'Prelates in Parliament', *Parliamentary Affairs*, Vol. 24, No. 3, (1970), pp. 222-50. The twenty-six bishops in the upper chamber subscribe to a rota allocating responsibility for conducting prayers at the start of daily sittings. For many of them, appearances in the House are largely confined to the period when they are expected to perform this task. Not all bishops are members of the Lords and access to the available places is on the basis of seniority with a few exceptions.

21. See *Parliamentary Debates* (House of Commons). London: HMSO, 8 April 1981, cols. 959-64.

22. *Parliamentary Debates* (House of Lords). London: HMSO, 14 March 1980, cols. 1208-74, esp. cols. 1230, 1256.

23. Our interviews certainly point toward a high degree of episcopal agreement on such matters and a high priority for intervention in this sphere.

24. Several bishops we interviewed stressed that on national political issues, including race, immigration and citizenship, the Anglican Church should eschew its own separate initiatives in favour of cooperation with, at the least, other Christian bodies, particularly as represented in the British Council of Churches.
25. See *The Church Times*, 18 February 1981.
26. See *The Church Times*, 13 February 1981. See also *Unemployment—What Can be Done?* (GS 477), London: Church of England Board for Social Responsibility, 1981; and a letter from eight bishops in *The Times*, 25 July 1981.
27. See *The Church Times*, 26 December 1980.
28. Ibid.
29. Cf. Giles Ecclestone, *The Church of England and Politics: Reflections on Christian Social Engagement*. (A Report for the Board for Social Responsibility) London: Church Information Office, 1980. See also the article by Clifford Longley in *The Times*, 17 August 1981.
30. See Edward R. Norman, *Christianity and the World*. London: Oxford University Press, 1979.
31. On abortion in 1967, see Keith Hindell and M. Simms, *Abortion Law Reformed*. London: Peter Owen, 1971, esp. p. 142.
32. See note 18 above for the issues at stake.
33. For a discussion of divisions within the General Synod, and particularly of those 'liberals' with whom many bishops appear to identify, see our article, 'The Open Synod Group' in Kathleen Jones (ed.), *Living the Faith*, London: Oxford University Press, 1980, pp. 132-50.
34. This somewhat negative evaluation is the view expressed to us by bishops who confessed to a lack of relevant expertise. In some other cases, it appeared as if an appropriate use of the media has received relatively little systematic attention. With few exceptions, those with a keen interest in this sphere concentrated chiefly on religious broadcasting conceived in conventional terms.
35. A number of bishops testified to close and informal conversations with some very prominent individuals located within all the major political parties, within the senior ranks of the academic and business communites and, to a lesser extent, within the trade union movement. These contacts do form part of a process of long-range thinking about contemporary issues, and provide the Church with opportunities for informing itself about long-term trends, and also for influencing the thinking of others. It is in this sense, not least, that the Church may help to create 'climates of opinion'.
36. On this subject, see Lord Longford, 'The Permissive Society', in N. Autton (ed.), *Christianity and Change*. London: SPCK, 1971. For abortion legislation, the effect of thalidomide on public opinion was substantial (see Hindell and Simms, op. cit., Ch. 5).
37. On this point, cf. our article in *Government and Opposition*, op. cit.
38. Cf. G. Ecclestone, op. cit.